A GUIDE TO TRAINING
AND
HORSE MANAGEMENT IN INDIA

A GUIDE TO TRAINING

AND

HORSE MANAGEMENT IN INDIA

WITH

A HINDUSTANEE STABLE AND VETERINARY VOCABULARY AND THE CALCUTTA TURF CLUB TABLES FOR WEIGHT FOR AGE AND CLASS

M. HORACE HAYES

GYAN

Published by

Gyan Publishing House
5, Ansari Road
Daryaganj, New Delhi-110002
Phone: 011-47034999, 9811692060
E-mail: books@gyanbooks.com

Distribution Network
gyanbooks.com
India, USA, Canada, UK, Australia, France

ISBN : 978-81-212-9673-1 (PB)
First Published, 1878

2nd Impression 2023

Printed at: Gyan Press, Delhi.

A GUIDE TO TRAINING AND HORSE MANAGEMENT IN INDIA
Author: M. HORACE HAYES

A GUIDE TO TRAINING

AND

HORSE MANAGEMENT

IN INDIA;

WITH

A HINDUSTANEE STABLE AND VETERINARY VOCABULARY AND THE CALCUTTA TURF CLUB TABLES FOR WEIGHT FOR AGE AND CLASS.

BY

M. HORACE HAYES,

Capt., Bengal Staff Corps,

AUTHOR OF "VETERINARY NOTES FOR HORSE OWNERS."

NEW EDITION.

Re-arranged and much enlarged.

1878.

Dedicated to

COLONEL MONTAGU JAMES TURNBULL

ON HIS APPROACHING DEPARTURE TO ENGLAND

AS A SMALL TRIBUTE OF RESPECT

FOR THE POSITION HE HAS HELD FOR MANY YEARS

THAT OF OUR FIRST AUTHORITY ON HORSES AND RACING

AND THE ACKNOWLEDGED LEADER OF

ORIENTAL SPORTING LITERATURE.

M. H. HAYES.

Cawnpore, 20th August, 1874.

PREFACE TO THE NEW EDITION.

In the previous edition of this work, which was intended chiefly for the use of racing men, the subject of Horse Management was made subservient to that of Training, while the principles of the former were enunciated with but little attempt to reason out their correctness. The favourable notice which the work received from the Public, convinced the Author of the advisability of treating, in detail, these two subjects under separate headings, and of giving, in popular language, a concise *résumé* of the theoretical points affecting the Horse, so that the reader might draw his own deductions, without having to accept the mere *ipse dixit* of the Author as sufficient authority for his teaching. By this, the practical utility of the work is in no way prejudiced, for these chapters are complete and distinct in themselves, so that the reader may skip them or not as he chooses, while the inferences to be drawn from them are separately summed up.

The chapters on Bitting and Riding have been carefully re-written and illustrated.

The additions to the Hindustanee Vocabulary have been compiled chiefly from the *Hidayut Namah* of Farrier Major Bunnay Khan and *The Bengal Pharmacopœia*, with a few words from a *Glossary* by Hem Chunder Kerr, and from a *Manual of the more Deadly Forms of Cattle Disease in India* by H. B. H.

I beg to thank the Stewards of the Calcutta Turf Club for their kindness in allowing me permission to print their tables for "Weight for Age and Class."

CONTENTS.

—:o:—

Part I.

HORSE MANAGEMENT IN INDIA.

CHAPTER VII. PAGE

Grooming and Stable Routine.

CHAPTER VIII.

On Bitting and Saddling Horses.

CHAPTER IX.

Racing Saddlery.

CHAPTER X.

Riding.

CHAPTER XI.

CHAPTER XII.

Servants.

CHAPTER XIII.

Shoeing.

Part II.

TRAINING AND RACING.

ERRATA.

Page 36, line 6 from bottom, *dele* "Starch or."

Page 71, line 12, for "Alongside each hair, where it pierces the skin, a small tube opens, which gives," *read* "Into each hair follicle open two tubes, which give."

Page 90, line 16, for "2½" *read* "1½."

HORSE MANAGEMENT
IN INDIA.

HORSE MANAGEMENT IN INDIA.

CHAPTER I.

Stables.

POSITION AND CONSTRUCTION OF STABLES—MANGERS—PICKETING HORSES—POULTRY NEAR STABLES—DISINFECTING STABLES.

Position and Construction of Stables.—In the plains stables should be built on high ground devoid of trees in their immediate vicinity; while their direction should run at right angles to the prevailing winds, so as to obtain free circulation of air through the building; the object, here, being to provide against the baneful effects of heat, and not against those of cold, which can always be obviated by warm clothing. In this country, experience proves that the chief requisites, for good stables, are airy positions, thick roofs overhead, lofty and spacious stalls, and perfect circulation of air. As long as men or animals are protected from the direct rays of the sun, while the air blows freely through the habitation, whatever it may be, there is little danger from the effects of our tropical sun. The best proof of this important principle is afforded by the fact, that however powerful the noonday sun may be, and however fiercely the hot wind may blow, neither man nor beast will suffer from the high temperature, when out in the open, if they be under the shade of a tree with thick foliage. But if, in such a case, the current of air become impeded by a wall, screen, or other object, the distressing effects of the heat will be felt in a moment. Stagnation of air, in nine cases out of ten, is the cause of the many cases of fever which occur during the hot weather, especially in large cities like Calcutta, where houses are crowded together. I have seen, on different occasions, horses, that were almost dying from the effects of heat in stables situated on low and confined positions, recover their condition and health, in a very few days, after being removed to others on high and airy ground.

I have tried the experiment of keeping a race-horse in my own house during the hot weather, but he suffered far more, even under a punkah, from the confined atmosphere inside, than he had done in his stable, which was actually many degrees hotter, but through which there was a free current of air.

If valuable horses be kept during the hot months in the plains, punkahs may be used with advantage; but if they cannot be conveniently fixed, and the horses feel the heat much, a couple of coolies may be told off to each animal, to keep him cool during the mid-day heat with a large hand-punkah.

I have always found that, when proper precautions have been adopted, horses, in dry climates, such as those of the North-West, Oudh, and the Punjaub, have retained their health and condition during the hot weather, quite as well, as they did during the cold months. This is in conformity with the fact that the horse is a native of a dry, hot climate.

In order that the stable should be kept as dry as possible, its walls should be constructed of some material which will not absorb moisture, such as fire-burnt bricks or stone; the former is, I think, the more preferable material. Wood, also, might be employed, though stables made of it are not nearly so cool, during the hot weather, as those constructed of either of the other two. Throughout Eastern Bengal, strong screens made of bamboo are used; they suit admirably. In the case of a kicker, the horse may be saved from injury by placing matting (Hind. *chitai*), say three feet high, about six inches from the wall, while the interval is filled up with dried grass. This will give to the blow, and will act as a padding to the wall.

The floors of the stable should, if possible, be laid down with concrete, or some other material, which will not absorb water. In many parts of India, *kunkur* may be obtained, and then can be applied in the same manner as it is used for metalling roads. In default of it, pounded bricks, which are employed for the same purpose, may be substituted. After these floors are laid down, the stables should not be used, until they are thoroughly dry, and the *pucca* has become hard and solid.

If it be not practicable to have the floors made of water-proof material, they should be kept covered with five or six inches of sand, the tainted parts of which should be daily removed, and replaced by a fresh supply.

Damp stables are the sources of many serious ailments to the horse, who can keep health and condition alone in a dry habitation. This most important fact should never be lost sight of by the horse-owner.

Only on rare and exceptional occasions should stables be washed out.

The ground around stables should be thoroughly well drained.

The form of stables, I prefer, is one with a single row of boxes, having a passage, between them and the outside wall, 10 or 12 feet wide and provided with a window at each end.

If possible, each horse should have a large loose box, at least 12 feet by 16 feet, in which he may move freely about.

The smallest size for a comfortable box is 10 feet by 12 feet. If less space than 8 feet by 12 feet be available, stalls must be used. For large horses, they should be 6 feet by 12 feet, while ponies may be contented with a foot less, each way. When stalls are used, the syce should never attempt to turn the horse round, when removing him, but should back him out.

A stable should not be made to hold more than five or six horses.

With a number of horses it is advisable to have a loose box — forming a separate building if possible — provided with slings, set apart in case of illness.

The roof of the stable should afford perfect protection from the direct rays of the sun; for which object thatch will be found to be the best material. Flat *pucca* roofs may be protected by having *gurras* (earthen vessels) filled with water, placed on them; while tiled roofs may be covered with dried grass (Hind. *phoos*) attached to bamboo frames. If expense be not an object, double roofs may be employed with great advantage.

The stable may be admirably ventilated, by a space

of a few inches being allowed, all round, between the roof and the top of the outside walls.

During the hot weather, the outer walls of the stable should be protected by thick *chhuppur* (frames covered with thatch). The outside of the stable should be white-washed, while the walls inside should be dark coloured.

When flies are troublesome, *surkunda* (a variety of cane-like grass) or bamboo screens should be placed in front of the door-ways and windows. They should be kept down during the hours between sunrise and sunset. I may here mention, in passing, that the cleaner and darker stalls are kept, the freer they will be from flies.

I think that hard-worked horses rest and thrive far better when completely separated from each other, than they do when kept apart simply by bails, or by low partitions. I would therefore advise that, for them, the walls between the boxes should be made about 6 feet high, just sufficient to prevent the animals smelling each other over them. With ordinary hacks such a precaution is not necessary. Some few horses thrive best in company.

At the head of each box or stall, there should be a window, say a yard square, and a yard and a half from the ground. The space below the window may be occupied by a moveable door, which, during the hot hours, may be taken away, and a thin bamboo screen hung across the opening.

In many stables in India, covered receptacles for urine are made in the centre of the stalls, which the syces are supposed to bale out every day. This is, obviously, a most objectionable arrangement. A common trick of those servants is to teach their horses to stale into an earthen pot, which they hold for them, and thus get rid of the fluid without it soiling the bedding. This is also a most reprehensible practice, for horses, that are accustomed to it, will often, if the syces be not ready to hold the vessel, abstain from staling for an injurious time. The system of drainage, adopted in England, is not applicable to India. The litter should be taken up twice a day, every soiled particle of it should be removed, and the floor should be thoroughly cleaned and dried. The less tainted portions of the bedding may be dried in the sun for further use.

The door-ways of the stalls are usually barred across by two poles—generally bamboos— that are let into the walls at each side, the upper one being fixed about four feet from the ground. These bars are sometimes made to slide through boarded passages in the walls, an arrangement that will save the latter from becoming broken. The best and neatest plan is, I think, to plant two strong upright posts—in which are bored holes for the reception of the horizontal poles—10 or 11 inches from each side of the walls at the door-way. The walls will then be free from injury, and there will be no occasion to remove the bars, unless, when the horse is taken out or in, for there will be quite sufficient room for a man to pass sideways between the walls and the upright posts. The bars are secured by being lashed together with a piece of rope.

Moveable half-doors —as well as bars—may be provided, to be used when the nights are cold.

I attach great importance to allowing the horse freedom to move about in his stall, and opportunity and inducement to lie down when he chooses, so that stagnation of blood in his feet may be avoided, both by movement, and by the assumption of a horizontal position, and that his legs and frame may obtain the rest which is essential to their well-being: hence I recommend large loose boxes well bedded down and partitioned off, moderately darkened stables, and the absence of all noise and disturbing influences between grooming hours.

The blood vessels in the foot of the horse, unlike those in other parts, do not possess valves; because the almost constant movement—except when the animal is lying down or sleeps standing—that he, in a natural state, takes in the search for his food, prevents stagnation of blood by gravitation while he assumes the erect position, for on the foot being raised, blood rushes into and fills these vessels, which, at the next moment, are emptied by the effect of pressure, the instant the foot is brought to the ground and weight is thrown on it.

I thoroughly agree with Admiral Rous' remark that, "The windows of a stable ought never to be shut by night or day; in cold weather, add to the clothing, but never deprive them of the first great source of vitality, 'fresh air.'"

In India, during the cold weather, the air is generally so dry that precautious to be taken against draughts are not nearly so necessary as in England. Respecting the latter country, Professor Williams writes, "Horses kept in ill-ventilated stables are undoubtedly rendered susceptible to many diseases, and to pneumonia among the rest, but they will bear impure air even better than cold draughts blowing directly upon them. I have repeatedly observed that the slightest cold contracted by a horse kept in a draughty stable has almost invariably been succeeded by pneumonia, and, that if the animal was not removed to a more comfortable situation, the disease tended to a fatal termination."

Grooms in England have a strong prejudice in favour of warm stables, on account of the good effect they have on the animals' coats, while these men naturally ignore the increased susceptibility to catching cold, which horses kept in such places acquire, as well as the very marked tendency the legs and feet have of "going to pieces;" for a horse, that is laid up with a cough, or a filled leg, gives far less trouble to the groom, than one which is in full work. In winter, horses undoubtedly thrive better in comfortable stables than in cold bleak ones. The owner, trainer, or groom can personally satisfy himself as to the proper degree of warmth by regulating it according to what he would consider agreeable to his own feelings, were he to make the stable his own abode; always remembering that its atmosphere should be pure, and free from the slightest suspicion of "closeness."

With hard-worked animals—such as race-horses, &c.—I have found the best results attend the practice of keeping the stables moderately dark, in order to induce the occupants to lie down, and, during hot weather, to keep the abode cool, by preventing the admission of rays of light, which are always accompanied by rays of heat. I here take for granted that the free circulation of air is not interfered with.

On all occasions, when the stables are empty, they should be thrown open for the admittance of sun-light, which is a powerful disinfectant.

Mangers.—Many years ago, Professor Coleman directed, and I think with reason, that the feeding trough should be placed on the ground, as that arrangement makes the horse assume the natural position in which he was intended to feed. I advocate this practice, because it obliges the animal to eat much slower than he would do, were the manger in the usual position; hence he will masticate his food more thoroughly. In order to carry out this principle still further, I would advise that a broad feeding-box be used, in which the grain should be spread in a comparatively thin layer. Some horses, from infirmity, &c., will require the manger to be slightly raised, say, a foot from the ground.

Picketing horses.—Head and heel-ropes are admissible only with animals—like those in the Artillery and Cavalry—that may be called upon to camp out at any time. In such cases, if there be any probability of rain, great care should be taken to render the pegs secure, for, if a shower falls, it will both render the horses fidgetty, and will loosen the hold the pegs have in the ground.

Natives, when they use head and heel-ropes, are very prone to tie up the horses far too tightly.

Horses should never be picketed by a fore-leg, for then they will be very apt to screw themselves by straining at the rope, in the event of being startled, or when jumping about in play.

During the hot weather, in the plains, the horse may, with advantage, be picketed to a pole fixed vertically in the ground, round which his bedding should be spread. The head-rope should be attached to a moveable iron ring, which works round the pole. No heel-ropes are necessary.

Poultry should never be allowed about a stable, nor should they be kept near it, for the louse, that often infects fowl, proves excessively irritating to the horse, when they are allowed to settle on him. Removal of the poultry will soon cure the animal attacked, for these parasites cannot live, beyond two or three days, away from their proper "host."

Disinfecting Stables.—When the floors of stables are formed simply by the surface of the ground, they should be dug up, from time to time, the tainted soil removed, and fresh, dry mould substituted.

This proceeding is particularly necessary after the appearance of Loodiana Fever.

To purify metalled floors, and drains, a solution of 1℔ of sulphate of iron (Hind. *hurree kussees*) to the gallon of water may be used.

Crude carbolic acid may be applied to the iron and woodwork of the stable.

Carbolized sawdust may be sprinkled here and there in a stable, occasionally, in order to keep it fresh and sweet. This preparation is made by steeping sawdust in as much crude carbolic acid and water—using a solution of equal quantities—as it will take up (*see Veterinary Notes for Horse Owners*).

CHAPTER II.

Clothing—Bedding—Stable Gear.

CLOTHING—BANDAGES—BOOTS—CLOTHS—BEDDING—STRAW—SAW-DUST—SAND—TAN—NOSEBAGS—FOMENTING BUCKETS AND SHOES—OAT-BRUISING MACHINE—ARTICLES USED IN GROOMING.

Clothing.—For the maintenance of high condition in the horse, it is requisite that he should be supplied, in the stable, with an ample quantity of warm clothing—short of causing him to perspire. Clothing not alone stimulates the skin to act, and guards the animal from the ill effects of chill, but also aids in maintaining the internal temperature of the body, thereby supplementing one of the most important offices of food. To avoid overweighting the horse too much, it is advisable to use only good English clothing of close material and not too heavy. During the cold months, a suit of warm clothing by day, with an extra rug at night, will generally be sufficient. As a rule, hoods may be dispensed with, though a "night cap" may be put on at night. This article is a short hood about a foot long, and is made to fit close round the throat. Ordinary hoods, if buckled to the body-piece, are apt during the night to prove uncomfortable to the horse; while, if unattached, they usually fall over the animal's head, on his lowering his neck. The head-collar should be put on over, not under, the hood, or "night cap."

Horses, that are used for rough work in all weathers, should naturally be clothed lighter, so that they may not be liable to be affected by change of temperature. On this point the owner should exercise his own judgment.

Clothing, with the breast and quarter piece in one, will do for night use, but if it be worn by horses when they are exercised, it will wear the hair off their shoulders, thus giving them the appearance of having been worked in harness.

If hoods be made of country blanketing, they should be lined with cotton cloth, so as to save the manes from being frayed by the coarse woollen material.

A suit of warm clothing can be made from an English pattern, for about Rs. 10.

The use of warm clothing often irritates a horse having a thin, delicate skin; in such a case, a light cotton sheet should be placed under the woollen suit.

With well-bred horses, rollers should be provided with breast-plates.

Bandages.—Horses that have done much work, and whose legs are inclined to fill, will generally require the aid of bandages to keep them fine. Their uses are to encourage insensible perspiration from the skin, to afford support to the tendons and ligaments, and, by pressure, to cause absorption. These bandages should be made of close, thick flannel—not of serge—and should be about 2½ yards long and 4½ inches broad.

The usual way for putting them on—for stable use—is to begin at the middle of the cannon-bone, and go down to the fetlock, round which a couple of turns will make the bandage fit neatly, and then work up to a little below the knee, finally ending where one commenced.

To give support during work, the best bandage is an elastic one, made from the material used for side-spring boots, and of the same form as an ordinary bandage, but somewhat shorter, so as to allow of its stretching. In my *Veterinary Notes for Horse Owners*, I have given a drawing to show its mode of adjustment; the description is as follows:—"Commence by laying the loose end diagonally across the fetlock, with its extremity a little below that joint; then take about four turns round the leg so that the bandage may come close below the knee, take another turn in a downward direction, bring the loose end up and lay it flat against the bandaged part, and continue the turns over it. The loose end will now be firmly secured between the cloth on both sides. When put on according to this plan, the bandage cannot become undone unless the tape breaks."

Flannel or crape bandages may also be used for the same purpose. The former should be about three inches broad; and, for exercise, should always be put on in the manner just described, so as to obviate the possibility of the loose end working free.

When a wet bandage is used to obtain cold by evaporation, it is best to employ a single fold of thin cotton, and to keep it constantly moist with cold water, or with a lotion like the following one recommended by "Stonehenge:"—

Sal ammoniac	... ...	1 ounce.
Vinegar	... ...	4 ounces.
Spirits of wine	... ...	2 "
Tincture of arnica	... ...	2 drachms.
Water	... ...	½ pint.

Unless an owner looks personally after the syces, it is difficult to make them keep the bandage constantly wet; hence it is generally much the best plan to get a *bheestie* (water-carrier) to keep a fine jet of water, from his *mussuck* (water-bag), on the injured part, for a quarter of an hour or so, five or six times a day. If the horse be too fidgetty to bear this, and a running stream be near, he may be made to stand, up to his knees in it, for half an hour, three or four times a day.

The following plan may be adopted for putting on a bandage that is intended to be employed as a poultice:—Make a pad of four or five folds of soft cotton, and large enough to wrap round the leg; wet this pad thoroughly, apply it, wrap over it a piece of oil-silk, and then roll a moderately tight flannel bandage round the whole. In cases of sprain, the application may consist of either plain water, or of a lotion consisting of a wine glass full of the tincture of arnica to a quart of water. Arnica appears to act by stimulating the small blood vessels of the skin.

Boots are worn to give support like bandages, and also to prevent the horse from hurting himself by "brushing," or by otherwise striking his leg. For the former object, the boot may be made of two thicknesses of boot elastic, and to lace at the side. The laces may be made of whipcord, or, better still, of strong waxed hempen thread. For "brushing," or "speedy-cutting," leather guards should be sewn on to the inner side of the cloth. The same precaution may be used to protect the back tendon with cross country horses, especially when schooling.

When putting on boots, care should be taken that the upper and lower straps should be buckled looser than the middle one, or pair, according as there are three or four of them.

Bandages are best for support, boots for protection.

Cloths are commonly employed in England instead of bandages; they are formed of stout woollen material, sewn down the side of the horse's leg, and are not removed. I think bandages, which are properly put on, are much superior to them in every way, especially in the facility they afford for hand-rubbing, or fomenting the legs.

Bedding.—Long wheaten straw furnishes the softest and most comfortable bedding for the horse, especially if he be without clothing. Barley straw is objectionable, because it is very indigestible, while the horse will eat it readily. Oat straw is brittle, so does not last as well as that obtained from wheat; there is little or no harm in the horse eating a moderate quantity of either of these two last mentioned kinds, especially the former. Horses rarely care to eat rice straw.

If the animal be addicted to the practice of eating his bedding, the straw may be damped, and kept in the sun a few days before using, so that it may become too sapless and unpalatable to be chosen in preference to grass, while a layer of old bedding may be kept on the top. Such cases of morbid appetite will generally call for medical treatment, if a full supply of salt and green meat fail to correct the habit.

The bedding should be carefully spread, so as to be as comfortable as possible for the horse; and should be banked up around the walls, so that the animal may not hurt himself when lying down, or when rolling. At the entrance of the box or stall, for appearance sake, the bedding should be arranged in a straight line, and its edge finished off by plaiting the ends of the straw together.

Hard-worked horses should, if possible, have the bedding under them by day as well as by night, so that they may have every inducement to lie down and rest themselves, when they choose. Besides this, when the horse stands on the bare ground, he will abstain from staling longer than he ought to do, often to an injurious extent. Most of us old Indians know that a straw mat, expressively called, in Hindustanee, a *seetul patee* or cold mat, is the coolest thing on which to lie during the hot weather; so we may infer that straw forms an equally grateful couch for the horse. While he is out at morning and evening work, the bedding should be removed, and dry straw should be substituted for any that may have become soiled or wet.

A slight additional expense is the only objection to keeping the horse bedded down by day.

Sawdust.—I have found that *sawdust* makes a good substitute for straw, though I am inclined to think it takes some of the polish off the coat. "Stonehenge" remarks, "that it soon heats when wetted with urine, and ammonia is given off profusely, so that great care must be exercised to change it as soon as it becomes soiled."

When a horse has on a high-heeled shoe—as during treatment for sprain of the back tendons or suspensory ligaments, &c.—sawdust makes the best bedding, as it will not catch in the long calkins. Alone, without a raised shoe, it enables a horse to assume a comfortable position for the injured limb.

Sand—Forms a very cool bedding for horses; while they generally show that they like having it under them by frequently rolling on it. Its use spoils the look of the coat, for the time being, on account of its absorbing a considerable part of the oil, which is secreted by the glands of the skin in order to keep the hair soft and pliable.

Tan—Is an excellent material to put down in a loose box, for a horse that is at all inclined to inflammation in the feet, provided that the syce is most careful in removing the wet portions immediately they become tainted.

Nosebags.—These articles should never be used, except when a proper manger is not obtainable, as on the march, &c., because they are uncomfortable to the horse, who with one on, is apt to bolt his food or chuck it out, while he taints his corn with his breath and rejected saliva; besides this, it is difficult to keep nosebags clean and sweet. When used, they should be made of canvas or sacking, and not of leather, should be deep, not too wide, and should narrow off to the bottom, so as to allow the animal, towards the end of his feed, to readily pick up the remaining grains of corn without having to chuck the bag up.

A common plan for preventing a horse from throwing corn out of his nosebag, is to tie a string at the place where either end of the head-strap is fixed to the bag, and then attach it just above the knee of one of the animal's forelegs, at such a length that he cannot chuck up his head.

When nosebags are used, horses should have something on which to rest them, for instance, a low wall, or a bundle of hay. Dray horses may often be seen supporting their bags on their companions' quarters. Without some such aids the animal will be liable to spill his corn, in his attempts to get it into his mouth.

Fomenting Buckets and Shoes.—A couple of long narrow leather buckets for applying warm water to horses' legs are most useful in cases of accident. They should reach up to the knee, should be made of stout hide, and should be provided with wooden bottoms to preserve them from injury. I may here mention, in passing, that water, at a temperature higher than what the hand can comfortably bear, should never be used in fomenting the horse's skin. A pair of shoes, with wooden bottoms, made of pliable leather, and reaching only to a little above the fetlock joint, should be kept for poulticing the feet, when required. Each shoe should be provided with a leather thong to close the mouth round the leg. Mashed turnips or carrots form an excellent poultice.

Oat-bruising Machine.—Machines which are provided with circular rollers should be employed when oats are used. Those made by Turner of Ipswich are excellent. A small one, with packing case, which also answers for a stand, will cost about Rs. 75 in India.

Articles used in Grooming.—Each horse should be provided with a brush and curry-comb, a hoof picker, manecomb, and three or four cotton rubbers; while one pair of scrapers will be enough for a small stable.

English brushes should be used in preference to those of country make. The bristles should be closely set, long, and moderately soft, so as not to hurt the skin while cleansing it from scurf. The teeth of a curry-comb should be blunt, not sharp, in order that they may not unduly wear out the bristles of the brush. Long, thin, copper scrapers, made with handles at each end, are much to be preferred to those of a semi-circular form, constructed with only one handle, as the latter are hard and unyielding to the skin.

Capital wisps may be made from unprepared hemp (Hind. *sun*).

CHAPTER III.

Varieties of Food.

OATS—GRUEL—GRAM—KULTHEE—URUD—BARLEY—INDIAN CORN—WHEAT—BRAN—BRAN MASHES—BRAN AND LINSEED MASHES—LINSEED—LINSEED TEA—RICE—RICE-WATER—ROOTS—GRASS AND HAY—BAMBOO LEAVES—LUCERN—MILK—STOWAGE OF GRAIN.

Oats.—This grain, when grown in India, possesses a far larger proportion of husk to flour than that produced in England, hence its lower value as an article of food. As the measure of the horse's appetite is by bulk, and not by weight, the heavier the oat, the more valuable it becomes. Samples, at 47lbs., 42lbs., and 32lbs. to the bushel, will respectively yield about three-fourths, one-half, and one-third flour, which proportions approximately give the nutritive values. Mr. Stewart *(Stable Economy)* tersely describes sound English corn as follows :—

"*Good oats* are about one year old, plump, short, hard, rattling when poured into the manger, sweet, clean, free from chaff and dust, and weighing about 40lbs. per bushel." Although our Indian oats are far below this standard, still they are much superior, as a food for horses, to any other grain which we can procure. This is especially the case with hard-worked animals, because they can eat an almost unlimited quantity of oats without it disagreeing with them; while, on the contrary, gram, *kúlthee*, barley, &c., given in adequate amounts, almost always upsets the digestion, inducing diarrhœa, and a general "heated" state of the system.

In order to make up for the inferior quality of the oats, we may, with great advantage, supplement them by an addition of gram, or *kúlthee*, which should not exceed a third of the whole amount. This practice is in accordance with that, in England, of adding beans to the corn, and is particularly applicable to old horses whose powers of assimilation are impaired. In England, new oats are rightly considered to be indigestible—an objection which may be removed by having them kiln-dried; but, in this country, they do not appear to be injurious to any great extent—a fact which may be accounted for by the extreme heat of our tropical sun. New Indian oats never present the soft, pulpy appearance seen in new English corn.

Oats should be given in a bruised state, for then, not alone is the possibility of the grain passing through the horse in an undigested state avoided, but also, the animal is obliged to chew it more thoroughly than were it given whole.

This grain is principally grown in Tirhoot and Dehra Doon.

Gruel is best made by mixing a pound of oatmeal well up with a quart of cold water, to which should be added three quarts of boiling water, the whole being put to simmer over the fire—occasionally being stirred up the while—till it thickens. It should then be removed and allowed to cool.

Gruel should be given to the horse in a lukewarm state, while its consistency should be little greater than that of milk. It may be flavoured with salt or sugar according as the horse may like it.

Gram.—This grain, known as *chunna,* is very commonly used throughout Northern India and the Bombay Presidency. It is objectionable on account of its tendency to cause diarrhœa, and to induce a "foul" and "heated" state of the system, when given in large amounts, say, anything above 10lbs. daily. It is best used in combination with oats, Indian corn, barley, or rice in husk.

Gram a year old should be chosen in preference to new. It should be given in a broken state and always *dry.* The practice of steeping gram in water is injurious.

Kúlthee is extensively employed throughout Madras and Bombay. It seems superior, as a food for horses, to *chunna,* when either grain is used alone; and, in limited quantities, has an excellent effect on the general condition and coat. On account of the hardness of the husk, it has to be given in a boiled state. Only just enough water to cook it should be used, so that, when fully done, the fluid, which remains over in the pot, may be absorbed on cooling. The steam should be allowed to escape, so that the *kúlthee* may become as dry as possible. It is very similar in its composition to gram, and may be used in the same combinations with oats, &c.

It is readily procurable at Hajeepore, which is near Patna, and also at different places in the North-West Provinces. *Kúlthee*, which is grown in those parts, does not appear to be as good as that produced in Madras.

Urud.—This variety of *dal* is commonly used throughout Eastern Bengal, and, more or less so, in other parts of India. It is extremely like *kúlthee* in composition and qualities, and is prepared in a similar manner.

Both *kúlthee* and *úrud* are valuable when a change of food is necessary, especially when the animal is in poor condition, and his skin out of order.

Barley.—Next to oats, this grain is, in my opinion, the most suitable one for horses, which should be gradually accustomed to its use, for it is apt to disagree with them at first. It may be given raw and in a bruised state, or parched, which is probably the better plan, as the husk seems to possess an acrid principle, whose effects appear to be obviated by the process of parching. Boiled barley is also used.

A mixture of parched barley and gram, known as *ardawa*, is commonly sold in India. It is usually made of inferior grain, and is always more or less adulterated with dirt and chaff.

A native parcher (*bhurbhúnja*) will charge two or three annas a maund (82lbs.) for parching.

Indian Corn.—This grain, known as *mukaee*, is very cheap and plentiful in some parts, the Punjab for instance. Given by itself it is not suitable for working horses, but an excellent food may be made by mixing it with equal quantities of bran and gram.

Owing to its hardness it requires the addition of bran, chaff, or chopped hay to make the animal chew it properly. When given alone, it is very apt to cause colic.

It should be given raw, and in a roughly broken state.

Owing to its cheapness, it was very generally used, in England and Ireland, during the years 1876 and 1877.

Hiram Woodruff, the celebrated American trainer, thus writes :—"The grain should be oats of good quality. I do not let colts have corn at all when young; and even to old horses I think it should be fed very sparingly. . . . . Above all, avoid Indian corn in all shapes for young colts. . . . . . . Keep the corn for the bullocks and hogs, and give oats to the horses."

Wheat.—This grain is difficult of digestion, probably owing to the viscid nature of the gluten, which it contains, preventing the different digestive fluids—saliva, gastric juice, pancreatic juice, &c.—from permeating through its substance. This objection might be removed by the process of parching.

Raw wheat is very apt to gripe the horse.

That most reliable authority, Mr. Stewart *(Stable Economy)*, mentions that a quantity of wheat, not exceeding 4 lbs., may be substituted for the same, or a slightly larger amount of oats; that it should always be given mixed with bran or chaff; and that it should be bruised in the same manner as oats. For instances of its combinations, see Chapter VI.

A couple of pounds of boiled wheat, mixed with a

little salt, may be given at night when soft food is required.

Bran.—English bran consists of the envelope which surrounds the grains of wheat, while the flour is almost completely separated. The outer portion of this envelope is indigestible, and acts, mechanically, as a gentle laxative; while the inner layer (according to Mège Mouriès) has the same property as diastase in converting starch into sugar, and consequently aids in the process of digestion. English bran is therefore of itself unsuitable as a food. Indian bran, on the contrary, owing to imperfect manufacture, retains a considerable portion of the flour, which supplies nutriment; so that horses, doing slow work, may be kept in good condition on 10 or 12lbs. of it alone, without other grain. Given even in these quantities, it hardly ever purges a horse; on the contrary, if an animal gets "foul" and "loose" from too much corn, nothing is better than to keep him simply on dry bran and grass for a few days; after which time his dung will become well formed and healthy looking.

Dry bran seems to have a binding effect, or at least, one opposed to a lax condition of the bowels. This is probably owing to a healthy action of the stomach and intestines being induced by bulk being given to the food, without the addition of a large proportion of nutriment which would have a stimulating effect.

Wet bran, in the form of mash, is a laxative.

I am very partial to the use of bran with hacks and ordinary horses when oats are not used, and would advise that 3 or 4lbs. of it be given daily in a dry state,

With race-horses and others, the custom is to give a bran mash every Saturday night, or oftener, as the case may demand.

Instead of a simple bran mash, I much prefer one to which linseed is added.

Bran Mashes—Are made as follows:—After scalding a stable bucket with boiling water, put into it about 3lbs. of bran, with an ounce of salt, and pour in as much boiling water as the bran will take up, which will be about equal to the weight of the bran itself, calculating the gallon of water to weigh 10lbs. The mash should then be well covered, so as to keep in the steam, and should be left to stand for a quarter of an hour, or 20 minutes.

Bran and Linseed Mashes.—Boil slowly from 1 to 1½lbs. of linseed, for two or three hours, till the grains are soft, allowing only sufficient water, so that at the end of the time, it may be just sufficient to soak up a couple of pounds of bran, which is then mixed in and covered up, as before described.

The thicker the mash, the readier the horse will eat it.

Linseed.—This grain, which is the seed of the flax plant, containing as it does a large percentage of oil, is most useful for fattening horses that are low in flesh. It improves the condition of the coat in a marked manner, and has a peculiarly soothing effect on the urinary organs. A linseed mash is the usual form in which it is given. If the making of this cause too much trouble, a quarter of a pint of the oil, mixed through the corn daily, may be substituted. Linseed is most beneficial in cases of a disordered state of the skin, difficulty in staling, bloody urine, and diseases of the organs of breathing.

Linseed Tea.—This is convenient form to be given in illness, when it may replace water as a drink. It may be made by boiling half a pound of linseed in two gallons of water, for a couple of hours. The fluid should then be strained off and allowed to cool.

Rice.—In some parts of India, especially in Eastern Bengal, rice in husk, commonly called paddy (Hind. *dhan*), is much used. It is given raw and in a broken state. It forms a fairly good food. A mixture of one part of gram to two of rice is an excellent one for feeding purposes. Rice, without the husk, is quite unsuitable for horses.

Rice-water.—This fluid (Hind. *kanjee)* is most useful in cases of superpurgation, &c. It may be prepared by boiling a pound of rice in two gallons of water, for a couple of hours. If time be of consequence, and boiled rice be at hand, a sufficient amount may be taken, and well macerated between the fingers in warm water, the whole being brought to the boil, and then allowed to cool.

Suttoo.—This, mixed with water, is the Indian substitute for gruel. It is usually composed of finely ground parched gram and barley; but is sometimes made from Indian corn alone. It is given always in cold water, 1lb. to half a bucket being the usual proportions. The horse gets his *suttoo* and water usually before his morning feed. I have never been able to discover any benefit to arise from its constant use

Syces are very partial to the practice of giving it, but more for their own sakes than that of their horses.

Carrots—Contain but a small amount of nutriment compared to their bulk, hence they are inapplicable for forming a large proportion of the food of horses, which are called upon to do fast work. The good effects they produce on an animal's general health recommend their use. They come into season during the autumn, and may, with great benefit, be given in quantities of 6 or 7lbs. daily; 2 or 3lbs. will be sufficient for race-horses. Parsnips are almost as good as carrots. No other roots seem to be suitable to the horse, unless when given, in a boiled state, to animals used for slow draught.

"Carrots also improve the state of the skin. They form a good substitute for grass, and an excellent alterative for horses out of condition. To sick and idle horses they render corn unnecessary. They are beneficial in all chronic diseases of the organs connected with breathing, and have a marked influence upon chronic cough and broken wind. They are serviceable in diseases of the skin. In combination with oats, they restore a worn-out horse much sooner than oats alone." (Stewart.)

Dr. Vóelcker points out, that the nutritive value of different root-crops depends largely upon their state of maturity; that unripe roots are not alone poor in sugar—hence their decreased value—but also contain a number of organic acids (notably oxalic acid), and imperfectly elaborated nitrogenous substances, which appear to be the cause of their unwholesomeness; that the leaves of roots contain a far larger proportion of oxalic acid than does the root itself—hence the scouring effect produced by this poisonous acid when the leaves are given; and that moderate sized, well matured roots are infinitely more nutritious and wholesome than monster ones.

Grass and Hay.—I am convinced from long experience that the maintenance of good condition in the horse is much more dependant on the proper supply of grass, than on that of corn. If possible, only *doob* grass—called *hurryalee* in Madras—should be used. It is that peculiar root-grass that grows on, or rather in the surface of most sandy soils, spreading itself as a creeper, so that it cannot be cut like the ordinary kind, but has to be rooted up *(cheeled)* with a sort of trowel, called in Hindustanee a *kurpa.* One or two days' drying in the sun will be sufficient to prepare it for horses doing fast work. In some districts it is necessary to convert a quantity of it into hay for consumption during the rains.

The grass, before being given, should be carefully picked, and beaten in order to get rid of the dust and earth that may adhere to its roots. The grass-cutters should not be allowed to wash it, as they often do, before bringing it in, with the object of making it look fresh and green, and sometimes, to make it weigh heavy.

I have abridged the following remarks on grass and hay from a paper by M. L. Grandeau, which appeared in the "Journal d'Agriculture Pratique," and which was translated in the "Mark Lane Express."

Growing grass possesses a waxy envelope which protects the sugar, albumen, and other soluble compounds contained in it from being dissolved by moisture and rain. When the grass is cut, this varnish gradually wears away, and if the grass be exposed to wet, it will then lose a considerable portion of its nutritive elements, especially if this envelope be bruised in any way. As long as the plant lives, fermentation cannot take place, which process is caused by the nitrogenous matters coming in contact with the sugar and water, on the breaking up of the different cells which compose the substance of the grass. During fermentation, the non-nitrogenous matters are turned into sugar, then into alcohol, and finally into carbonic acid, which is set free into the atmosphere in the form of gas. Thus "fodder which has been submitted to active fermentation generally loses its nutritive properties, because the materials destined for the production of flesh in animals is transformed into sugar, which destroys itself soon after." When grass is cut, "if the weather is fine and warm, so that desiccation takes place rapidly, the rate per cent. of damp soon falls so low that fermentation cannot take place. The hay remains upon the ground and cannot easily become heated, even though in reality it contains more water than fodder harvested in bad condition. The more rapidly hay is turned to the sun, the less it will be bruised, and the greener it is, the better it will resist fermentation when it is stored; nevertheless, it often happens that a too rapid preparation injures fodder, and in a good year hay appears to be saved in fine condition, when in reality it is not. If hay be completely dried in the sun it never heats; a slight fermentation, far from being deleterious, is often very useful; in fact, we know that, in such a case, certain aromatic principles are produced which render fodder more sapid, and perhaps even more nourishing. As long as the green colour remains, the hay has lost none of its quality; when it is much heated, it turns brown. Some cultivators prefer brown to green hay, and it is certain that the former frequently has more flavour and smell than the latter; but, though cattle prefer brown hay, it is not at all desirable to have sufficient moisture in the fodder at the time it is housed to turn it brown, because the loss resulting from fermentation is not counterbalanced by the slight aromatic smell it acquires."

Grass lands, unless of exceptional richness, require to be manured in order to keep up the quality, as well as the quantity of the grass produced. Poor and impoverished land produces but very inferior fodder. On the other hand, as pointed out by Mr. H. S. Thompson (Journal of the Royal Agricultural Society, 1872), if land be treated with an excess of manure rich in nitrogenous matters, as guano and nitrate of soda, the luxuriant grass thus produced will be of inferior quality, and will prove unwholesome. The same remark applies to carrots and other roots.

Bamboo Leaves.—In some parts of Eastern Bengal these leaves are used as a substitute for grass; they seem to answer fairly well.

Lucern.—Lucern forms the best green crop for use during the hot weather: the seeds are readily procurable, and the plant, as a rule, grows well in India, provided it gets a sufficiency of water. When out of work, 8 or 9lbs. of it will be a good allowance for each horse, half to be given after the morning feed, the rest during the afternoon. It is advisable to dry it, for half an hour or so in the sun, before the horse eats it.

Milk.—For sick or delicate horses, milk is often most valuable, and they will seldom refuse it. Sweet skim-milk is preferable to new milk, which, from being too rich, is very apt to purge the horse. A couple of gallons may be given daily. To correct any tendency it might have to produce diarrhœa, the milk might be brought to the boil in a clean vessel, care being taken that it be not smoked during the process. Sugar or salt may be added.

Stowage of Grain.—Grain may be kept sweet, and free from the attacks of rats and mice in large earthen jars (Hind. *mutka*). They will hold 7 or 8 maunds, are very cheap, and can be readily procured.

Bags, capable of holding 25 to 30 maunds, may be employed. Each bag will cost about 7 or 8 rupees, and should be placed on a wooden stand. There is generally some difficulty about protecting them from the attacks of vermin.

Native grain-sellers generally use receptacles (Hind. *kothee*) made of thin bamboo wicker-work plastered over with clay, or with clay and cowdung.

If a large quantity of grain has to be stowed away, a granary may be constructed as follows:—Trace on the ground a circle of about 16 feet in diameter, and build on its circumference twelve or thirteen brick pillars, say, 18 inches square and $2\frac{1}{2}$ feet high, and at its centre a circular pillar of the same height, and about 3 feet in diameter. On these pillars construct a boarded floor, and build on it a strong bamboo wicker-work house, 9 or 10 feet high. This is plastered over, a small door is left at the top, and a light thatched roof is put over the whole. A house, such as I have described, would cost, say, 25 rupees, and would hold about 700 maunds of oats.

CHAPTER IV.

Sketch of the Theory of Food and Nutrition.

COMPOSITION OF THE BODY—WASTE OF TISSUE—REPAIR OF WASTE—ANALYSIS OF GRAINS AND GRASSES — NITROGENOUS FOOD — FAT, STARCH, AND SUGAR IN FOOD — HEAT SUPPLY — MINERAL SUBSTANCES—HUSK OF GRAIN—BULK IN FOOD—SELECTION OF FOOD—HAY AND GRASS—GREEN MEAT—VARIETY IN FOOD—SALT—RELATIONS OF COLD, HEAT, AND CLOTHING TO FOOD — MASTICATION AND DIGESTION—FUNCTIONS PERFORMED BY THE BLOOD—APPETITE—INFLUENCE OF AN ARTIFICIAL STATE OF LIFE—PREPARATION OF FOOD.

Composition of the Body.—Nearly four-fifths of the body of the horse is composed of water, while the remainder is made up of various organic and inorganic compounds. The former may be subdivided into substances that contain nitrogen—a gas, that mixed with oxygen, forms atmospheric air,— and substances which are wanting in that element; while the latter comprise the different mineral matters of the system, such as common salt, the carbonate and phosphate of lime, and carbonic acid, with traces of ammonia. The non-nitrogenous compounds may be put under two classes, namely, fats, and saccharine substances, such as milk and sugar.

Every tissue of the body which is employed in the performance of labour—such as the muscles, tendons, nerves, glands, &c.—is composed of substances that come under the nitrogenous group; "even the non-cellular liquids passing out into the alimentary canal at various points—which have so great an action in preparing the food in different ways—are not only nitrogenous, but the constancy of this implies the necessity of the nitrogen, in order that these actions shall be performed" (Parkes). Albumen is a familiar example of this group. These substances consist of carbon—of which charcoal is a well known form—hydrogen and oxygen—the two constituents of water—combined in various proportions with nitrogen, and, in the case of albuminous substances, with a small amount of sulphur.

Both the fats and saccharine matters are composed of certain combinations of carbon, hydrogen and oxygen. In the latter, the two last mentioned elements are united in the proportion that forms water, so that sugar and starch may be regarded as a combination of carbon with that fluid; while in the former, there is a smaller amount of oxygen. The fat, which is deposited as a layer immediately under the skin, serves to maintain the internal temperature of the body, by the fact of its being a bad conductor of heat. Fat also acts as a natural elastic cushion to various parts of the system, as, for instance, at the back of the eyeball, above the horny frog, and around the joints.

Dr. Carpenter remarks, that "the muscular, nervous, and glandular tissues are not composed of albuminous substances alone; they contain, as an essential constituent of their structure, a certain portion of fat, without which their composition would be imperfect, and the performance of their functions impossible." Such fat, he points out, must, therefore, be regarded as a tissue former, and not alone as a supplier of heat, although it will serve in the latter capacity on becoming broken up.

Waste of Tissue.—Every tissue of the body has a certain limited time for existence (a period which is directly shortened by exercise) after which it becomes broken up, and is absorbed into the blood. In order to remove these effete and deleterious matters, the system is provided with various excretory organs, such as the lungs, kidneys, &c. During respiration, the oxygen, which is absorbed from the air by the blood-vessels in the air-cells of the lungs, is carried through the various parts of the body, so that it may break up the effete tissue by combining with its carbon to form carbonic acid, which the blood, at the completion of its circuit, conveys to the lungs, to be by them expelled into the atmosphere.

A small amount of carbonic acid is eliminated by the skin.

We may roughly express the oxidation of the various tissues as follows :—

1. Fat + oxygen = carbon + hydrogen + oxygen + oxygen = carbonic acid + water.
2. Starch (or sugar) + oxygen = carbon + water + oxygen = carbonic acid + water.
3. Albumen + oxygen = carbon + hydrogen + nitrogen + oxygen + oxygen = carbonic acid + water + degraded nitrogenous matters, such as urea ($C_2 H_4 N_2 O_2$), &c.

The carbonic acid, as we have already seen, is got rid of by means of the lungs, which, together with the kidneys and skin, eliminate water; while the degraded nitrogenous matters, and broken up mineral substances are excreted by the kidneys.

Repair of Waste.—In order to supply material for the repair of the constant waste experienced by the system, the animal must have food which shall answer the following conditions:—

1. It must contain a proper proportion of the elements necessary for the building up of new tissue.
2. It must be digestible.
3. It must be of sufficient bulk for the stomach and intestines to act on it.
4. It must be palatable.

Grain, grasses, and roots, used in suitable proportions, answer the above conditions. As chemistry enables us to analyse these foods, we may, by its aid, approximately judge of their respective nutritive values. The following tables may serve as a guide to the reader:—

Analysis of Grains, &c.

	Nitrogenous matters.	Starch and Sugar.	Fatty matters.	Mineral matters.	Woody Fibre.	Water.
Indian Corn (Parkes) ...	9·9	64·5	6·7	1·4	4	13·5
Oats (Stonehenge) ...	11·4	53	·6	2·5	20	12·5
Wheat (Kensington) ...	11·64	68·74	......	1·75	2·6	15·27
Bran (ditto) ...	12·44	27·94	2·82	2·52	43·98	10·30
Barley (ditto) ...	13·2	56·9	2·6	2·8	11·5	12
Linseed (Stonehenge) ...	20	35	20	6	9	10
Gram (Parkes) } not including husks	22·70	63·18	3·76	2·60	......	11·39
Kúlthee (ditto) } not including husks	23·27	59·38	2·20	3·19	......	12·03
Urud (ditto) } not including husks	24·73	58·76	1·36	3·17	......	12·44
Peas (Stonehenge) ...	24	48	2	3	9	14
Beans (ditto) ...	26	40	2·5	3	14·5	14
Milk (Voelcker) ...	4·04	4.62	3·08	·71	......	87·55
Locust Meal (Kensington) ...	5·87	70·43	1·08	2·87	7·14	12·61
Rice (ditto) ...	6·40	75·70	......	·69	3·01	14·20
Rice husks (ditto) ...	4·18	44 94	1·10	13·18	26·80	9·80
Rye (ditto) ...	8·8	65·5	2	1·8	6·4	15·5
Bread (ditto) ...	8·8	57·6	......	1·1	......	32·5
Dates (ditto) ...	10 93	*63·40	·19	1·50	2·38	21·60
Eggs (ditto) ...	14·08	......	10·25	1·65	......	74·02
Brewers' Grains (ditto) ...	5·87	15·24	......	1·98	7·21	69·70

* Dates contain 56·41 per cent of sugar.

Analysis of Grasses, Roots, &c.

	Nitrogenous matters.	Starch and Sugar.	Fatty matters.	Mineral matters.	Woody Fibre.	Water.
Italian rye grass (Kensington) ...	2·45	14·11	·8	2·21	4·82	75·61
Saintfoin (ditto) ...	3·52	17·43	......	1·73	Included under starch.	77·32
Lucern (Seller and Stephens) ...	3·83	13·62	·82	3·04	8·74	69·95
Clover (ditto) ...	4·27	8·45	·69	1·82	3·76	81·01
Vetches (Kensington) } calculated dry	8·25	49·03	1·32	5·68	35·72	......
Hay (Voelcker) } calculated dry	9·88	48·09	2·99	7·24	31·80	......
Clover (Kensington) } calculated dry	12·90	35·07	3·39	7·58	41·06	......
Oat straw (ditto) ...	2·75	36·87	1·69	5·42	39·57	13·70
Wheat straw (ditto) ...	2·93	23·66	1·74	4·21	54·13	13·33
Barley straw (ditto) ...	4·43	8·21	1·36	4·26	66·54	15·20
Sugar cane (ditto) ...	2·19	8·44	2·55	·97	4·05	81·80
Carrots (Voelcker) ...	·7	7·7	·2	·9	3·5	87
Parsnips (ditto) ...	1·3	7·7*	·5	·1	7·5	82
Turnips (ditto) ...	1·1	4·5	·2	·7	2	91·5
Swedes (ditto) ...	1·5	6	.2	·7	2·1	89·5
Potatoes (Kensington) ...	2·3	18·7	......	1	3	75

* Parsnips contain 3·5 per cent of sugar.

In the foregoing table, the analysis of oats is that of good English corn, which, I would say, does not contain more than half the amount of woody fibre found in the Indian variety.

The nutritive value of bran is not in accordance with its chemical composition, owing to its indigestibility. This want of agreement is also apparent in other foods, notably in wheat and potatoes.

The nitrogenous matters contain from 15·4 to 16·5 per cent of nitrogen (Parkes).

Nitrogenous Food.—The natural waste of nitrogenous tissue is accelerated by exertion, though to a far lesser extent than is that of fat. From the analysis of the urine of men, taken while they were undergoing violent exertion, it was observed that there was but a small increase in the waste of nitrogenous products, which, as before remarked, are excreted by the kidneys. Experience, however, demonstrates the necessity, in such cases, of an adequate supply of nitrogen, as may be seen by the good results obtained from the addition to oats of beans—in England—or of gram, or *kúlthee*—in India—especially, when, from old age, or illness, the horse's powers of assimilation are diminished. Such a diet, however, should be carefully regulated, for an oversupply is most apt to upset the animal's digestion, and to poison his blood-mass by causing it to become filled with an excess of deleterious nitrogenous products, which the excretory organs will be unable to eliminate with sufficient rapidity. We may often witness the baneful effects —in the form of diarrhœa, filled legs, and a general "heated" state of the system—of the consumption of too much gram, or *kúlthee.*

An excess of nitrogenous food, such as gram, or *kúlthee,* seems to hasten the oxidation of fat, probably by inducing a fevered state of the system, in which the temperature of the body is raised above its normal degree. Hence we find that an excess of such food retards the process of getting an animal into a fat condition.

Fat, Starch, and Sugar in Food.—These constituents are, by the process of digestion, utilized in the formation of adipose tissue; the first named being directly absorbed, without undergoing any organic change. Its excess is most apt, especially during idleness, to cause derangement of the liver, from its accumulating to an injurious extent, in the cells of that organ; and also tends to produce fatty infiltration and degeneration of various tissues, rendering them unable to bear the strain of violent exertion. Too large a supply of sugar also acts in a similar, but in far more limited manner; while an excess of starch appears to exert little or no injurious effect; for what is not required, seems to be harmlessly expelled with the dung. Thus we see that the bad results of an excess of either fat, sugar, or starch are in a direct proportion to the ease with which they are assimilated. When an animal is in poor condition, the *value* of these foods is in the same ratio.

Nitrogenous matters are also capable of forming fat, for in them we find the necessary carbon, hydrogen, and oxygen. This process probably, takes place to a far slighter degree among the herbivora, than among the carnivora, whose bodily weight and internal temperature can be sustained on a diet of lean meat alone.

When long distance walking and swimming came into vogue a few years ago, it was thought that concentrated food, of a highly nitrogenous nature, was the most suitable for the athlete while attempting such feats; the fallacy of this was proved by experience, for it was found that incomparably greater trials of endurance were performed under a regimen rich in fat, than under the old system of training on lean meat and dry bread. This was notably shewn in the case of Gale, while walking 1,500 miles in 1,000 hours, for his diet consisted of ordinary meat, buttered toast and bread, eggs, &c. Weston, the pedestrian, was, I believe, one of the first to demonstrate, in England, the advantages of this system; Webb, too, was another instance. The Indian wrestlers, on the contrary, have for ages practiced what European physiologists are just beginning to understand. I am thoroughly convinced that the fact of modern feats of endurance, so totally eclipsing the performances done in former days, is mainly owing to a larger supply of fat and starch having been introduced into the diet of athletes. This lesson we should utilize in the case of hard-worked horses. Unfortunately our choice in the matter of food is here but small, when we are limited in the matter of expense, except in the case of linseed, which is a most suitable article; we might, however, in some cases, supplement it with milk, eggs, *ghi* (clarified butter), and *goor* (unrefined sugar).

We find that, for the maintenance of health, a man requires, in his food, a supply of fat as well as of starch, and that the former cannot be replaced altogether by the latter. The horse, it appears, is far more independent of a supply of fat in his diet, than is man; but whether it can be dispensed with altogether or not, is a question I am unable to answer. The fact, however, of a certain, though varying proportion of fat, in the natural food of the animal, indicates, I think, its value, if not its absolute necessity. In the daily diet, given by Dr. Parkes, for a man performing very laborious work, we find that the fat is to the starch and sugar, as one is to four; while the proportion for a horse, on a full supply of oats and hay, is about one to sixty.

In equine food, it appears that sugar may be entirely replaced by starch, though the converse of this does not hold good.

Heat Supply.—The constant oxidation of carbon and hydrogen—attended by the formation of carbonic acid and water—in the various tissues, is attended by the evolution of heat, which serves to sustain the internal temperature of the body at about 99·5° F. During exercise, there is a proportionate increase in the amount of tissue broken up by these chemical combinations taking place, but the greater portion of the excess of heat, appears to be utilized by its becoming converted into motion; for we find that after rapid movement, which is necessarily accompanied by considerable waste of tissue, there is but a very slight increase to the temperature of the body. This is in accordance with the generally accepted view, that heat is an allotropic form of motion.

Mineral Substances.—These, with the exception of common salt, are obtained in ample sufficiency from the various grasses; while corn contains them in a far smaller proportion; hence the necessity of the former food. The following analysis, taken from *The Composition of Foods, &c.*, compiled by Dr. Kensington, will give an idea of the proportions in which they are found:—

Ash of Grass.

Potash	25·40	Phosphoric acid	5·45
Lime	15·21	Sulphuric acid	7·08
Magnesia	5·30	Silicic acid	24·30
Soda	6·24	Chlorine	4·76
Oxide of iron	·18	Carbonic acid and loss ...	6·08
			100·00

The phosphates of lime and magnesia, the carbonate of lime and silica are the chief agents that give solidity to the bony skeleton. The phosphate and carbonate of soda "would seem to have as their chief purpose the maintenance of the alkalinity of the blood, on which depends not merely the solubility of its albumen, but the facility of its passage through the capillaries, and the readiness with which its combustive materials are oxidized, whilst they also increase the absorptive power of the serum for gasses, and thus play an important part in the respiratory process. The salts of potash appear to be specially required for the nutrition of the muscles and nerves, since they are largely present in the fluids and ashes of these tissues, but they probably exert the same general influence as those of soda......The presence of the earthy salts, on the other hand, would seem to have reference almost exclusively to the composition of the tissues, into which some of them enter very largely" (Carpenter). Iron is principally found in the red corpuscles of the blood, in the muscles, and in the hair.

Husk of Grain.—The office of the husk of grain appears to be to furnish mineral matters, and to give bulk to the food. It also seems, by mechanical irritation, to increase the vermicular motion of the bowels, in order to obviate the ill-consequences which might arise from the decomposition, in the intestines, of the unassimilated nitrogenous matters of the corn, a possibility likely to occur owing to the unstable nature of the compounds of nitrogen. Both from theory and practice we may safely conclude, that the husk should not be removed from the grain which the horse is to consume.

We may see, from the foregoing observations, that the working parts of the animal machine are formed of nitrogenous and mineral substances, with a small amount of fat; while the motor power is obtained from heat generated by the oxidation of fat, and also of the component parts of the machine itself.

Bulk in Food.—The fact of the large capacity of the horse's intestines indicates that his food should be of a bulky nature, so that they may be able to act properly on it by their wormlike (peristaltic) motion, which causes it to become thoroughly mixed with the intestinal juices, its various particles to be presented to the absorbants—which take up the nutrient matter—and the remainder to be expelled onwards. If this condition of bulk be not complied with, the digestive apparatus will get out of order, however accurately materials for bulding up tissue be supplied. Indigestible woody fibre—contained in large quantities in the various grasses—and unassimilated starch, chiefly serve the required purpose. That, within certain limits, the measure of a horse's appetite is by bulk and not by weight, is evidently due to the necessity the animal feels of having his intestines filled. We see the same craving for bulk evinced by human beings. "The Kamschatdales, for example, are in the habit of mixing earth or saw-dust with the train-oil, on which alone they are frequently reduced to live. The Veddahs or wild hunters of Ceylon, on the same principle, mingle the pounded fibres of soft and decayed wood with the honey on which they feed when meat is not to be had; and on one of them being asked the reason of the practice, he replied, 'I cannot tell you, but I know that the belly must be filled'" (Carpenter).

Selection of Food.—For all practical purposes, we need not consider grain beyond its use as a former of fat, and of nitrogenous tissues—such as the various muscular and nervous structures — while to give bulk to the food (except in the cases of horses getting as much oats as they can eat), and to supply the required mineral matters, we must principally depend on grass. As exercise directly increases the waste of tissue, we must add to the amount of grain according to the degree of labour, though, at the same time, allowing an unlimited supply of hay, in order to comply with the conditions just stated. The exceptions to this rule will be, when the horse is in a state of enforced idleness, when his appetite is in a depraved or abnormal condition, and when he is required for immediate work. When a horse's powers are fully taxed, he should be allowed as much hay and suitable corn as he chooses to consume. This now leads us to the pertinent question, "what proportion should the nitrogenous matter in grain bear to the starchy constituents?" From the teaching of experience, which here can alone direct us, we may learn that for moderate work, it should not exceed that which is contained in oats, namely, 10 to 47 (about). To find the maximum, we may assume a diet of four parts of oats and one part of beans — as given in England to hardworked animals; this will give us the proportion of 10 to 38 (about).

To determine the maximum amount of nitrogenous food, I think, we may safely assume it to be about that contained in 20 lbs. of oats, namely, 2¼ lbs. (about). If we are forced, by circumstances, to use a grain, such as gram, or *kúlthee,* which is too rich in nitrogen, we should do so at the expense of the starch, but should, on no account, exceed the amount of nitrogen already laid down, for if we do so, the excess will tend to produce the derangements of the system, which have been already mentioned.

Respecting the supply of fat, I am unable to say anything more definite than I have done in the previous pages of this chapter. Dr. Parkes' proposition, that "if men are undergoing great exertion, they take more food, and if they can obtain it, the increase is especially in the classes of albuminates and fats," holds equally well with regard to horses.

Hay and Grass.—We may consider these two to be identically the same food, except that the former contains a less proportion of water than the latter.

I have previously argued that a horse should get a full supply of hay under all circumstances, except when he is unable to take sufficient exercise.

A horse—omitting exceptional cases—evinces a marked preference for corn compared to hay; hence we may assume that, when he turns from the former to the latter, he does so from the natural prompting of an instinct, which is intended by nature to guide him in the selection of the food most suitable for the requirements of his system. We need hardly dwell on the not uncommon folly of stinting a horse of his hay, when the object is to get him to eat as much corn as possible, in order to enable him to sustain violent and continued exertion, such as that demanded during the training of race-horses, &c. I have always found that such animals eat more corn and digest it better when their supply of hay is unlimited at all times, than when it is curtailed, and especially so when they are deprived of it during feeding hours. The idea, that a trainer, or owner, can tell to a pound, how much hay his hard-worked horse should eat, is too palpably absurd. The case of corn is very different, for a horse, unless his powers are fully taxed, is almost always prone to eat too much of it, while its bad effects are patent to the most careless observer. Colonel Sir F. Fitzwygram justly remarks that, "practically it will be found that horses, which are not limited as regards oats, will not usually consume above 6 lbs. of hay per diem." Surely no one could say that this was an inordinate amount? As regards training, I have often been met with the objection that horses would gorge themselves, and would even eat their bedding, unless muzzled; but I have never found this to occur, when a full supply of oats has been given, although I have had several horses in training that came to me with the character of being insatiable gluttons.

I desire to lay considerable stress on the subject of allowing horses hay during feeding hours, as I have always found this practice to be attended with the best results, for not alone is the condition of bulk complied with, but also irritation to the alimentary canal, resulting from the presence of the stimulating food, is avoided, as much as possible, by the corn becoming diluted by the hay. To see how reasonable this practice is, we need but apply the case to ourselves with respect to the meat and vegetables we consume at our meals.

Green Meat.—Although the necessity of a supply of *fresh vegetables*, as a part of human food, is clearly recognised, still, up to the present time, physiologists have been unable to explain the *rationale* of the fact, and have been obliged to accept it simply as a result of experience. In the same manner we find that "green meat" is almost equally as indispensable for horses. This is especially the case when the hay, which is used, has been subjected to a process of fermentation, which gives it a brown appearance, and often increases its sweetness, although it diminishes its value. This method of curing hay is little pursued in India, where an ample supply of *doob* grass will fairly fulfil the conditions supplied by "green meat" and ordinary hay.

Variety in Food.—As far as my experience goes, I have been unable to notice any marked good arising from a change of food, unless when the new article of diet contained elements of nutrition deficient in the other.

Salt—Is the only necessary food, that is not supplied in sufficient quantity by the grain, grass, and water consumed by the animal. A moderate excess of it can, in nowise, prove injurious, for it will be speedily eliminated by the kidneys, after the system has taken up sufficient for its own requirements. It furnishes the elements for the supply of the hydro-chloric acid, which is a constituent of the gastric juice. It also plays a most important part in the whole nutrition of the body. "It was demonstrated by Boussingault, that when, of two sets of oxen, one was allowed the unrestricted use of salt, whilst the other was as far as possible deprived of its use, a marked contrast was observable in the course of a few weeks between them, and manifestly to the advantage of the former. The desire for common salt on the part of animals and man is extremely powerful, leading the former, especially if they be vegetable feeders, to traverse great distances to reach saline deposits." (Carpenter.)

Relations of Cold, Heat, and Clothing to Food.—When the temperature of the surrounding air falls much below its normal degree, a proportionate increase of starch and fat, to keep up the natural temperature of the body, should be made to the food of the animal, if it be unsupplied with warm clothing, which, by preventing radiation, supplements the action of the fatty layer that lies immediately underneath the skin. Hence a judicious addition of clothing may be practically regarded as an addition to the food; so that, when it cannot be made, the latter ought to be given. In hot weather, the animal will naturally require less food.

Mastication and Digestion.—The long hairs about the horse's muzzle serve him as feelers in the selection of the food, which his lips convey into his mouth, aided, when the fodder offers some resistance, by the *nippers* (incisor teeth). The mouthful is then conveyed to the grinders, and is ground by them into a pulp. During this operation it becomes mixed with saliva, which, under the stimulus of the food, flows into the mouth from the different salivary glands. This secretion contains the active principle *ptyalin*—a species of ferment—whose office is to convert starch into dextrine (a kind of mucilaginous starch) and subsequently into grape sugar, in which form it is absorbed by the system. "A large proportion of this albuminous principle is present in the saliva of the horse, but only traces of it exist in that of man" (Carpenter). The amount is proportional to the hardness and dryness of the fodder. Lassaigne gives, from experiment, the following results:—

100 parts of	dry hay	requires	406	parts of saliva.
„	barley	„	186	„
„	oats	„	113	„
„	grass	„	49	„

"Bernard was led to suggest that the submaxillary gland ministers to the sense of taste, whilst the parotid is connected with mastication, and the sublingual with deglutition. The size of the parotid in animals is proportionate to the degree in which the mastication of their food is performed. It is large in the horse, which lives on comparatively dry food, less in carnivora, and still less in the aquatic mammals, as the seal. It is absent in birds which swallow their food whole." (Carpenter.)

The presence of saliva in the food materially aids

its digestion in the stomach. "Among the experiments are those of Spallanzani and Reamur, who found that food inclosed in perforated tubes, and introduced into the stomach of an animal, was more quickly digested when it had been previously impregnated with saliva than when it was moistened with water. Dr. Wright also found that if the œsophagus [gullet] of a dog is tied, and food mixed with water alone is placed in the stomach, the food will remain undigested though the stomach may secrete abundant acid fluid, but if the same fluid is mixed with saliva, and the rest of the experiment similarly performed, the food is readily digested." (Kirkes.)

Saliva is alkaline, gastric juice acid, while the pancreatic juice and bile are both alkaline. This alternate character seems to have been given to these fluids, so as to regulate their action.

The frothy nature of saliva seems to aid digestion, for "the numerous air bubbles for which saliva is remarkable have their special purpose; since the presence of atmospheric air in the stomach is accessory to digestion." (Leared.)

I submit that the foregoing observations indicate, as a general rule, the advisability of giving grain in a dry state.

The presence of salt in the food excites the flow of saliva into the mouth; hence, if boiled, or steeped food be used, it should be given mixed with that condiment; because, owing to the moist and soft state of the grain, a deficient amount of saliva will be secreted.

Having reached the stomach—whose capacity is from

3 to $3\frac{1}{2}$ gallons—the food becomes mixed with the gastric juice, whose flow at first is slow. This secretion is liable to be checked by violent exercise, or by the stomach becoming unduly distended. If it be largely diluted with water, its action will be arrested, until the excess of that fluid be absorbed. Cold also stops the performance of its functions, for it will not act at a temperature much below blood heat. A moderate supply of hot spices stimulates its secretion. When the supply or action of the gastric juice—which is a natural antiseptic —is checked, the food, that is in the stomach at the time, is most apt to become decomposed, with the probable result of indigestion, flatulent colic, and even rupture of the stomach, caused by the evolution of gas. Hence we may conclude that horses ought not to be watered soon after being fed, and that they should not be given large supplies of boiled food, which is very bulky in comparison to the amount of nutriment it contains, while it can be rapidly swallowed. Besides, exciting but a small secretion of saliva, it arrives in the stomach in an unprepared state, and is consequently liable to become decomposed, before the gastric juice can properly act on it.

The antiseptic properties of gastric juice is well shewn by the immunity with which many races of men eat putrid flesh and fish.

The active principle of gastric juice—*pepsine*—converts the nitrogenous matters of the food into a soluable form—*peptone*—and also serve to split up the fat into a state of fine division, by dissolving the nitrogenous envelopes, which enclose the globules. When the food—now called *chyme*—leaves the stomach and enters into the small intestine, it becomes mixed with bile and pancreatic juice which flow from a common duct. The secretion from the pancreas (sweetbread) is very similar in its nature to saliva, whose action, in converting starch and cane sugar into grape sugar, it completes. It also, by virtue of its alkaline nature, makes an emulsion, or soap, with the fat contained in the chyme, which consequently assumes a white appearance, and is then termed *chyle*. The particles of fat are thus split up into a very fine state of division, so as to be readily absorbed. The bile acts as a natural purge, the bowels becoming constipated when it is deficient in quantity; it also, by reason of its antiseptic properties, prevents decomposition of the ingesta, prior to their being expelled. In the absence of bile, deleterious gasses are evolved in the intestines, and are absorbed into the system, to the detriment of the health of the animal; in such cases the dung has a foul smell. Bile is constantly being excreted by the liver. We find that certain of the higher animals, such as man, are provided with a gall-bladder, into which this fluid collects, to be poured out into the intestines during the process of digestion, which is, in these cases, one intended by nature to take place at certain intervals. The horse, however, possess no gall-bladder, which fact clearly indicates that he should be, more or less, constantly supplied with food. The small capacity of his stomach and large size of his intestines point to the small thing.

On leaving the small intestine, which is about 72 feet long, the food becomes collected into a capacious *cul-de-sac*—the cæcum—formed by the large intestine, whose length is about 20 feet. The cæcum appears to be a kind of supplementary stomach, in which is collected the pulpy mass of still unassimilated food, mixed with the water, which the stomach and small intestines failed to take up. Here the remaining nutritive particles are dissolved out and absorbed. The cæcum can contain about 7½ gallons of fluid.

Functions performed by the Blood.—As the nutritive part of the food becomes changed into forms capable of being assimilated, it becomes gradually taken up by the minute vessels called *absorbants* that line the interior of the stomach and intestines, and is conveyed into the blood, which ramifies through the various tissues of the body, supplying them with materials for repair. Thus we see that the blood acts as the vehicle for removing the products resulting from the waste of tissue, and also for furnishing the elements required in the building up of new structures.

Appetite.—Appetite serves two purposes—(1) When the system requires new elements for repair, it prompts the animal to eat, so as to obtain them from his food. But, in order to avoid excess, the process of feeding should be carried on slowly. On this subject, Dr. Carpenter remarks—"To eat *when* we are hungry, is an evidently natural disposition; but to eat *as long as* we are hungry, may not always be prudent. Since the feeling of hunger does not depend so much upon the state of fulness or emptiness of the stomach, as upon the condition of the general system, it appears evident that the ingestion of food cannot *at once* produce the effect of dissipating it, though it will do so after a short time; so that, if we eat with undue rapidity, we may continue swallowing food long after we have taken as much as will really be required for the wants of the system; and every superfluous particle is not merely useless, but injurious." These observations apply equally well to horses as they do to ourselves. (2) Appetite guides the animal in its selection of food suitable for the repair of the waste that is going on at the time. As a general rule, when a horse's powers are fully taxed, he should be allowed as much corn and hay as he chooses to eat, provided always they are both of a suitable nature. The instinctive selection of food is well seen in the case of men who have to work hard, such as navvies and sailors, for they will eat, with benefit, a quantity of animal food and fat, from which a sedentary person would turn with loathing.

Influence of an artificial state of Life.—The horse is intended by nature to travel considerable distances when grazing; while his natural food is one of large bulk, containing a comparatively small amount of nourishment, his digestive organs being specially adapted for its consumption. The requirements of civilization, however, interfere most materially with these conditions. At times, long protracted rest deprives the animal of the exercise which is so essential to his health, and which he, in a state of nature, would be obliged to take in the pursuit of food. On the other hand, in order to develop his physicial system to its utmost extent, he is supplied with food of a far more concentrated form than he was naturally intended to consume. Hence we are unable to trust to the animal's appetite alone as a sure guide in the selection of food in all cases, so must regulate it according to the indications afforded us by the study of the anatomy and functions of his system.

Preparation of Food.—Oats, gram, Indian corn, barley, wheat, and rice in husk (*dhan, or paddy*) should be bruised or broken before being given to the horse, in order to oblige him to masticate them properly, so that the grain may become thoroughly saturated with saliva. If given in a whole state, it is liable to be swallowed, on its outer surface alone becoming moistened.

Heat, whether by the process of boiling or parching, causes the grains of starch in corn to burst, and the albumen to coagulate, so that the different digestive fluids are then able to penetrate easily through its substance. The objection to boiling is that it causes the food to become saturated with water, which decreases its digestibility, and greatly increases its bulk. Parching, however, is free from any such drawback, and may be most advantageously applied to the preparation of barley and wheat. The husk of the first mentioned grain has, to a more or less extent, an irritating effect on the intestines of the horse, and probably possesses some acrid principle. The process of parching not alone renders the grain porous, but also deprives the husk of its objectionable properties. The husk of linseed, *kúlthee*, and *úrud* is so hard that they require to the boiled before being given.

CHAPTER V.

On Watering Horses.

THE blood being the source from which the different tissues obtain materials for repair and development, and the vehicle which conveys away the effete products resulting from the constant waste that goes on in the animal economy, the whole question of nutrition depends on supplying the system with materials suitable for preserving that fluid in its normal and healthy condition.

The proportion of water in the blood varies from 700 to 790 parts in 1,000. Its presence is essential to the performance of the various functions. If its supply be curtailed, the secretions that are indispensable to the process of digestion are checked either wholly or in part, because the glands are unable to obtain a sufficiency of water from the blood. If, on the contrary, more water be drank than is needed for the requirements of the system, the excess is quickly eliminated by the kidneys, skin, and lungs, without doing any harm. We may conclude, therefore, that a full supply of water, given a short time before feeding, is essential for the proper digestion of food.

The stomach is furnished with a vast number of blood vessels, whose office is to absorb water for the supply of the glands that secrete the gastric juice.

As the amount of the secretion, necessary for digestion, varies from 10 to 20 gallons daily (Brinton), and as about 99 per cent of it is composed of water, we find that the process of digestion, during the day, demands the outpouring of double or treble the amount of water for the gastric juice, than there is blood in the whole body. Now, as this water is derived directly from the blood, its adequate supply can only be obtained by the constant reabsorbtion, in the stomach, of the watery portion of the effete gastric juice, as well as of that of other fluids which may be present. Considering the enormous quantity of water required for the secretion of the gastric juice, we may accept the fact that drinking a small quantity of water with the food is not alone free from objection, but may be actually beneficial. On this point we may safely trust to the instinct of the animal in leaving a supply of water before him while he is eating, provided always that he has had a full opportunity of drinking shortly before being fed.

If (as we have seen in the preceeding chapter), while digestion be going on, a large amount of water be taken into the stomach, it will dilute the gastric juice to an extent that will probably arrest its action until the excess of water becomes absorbed. During this interval, decomposition of the food, with consequent derangement of the digestion, may ensue, followed, perhaps, by colic, or even by rupture of the stomach, owing to the pressure exerted by the evolved gas. Hence, we may conclude that the horse should be watered *before* being fed. But if, as in case of want of time, this precaution has not been observed, only small quantities, with reasonable intervals to allow of its absorption, should be allowed; say 10 "go downs" at intervals of five minutes, assuming 20 "go downs" to the gallon. Considering the quickness with which a horse digests his food, I think we may assume that he may be watered, 2½ hours after being fed, without any ill consequences. The reason that soft is better than hard water for horses—a fact known to every careful stableman—is that the freer this fluid is of impurities, possessing astringent properties, the more readily will it become absorbed into the blood.

Respecting the celerity with which water is assimilated, I cannot do better than quote the following extract from Seller and Stephens' *Physiology of the Farm*:—"That water passes with extreme rapidity from the stomach of the horse, as from that of mammals in general, is apparent from the well known fact that a horse will drink within a few minutes a much greater quantity than what his stomach can contain. It is commonly supposed that the excess passes at once into the highest part of the small intestines, namely the duodenum. But this supposition is hardly necessary, for it is proved that absorption of thin fluids takes place from the inner surface of the stomach with an almost incredible rapidity. This fact is established by many experiments; and moreover, that substances dissolved in the water taken in have been found in the urine within an incredibly brief period." The obvious lesson these considerations teach us is, that we should not be chary in allowing a horse to drink when he wants to do so, except indeed after feeding.

One of the popular errors about watering horses is, that they should be stinted of water for some hours before doing fast work, on the plea that it affects their wind. As the water, which becomes part and parcel of the blood, cannot by any possibility impede the organs of breathing, it follows that its unabsorbed portion alone can effect them; but we have just seen that the whole of the water is taken up with extreme rapidity, so that, after a short time, there is none left in the stomach or intestines to cause any impediment. On the contrary, stinting a horse of water will directly affect his wind, for the blood will then gradually become thickened, and, if the animal be put to violent exertion, will fail to circulate through the lungs with requisite freedom; besides that, the action of the heart will become impeded, and the whole nutrition of the system interfered with.

If a horse has been deprived of water for a considerable time, we should exercise some caution in watering him, lest he may drink a larger quantity than can readily be taken up, for the unabsorbed portion—especially if the fluid be given cold—may cause serious derangement. When a horse is heated by exercise, his system will absorb water far more readily than when he has cooled down; hence under the former condition there is far less risk in giving a liberal supply, than under the latter. Colonel Sir F. Fitzwygram remarks:—"It is a somewhat singular fact that horses may be watered with safety almost immediately after their return from work, even though somewhat heated." And points out that there is then far less risk of chill from horses drinking cold water, than when the system has begun to flag; and that, in the latter case, the water should be made slightly tepid, or a bucket of gruel should be substituted for the cold fluid. As the application of cold causes contraction of the muscular coats of the blood vessels, so does it retard the absorption of water which is taken into the stomach.

When a horse goes through violent and continued exertion without drinking, the amount of water in his blood falls below its normal quantity. If this loss is considerable, the thickened blood will be unable to circulate through the lungs with its wonted facility; in fact, more or less congestion takes place, while the action of the heart becomes laboured in its efforts to pump this abnormally dense fluid through the system. If a horse, in this state, be given a couple of gallons of water, they will be absorbed at once into the blood, and will restore it, more or less completely, to its normal fluidity; while the action of the lungs and heart will be almost instantaneously relieved, and the feelings of distress will rapidly subside. But had water been denied until the horse had cooled down, the prolonged distress, even if the congestion had passed off with no bad results, would undoubtedly tell on the animal's condition and spirits. In accordance with this principle, I have adopted, with the best results, the practice of giving half a bucket of water to race-horses I have had in training, immediately after their gallops.

Those who have had to ride long distances, in hot countries, are well aware of the advisability of allowing their mounts to drink frequently during a journey, at any good water near which they may pass, even when the horse is bathed in perspiration.

In Northern India the *ecka* (a small two-wheeled trap) ponies, which average about 13 hands 1 inch in height, frequently travel 50 to 60 miles a day over unmetalled roads during the hottest weather, when the noontide heat often exceeds 120° in the shade. Such performances can only be accomplished by watering the ponies every 7 or 8 miles: the system pursued being that they get at each bait from 1 to 2lbs. of *suttoo* mixed in a couple of quarts of water. This is in accordance with the practice—generally adopted by stokers and firemen on board steamers—of mixing oatmeal with the water they drink. These men, who are exposed to intense heat, and consequently are obliged to drink very large quantities of water, experience the greatest advantage from this precaution.

In the stable, I think the best system is to allow a constant supply of water: a practice which is not alone beneficial to "washy" horses that scour easily, to roarers and to broken-winded animals, but also is particularly well calculated to prevent and to cure the pernicious habit of wind-sucking.

CHAPTER VI.

Practical Rules for Feeding and Watering Horses.

FROM the theoretical considerations detailed in the two preceding chapters, and from the results of experience, we may draw the following conclusions :—

1. The horse's corn should be given dry; except when the grain—such as linseed, *kúlthee*, &c.—is too hard, in its natural condition, to be properly masticated; when, from old age and other causes, the animal's powers of chewing are impaired; and when the appetite has to be humoured in sickness.

The only way I can account for the practice—now happily falling into disuse—of steeping grain in water, before giving it to the horse, is that it is done with the idea of causing the grain to swell, as much as possible, before entering the stomach, in order that it may not do so after arriving there, especially, on the eventuality of the animal being subsequently supplied with water. Those who adopt such a precaution, entirely ignore the fact that it is the evolution of gas—resulting from the decomposition of the food—which produces flatulent colic and rupture of the stomach, and not any swelling of the grain, which, if it be given dry—as we have previously seen—will become saturated with a greater quantity of saliva than that of its own bulk, before it even reaches the stomach. The danger of a horse choking himself—if the stableman take the most ordinary precautions—is purely imaginary.

2. The different grains, before being given to the horse, may be prepared as follows :—

Oats and wheat, bruised.

Gram, Indian corn, and rice in husk, roughly broken; the last mentioned may be previously parched.

Barley, parched and roughly broken. If the parching be dispensed with, this grain should at first be cautiously given to the animal, as it is then apt to "scour" him.

3. The following forms a list of Indian foods, calculated to maximum amounts :—

1.	Gram or kúlthee	...	10lbs.
2.	Gram	...	7 „
	Bran	...	5 „
3.	Barley	...	17 „
4.	Barley	...	5½ „
	Gram	...	7 „
5.	Oats	...	20 „
6.	Oats	...	14 „
	Gram, kúlthee or úrud	...	5 „
7.	Indian corn	...	7½ „
	Gram	...	7 „
8.	Indian corn	...	6 „
	Gram	...	5 „
	Bran	...	4 „
9.	Gram	...	3½ „
	Barley (parched)	...	4 „
	Indian corn	...	5 „
	Bran	...	4 „
10	Oats	...	6lbs.
	Gram	...	5 „
	Bran	...	2 „
	Linseed	...	1 lb.
11.	Oats	...	9 lbs.
	Gram	...	6 „
12.	Gram	...	6 „
	Rice, in husk	...	10 „
13.	Gram	...	5 „
	Rice, in husk	...	8 „
	Bran	...	4 „
14.	Wheat	...	4 „
	Gram	...	7 „
15.	Wheat	...	4 „
	Indian corn	...	4 „
	Bran	...	4 „
	Gram	...	4 „

I have assumed Indian oats to contain about a quarter less nutriment than English corn.

Bearing in mind the difficulty there often is in procuring certain grains in many parts of India, I have varied the proportions, so as to suit horse owners who have but a limited supply of particular grains, such as oats for instance.

The reader may rely on these foods being suitable in practice, as well as correct in theory. Nos. 6, 8, 9, and 10 are those I would specially recommend. The first mentioned is the best for hard-worked horses, such as those used in racing; No. 10 for similar animals when low in condition; while the other two can be very generally procured, and at a cheap rate. The amounts are intended for a full sized Waler, or English horse. During ordinary work, we may give from two-thirds to three-fourths of them. One-half will be sufficient during idleness.

4. A 13 hand pony will eat about half as much as a large horse; while an Arab will, as a rule, require about 4lbs. less than the latter.

5. The amount of grain, given to the animal, should be proportionate to the work he is called upon to perform, remembering, always, that there is a constant waste of tissue going on which demands repair by food.

6. When a horse is comparatively idle, his food may consist of one-third to one-half of bran, and two-thirds to one-half of oats, Indian corn, barley, or *paddy*—in preference to gram or *kúlthee*, — say 8 or 10 lbs. altogether. The same practice may, with advantage, be observed during the hot weather.

7. Horses should not be allowed to run down in condition, even when out of work, for in India, especially, it takes a long time to put flesh on them again.

8. When a horse's powers are fully taxed, he should get as much *suitable* corn as he may choose to eat.

9. The corn should never be increased to an extent that will cause irritation of the intestines, which will be evinced by the dung becoming loose and sticky, on the contrary, it should be fairly formed, brittle, and devoid of bad smell. When gram and *kúlthee* alone are used, these conditions cannot be properly complied with. The offensive odour is due to torpor of the liver, while the diarrhœa is generally the result of an effort of the system to expel an excess of nutritive matter, which is absolutely deleterious to the health. In such cases, withdrawal of the corn, bran mashes, and, may be, a mild purgative are indicated.

10. When the amount of grain is limited, say to 8 or 9 lbs, and when the animal has to do hard work, gram, or *kúlthee* are more suitable than other grains.

11. Foods rich in fat and sugar, such as linseed, Indian corn, milk, *goor*, &c., are the most suitable for putting a lean horse into lusty condition.

12. Horses that get a full amount of corn should, as a rule, get a bran, or a bran and linseed mash once or twice a week—say on Wednesday and Saturday nights. It will tend to remove any irritation of the intestines caused by the grain.

13. In cold weather, if horses be not warmly clad, they should have an increase to the amount of their corn.

14. A horse should have a constant supply of salt, say two ounces daily; or he may be allowed a lump of rock salt in his stall.

15. If boiled food be given, salt should be previously mixed with it.

16. A horse's corn should be given at frequent and regular intervals. Say as follows, supposing 9 lbs. to be the daily amount :—

5 A.M.	..	...	1 lb.
8-30 „	...	...	2 lbs.
12-30 P.M.	...	...	2 „
4 „	...	...	1 lb.
8 „	...	...	3 lbs.
	Total	...	9 lbs.

17. When an animal's powers of digestion are impaired, spices or condiments may be given, in order to stimulate the system to take up an increased amount of nutriment from the food. Such articles have not the slightest dietetic value of their own.

18. In order to induce the horse to eat slowly, it is desirable to feed him from a broad box, or trough, placed not much above the level of the ground. On the bottom of the box, the corn may be spread out in a thin layer.

19. Greedy feeders may have a quantity of chopped hay mixed through their corn.

20. A horse should not be worked for at least an hour and a half after feeding.

21. A horse should always have a supply of hay, or dried grass before him while he is eating his corn, so that, by inducing him to vary his food, he may not consume it in too concentrated a form.

22. Horses, that are inclined to "scour," should have some hay given to them before being fed.

23. Unless in cases of enforced idleness, depraved appetite, &c., a horse should have as much hay, or dried grass, as he may choose to eat.

24. If procurable, the grass which is called *doob* in Bengal, and *hurryalee* in Madras, should be used in preference to all other kinds. It ought to be dried a day or two in the sun, before being given.

25. If possible, a horse should get daily, at least 2 or 3 lbs of green food, such as lucern, carrots, &c., as the time of the year may permit.

26. On a journey, a horse should be baited about every three hours, giving him, say, a couple of gallons of water—if he chooses to drink it—followed by about 2 lbs. of corn, with a little hay each time; or the corn may consist of *suttoo* mixed in the water.

27. The best plan, regarding the watering of horses, is to allow them a constant supply of that fluid in their stalls.

28. If this cannot be done, they should be watered *before* being fed, at least twice a day.

29. Immediately after violent exertion, a horse should have a moderate amount of water to drink, say, one gallon, and, if he be thirsty, another gallon in five or six minutes.

30. However hot and perspiring he may be, he should get this water *at once, before he cools down;* but if this cannot be done, he should be given a smaller amount, and some more at intervals of five minutes or so.

31. The "chill" need not be taken off water, except when the horse is very thirsty and the water unusually cold.

32. On long journeys, a horse should be allowed to drink very frequently, in fact, whenever he wants to do so. Taking an immoderate amount, at one time, should of course be guarded against.

33. Soft water should be used in preference to hard.

CHAPTER VII.

Grooming and Stable Routine.

ON THE THEORY OF GROOMING—WASHING THE HORSE—CLIPPING—GROOMING—DRESSING THE MANE AND TAIL—TAPEEING—MOULTING OF THE COAT—CARE OF THE FEET AND LEGS—TRIMMING THE MANE AND TAIL—BOTS—STABLE ROUTINE.

On the Theory of Grooming.—The skin of the horse is composed of two layers. The inner layer, or true skin, is tough and elastic, and is provided with nerves and blood vessels. In it exist a vast number of narrow, minute depressions—hair follicles—which secrete the hair that covers the body. Alongside each hair, where it pierces the skin, a small tube opens, which gives exit to an oily fluid, whose office is to keep the hair and skin soft and pliable. Where there is considerable motion of the skin, as at the back of the pasterns, these oil tubes exist independently of the presence of hair at the part. There are also a great number of other tubes which proceed from the glands that secrete the perspiration, and convey it to the skin which they pierce. The sweat of the horse is composed of a mixture of these two secretions, the former giving it a greasy character when he is fat, the preponderance of the latter, a watery appearance, when he is in poor condition, or when "drawn fine."

The inner layer secretes the outer skin in the form of scales, more or less—according to their distance from the surface—glued together. It lines the openings of the oil and sweat tubes, and surrounds each hair. Its presence affords protection to the skin and checks the outpouring of the oil and perspiration. Hence, when horses are turned out in the open, without adequate clothing, they should, on no account, be groomed. This process is intended to remove as much of the outer or scarf-skin as possible, and, by friction, to stimulate the secretion of the oily and watery fluids; the former of which protects the skin from the action of water, and also assists in maintaining the internal temperature of the body by rendering the coat bright and glossy,—a condition that checks the radiation, as well as the absorption of heat. Hence a horse, with a polished skin, will not be as liable to be chilled by wet or cold, nor to be as unduly heated by the rays of the sun, as he would be, were his coat dull. This immunity, however, will only last for a few hours, or until the weather affects the hair.

The skin acts as an assistant to the lungs in giving off carbonic acid gas, and thus aids in purifying the blood. The cold produced by the evaporation of perspiration materially assists in lowering the temperature of the body to its normal degree, when it has been raised beyond it by exercise. Hence the necessity of the free secretion of perspiration by the skin of hard-worked horses.

Apart from the foregoing considerations, we may see that the fact of the skin being in a healthy state will tend to induce a like condition of the stomach, intestines, and air passages; for the skin is continuous with the mucous membranes which line these organs; hence, owing to the sympathy which exists both between the various portions of these respective surfaces, and between themselves, we find that, in cases of derangement of the stomach, &c., the coat becomes dull and unthrifty. In like manner, a return to health will be marked by an improvement in the state of the skin, whose affections are more or less followed by an impaired condition of the digestive apparatus. Experience, as well as physiology, teaches us how much the horse's general well-being is dependant on his skin being clean, well polished, and healthy. (For further reference, see Professor Williams's *Veterinary Surgery* under heading *Laminitis.*)

From these considerations we may readily see how important the process of grooming is to the maintainance of high condition in the horse.

I may briefly sum up the objects, sought to be obtained by good grooming, as follows:—1, to remove the scaly part of the outer skin, in order to allow of ready exit to the fluids that flow from the oil and sweat glands; 2, to stimulate, by friction, these glands to increased activity; 3, to determine blood to the surface of the body, so as to relieve the internal organs; 4, to remove all superfluous hair, whose presence would tend to check evaporation from the skin; 5, to induce a healthy state of the skin itself, in which the mucous membranes of the digestive and respiratory organs will tend to participate.

The skin of the well-groomed horse will be in the best possible condition to play its allotted part, when the system is called upon to perform violent exertion, but not to resist the continued effect of cold during a state of inactivity; hence such an animal should, when he is at rest, be provided with an adequate supply of warm clothing to make up for the loss of protection, afforded by the scaly part of the outer skin, and by the increased amount of hair possessed by him in an ungroomed condition.

Washing the Horse.—This practice is most injurious, for it not alone removes the natural oil from the skin, thereby rendering the coat dull, but is also apt to produce chill, which, I need hardly say, is the fruitful source of many equine ailments. Water has no power to remove the scaly part of the outer skin, its effect being confined alone to any dust or mud that may have fallen on the coat. Our best authorities, Colonel Sir F. Fitz-wygram among the rest, are unanimous in condemning the custom of washing the animal. Mud-fever,—a form of inflammation of the skin, which extends more or less over the legs, and sometimes over the lower surface of the abdomen—is caused by this practice. It is a common complaint in England, though rare in India. Professor Williams writes as follows on this subject: "It will be generally known that the winter of 1871 was a very wet one, and consequently mud-fever, a very prevalent disease. Speaking one day to a large cab-proprietor and job-master in this city, and casually referring to the prevalence of sore legs from this disease, he informed me that none of his cab-horses were so affected, whilst his job-horses were all more or less so. The reasons he gave were that the cab-horses were never groomed at night; that they came in at all times, dirty and wet, were turned into their stables, but never groomed till the morning; the dirt was then dry, and was brushed off; whilst his best horses (out on job in gentlemen's carriages), which came in early and had their legs washed, dressed, bandaged, and otherwise made comfortable, were all affected with sore legs."

Mr. Broad, of Bath, alluding to the same disease, states, "I have never known it to occur when the mud has been allowed to become dry, and then well brushed off, without the application of water."

The following extract is from an editorial article which appeared in *The Field* of 25th December, 1875: "In many large establishments, where 'cracked heels' and 'grease' were constantly present among the horses while the system of washing the legs with warm or cold water was in vogue, a discontinuance of the practice of washing has been followed by the entire cessation of these annoying diseases."

The use of warm water, especially to the legs and feet, is still more objectionable than that of cold, for the heat is very apt to stimulate the oil glands, which lie deep in the true skin, to an abnormal degree of activity, while subsequent cold, brought on by evaporation, or by a current of air, may cause contraction of the superficial extremities of the oil tubes, so that the exit of the fluid may become obstructed; a state that will probably be followed by inflammation, as may be evinced by "cracked heels," "grease," or "mud-fever."

Clipping.—The presence of a thick covering of hair will check the free evaporation of perspiration from the skin; hence the horse that is intended for fast work, should, if his coat be long, have it clipped. If he be used in all weathers, it is advisable to leave the hair about his legs and pasterns untouched, for it will afford protection from chill to the skin of these parts, which is specially liable to inflammation. By doing this, the amount of perspiration given off by the system will be scarcely, if at all, affected. "With reference to the clipping of horses, I am of opinion that it is a great advantage; they work better after being clipped; thrive on less food; are less liable to disease; are stronger, healthier, and more cheerful; and when sick, recover in a much shorter time. It is not my intention to discuss the question; I merely wish to counteract a ridiculous idea propounded by Mr. Gamgee, that clipping is injurious to the horse.

"I strongly recommend the Irish method of clipping, namely, clipping all parts of the body except the legs. The hair that is left on the legs protects them from the irritation of wet and dirt; and when horses are used for hunting purposes, from the penetration of thorns, &c." (Williams.)

Horses in India, that are thoroughly groomed, well fed, and warmly clothed, will rarely have a coat long enough to require clipping.

As the bristles that grow about a horse's muzzle, eyes, and chin act as feelers—replacing to some extent the want of hands—they should not be cut or pulled out; the hair which lines the external ear should also be allowed to remain untouched.

Grooming.—Before grooming, the horse may be tied up by side reins running from rings fixed, about six feet high, at each side of the doorway of the stall, and attached to the rings of the watering bridle.

If he kicks badly, his hind legs may be confined by a short hobble, called by syces *mujuma*, placed on his hind pasterns. The use of heel ropes is apt to strain him.

When the horse returns from exercise in clothing, he should be tied up, his hood removed, and his neck and throat scraped, if there be any sweat visible.

The space between his jaws should be carefully dried with a dry cotton rubber, while a man on each side, with a fresh straw or hemp wisp, should go thoroughly over the exposed parts, working the wisp backwards and forwards well into his coat. The breast and body pieces are successively removed, and his chest, fore-arms, shoulders, back, loins, belly, quarters, thighs, &c., quickly rubbed down and dried in a similar manner. This done, the syces should set to and hand-rub him, beginning at his ears and ending at his hocks. The ears should be pulled gently between the fingers several times: a process that always seems to refresh the animal. When hand-rubbing, the stroke should be commenced by bringing the flat of the hand, each one to be used alternately, well under the belly, down the fore-hand, thigh or gaskin, or between the fore-legs, as the case may be, and it should then be drawn up with a steady pressure. As the hand is raised, the elbow should be turned out, and the under part of the bared forearm should be brought into play against the grain of the coat. In doing this, the weight of the body and the strength of the arm should be utilised.

With a valuable horse, one should put two men on the legs, and two on the rest of the body. The quicker the hand-rubbing is done, the more effectual will it prove.

On an average, the wisping down will take about ten minutes, the hand-rubbing somewhat longer.

If only two men be available, the legs below the knees and hocks should be left untouched until a later period of the grooming.

The hand-rubbing being finished, a syce on each side should go over the coat with the body brush, for the cleaning of which, only, should the curry-comb be employed.

The brush should have long and rather soft bristles, and should be used only in the direction in which the hair lies, and not against it, as it will then most effectually remove the dandruff, which is thrown off by the skin in the form of scales that are pierced by the hairs. The syce should place the brush lightly on the coat, so as to avoid hurting the skin, and should then press on it, as he makes his stroke downwards.

The chief object of brushing the coat is to remove the scaly dandruff; that of wisping and hand-rubbing to dry and stimulate it.

Dressing the Mane and Tail.—The brushing of the body being finished, the syce should brush out the forelock, mane, and tail, taking care, first of all, to commence at the ends of the hair, and to proceed upwards as each kink or knot becomes opened out. The hairs, by small locks at a time, should be brushed from their roots downwards, so as to remove all dandruff. The mane-comb should be used only when it is desired to keep the mane or tail thin.

It is the custom to make the mane lie to the off side, for, as we usually look at a horse from the near side, his neck and shoulders—if they be good—will then appear to greater advantage, than if the lines were broken by the mane.

The off-horse of a carriage pair may have his mane groomed to the near side.

Wetting the hair of the mane and tail will tend to make it grow fast.

If the mane does not hang properly down, it may be daily wetted and plaited, while small weights may be attached to its ends.

If a horse be inclined to rub his tail against the walls of the stable, a light leather case, to lace on, may, with advantage, be used to protect the part. In such cases, he will generally require some cooling medicine, while a soothing application may be smeared over the part (see *Veterinary Notes for Horse Owners* under heading *Prurigo*).

Some syces have a habit of washing horses' tails by means of a wet towel, which they rub with and against the grain of the hair. This practice should not be allowed, as it breaks the hair, and disarranges its set, thereby disfiguring the animal.

After the mane and tail have been adjusted, the syce should wipe out the horse's eyes, nostrils, sheath, and dock with a damp towel or sponge; and then smooth down the coat with a dry wash-leather or cotton rubber. After this, the clothing is put on, care being taken to throw the quarter-piece a little way in front of the withers, and then to draw it back, so that the coat may not be ruffled.

The feet should then be picked out and cleaned with a dry brush and rubber; the legs hand-rubbed, and bandages put on, if they be employed. If bandages be used during exercise, they should be allowed to remain on until the syce proceeds to hand-rub the legs.

The foregoing completes the description of ordinary grooming, to which I think, the following process may, with advantage, be added.

Tapeeing.—This essentially Indian practice is a species of shampooing done with broad circular pads, called *tapees*. Each one is about nine inches in diameter and three inches thick, and is stuffed with horse-hair. A strap is placed at the back of this pad to admit the hand placed flatwise. They are used one on each hand, and are brought down in quick succession, with the whole force of the arm, on the spot intended to be shampooed. The neck, shoulders, barrel, and hind-quarters are thus gone over—a syce being on each side of the animal—while the loins and flanks are avoided. The usual method is to strike first with the left hand, then with the right, again with the left, and then to bring the pads sharply together so as to knock out the dust. Tapeeing has an excellent effect on the skin and coat; and is much relished by the horse when he gets accustomed to it. If put into practice, it should be performed immediately after the animal is brushed down.

In all cases, when there is sufficient help and time, the grooming should be such as I have described in the foregoing pages.

When a horse comes in heated, and there be only one man to attend to him, the girths, if a saddle be on, should be slackened, and he should be walked about until he cools down, and then the wisp should be applied, beginning first of all at the part under the saddle.

I have never found the slightest ill-effect accrue from removing the saddle immediately the horse comes in, however heated he might be, provided always, the skin under it was thoroughly well dried without delay.

Moulting of the Coat.—The horse sheds his coat twice in the year—in the autumn and in the spring. At the former time, his fine summer hair moults, to be replaced by a thicker and longer covering, which, in its turn, gives place to the other. If, while the coat is changing in the spring, the brush, or other means be employed to hasten the process, the hair-follicles will become prematurely exposed to the action of the air, and consequently, will become stimulated to secrete a coarser form of hair than they would have done, had their natural protection remained on for its allotted period; hence the new summer coat will be rougher than it ought to be, and its appearance will, consequently, be more or less spoiled. On this account, when the coat is moulting during that time, the brush should not be applied to it, nor should it be hand-rubbed. The wisp and rubber will then be sufficient for grooming purposes.

In India, the moulting of horses, that are well groomed and warmly clothed, takes place to a far less extent than in England.

Care of the Feet and Legs.—The horse's feet should neither be washed nor "stopped," for the former practice is the fruitful cause of "cracked heels," while the latter induces thrush, and softens and weakens the sole, frog, and crust. The old idea of "thinning" the sole, and keeping the feet soft by stoppings of cowdung and clay, is an antiquated fallacy that hardly requires being combatted in the present day. In India, especially, we require the feet to be as hard and tough as possible, so that the horse may neither flinch, nor go short over hard and broken ground, nor become lame if he casts shoe, and has to proceed for a few miles bare-foot. Water applied to the feet renders them soft and weak, on account of the capillary attraction exerted by the fibres of the horn on any liquid with which it may come in contact. It is a significant fact that the drier the climate is, in which horses are bred and reared, the stronger and *better able to stand work* will their feet be.

No benefit is obtained by applying hoof ointment to the crust, unless, perhaps, to those parts from which the hard and varnished covering of the wall may have been rasped away by a careless or ignorant shoeing smith. The growth of the wall of the hoof can alone be hastened by stimulating the coronet which secretes it; hence, any hoof ointment, used as such, is powerless to effect this end.

In the preceding chapters I have dwelt upon the evils of washing the legs of the horse; hence I need not further allude to the subject, beyond saying that if the animal returns to his stable with his legs wet, or covered with mud, they should be dried by means of the scraper, wisp, and rubber, as the case may be, and then hand-rubbed.

One should avoid hand-rubbing the legs when they are wet, as doing so will tend to remove the hair.

The application of a little fresh butter or glycerine will tend to prevent the heels from becoming chapped. If they become rough and inflamed, oxide of zinc ointment may be applied with great advantage; or a little of the following—

Goulard's extract	... ...	1 part.
Glycerine, cream, or oil	... ...	4 parts.

(See *Veterinary Notes for Horse Owners.*)

Hand-rubbing the legs is a beneficial practice with the generality of stabled horses; for it not alone tends to prevent stagnation of blood in the legs and feet, but also, by the pressure exerted, promotes absorption of any effusions that may be present about the back tendons and suspensory ligaments.

Trimming the Mane and Tail.—The mane may be trimmed by pulling out the longest locks, a little at a time, having previously twisted them round the fore-finger or a stick. If this annoys the horse, the long ends may be divided by running a half shut scissors backwards and forwards across them, in the same manner as hair-dressers trim ladies' hair. The ends are held in the left hand, while the right uses the scissors.

A space about an inch and a half broad should be cut out of the mane, just behind the ears, for the passage of the head-stall of the bridle.

The practice of hogging the mane is confined to ponies.

A switch tail may be trimmed in the same manner as the mane.

It is not the fashion to bang the tails of Arabs; a fine

thin tail is considered to be a mark of high caste among them.

The object of banging a horse's tail is to add to the appearance of strength in his hind quarters.

Horses' tails ought not to be shortened after the beginning of April, as they will want them long in order to keep off flies. They should not be again trimmed before the month of October.

The usual length, at which a horse's tail is banged, is such that will enable the end of the tail, when pulled down, to reach the point of the hock.

The more "cobby" the animal, the shorter may be the bang.

The following are three methods for banging the tail.

1*st.*—Get an assistant to place his hand under the dock, and to hold the tail in a position, similar to which it would assume were the animal walking: then, with a strong pair of scissors, cut the hair level at the desired length.

2*nd.*—Bind the tail round, with a piece of cord, about six inches above the point at which it is to be divided. Then, with a sharp knife, cut so as to give the ends of the hair the required slope.

3*rd.*—Lay the tail, at the desired length, across the edge of a broad adze (Hind. *Busoola*), and divide the hair by a smart blow with a flat billet of wood. The adze should be held steady, the handle to the rear, the edge horizontal, and the blade sloped, so that the horse may carry his tail level at a walk. Any loose hairs may then be trimmed with the scissors. This is an admirable plan for troopers, dispatch and uniformity being matters of consideration. For use with a number of horses, a blade, resembling that of an adze, but broader, may be let into a block of wood 4 or 5 lbs in weight.

Bots.—During the autumn months, the bot-fly is very apt to lay its eggs on the chest and forelegs of horses, especially if the animals be kept much in the open, as when on the march. These eggs adhere to the hair, and, though very minute, may readily be recognised by their bright yellow colour, and by their position, which is chosen by the fly, so that the horse may easily lick them off, and thus convey them into his stomach. During these months, syces should be most careful to examine their horses after they come in from exercise, and pick off any of those eggs they may detect.

Stable Routine.—The system, applicable to race horses, should be the one pursued with all valuable animals, under the modifications that necessity or convenience may dictate. I may describe it as follows:

At day-break, the horse is given about a gallon of water, and after that a feed of about a pound of corn, his clothing is taken off, and he is groomed lightly over. The whole of the bedding should now be put outside, aired and dried, while the dung and fouled litter should be removed. The stable should be opened out for the admittance of air and sunshine. On the horse's return from work or exercise, say about 8 or 9 o'clock, he is watered, groomed, and clothed according to the season. His bedding is now neatly put down, and he is fed, and given a full allowance of grass or hay, at the same time as he gets his corn. The stable is now darkened, and he is left to himself for three or four hours. Between twelve and one he is watered, lightly groomed, and fed as before: and is not again disturbed till about four o'clock, at which time he gets a little water, a small feed of corn, and a thorough grooming. The bedding should again be removed, dried, and selected. On the horse's return to the stable in the evening, he is watered and lightly groomed over. His bedding is now arranged, and he is fed and given his grass or hay, and is left for the night.

Taking 10 lbs as the ordinary amount of corn a horse is allowed, I would divide it as follows :—

Early morning	1 ℔.
Morning	2 ℔s.
Mid-day	2 ℔s.
Afternoon	1 ℔.
Evening	4 ℔s.

If the horse gets only 9 lbs daily, 1 ℔. might be deducted from the evening feed.

Instead of watering the horse at fixed times, he may, with great advantage, have a constant supply of water at all times in his stall.

It is better to have horses groomed in the afternoon than in the evening, for then the syces will have plenty of light by which to do their work, while the owner will probably be able to superintend it, to some extent at least, without its interfering with his dinner.

To economise the bedding, it may be put down only at night.

I strongly advocate the system of feeding which I have described.

CHAPTER VIII.

On Bitting and Saddling Horses.

CURBS—PELHAMS—SNAFFLES—RUNNING REINS—CHOICE OF A BIT—ADJUSTMENT OF THE BRIDLE — REINS — NOSEBANDS — MARTINGALES — SADDLES—SADDLING THE HORSE—STIRRUPS—GIRTHS—SADDLE CLOTHS—CLEANING SADDLERY.

Curbs.—The proper method for restraining a horse with any species of bit, is to apply pressure, on some sensitive part, in a direction opposite to that in which he wishes to proceed; the most convenient spots being the tongue, and the bare spaces of the gums of the lower jaw. Had not nature formed the horse with a certain portion of his gums free from teeth, we could not use bits in the manner we do at present, but would have been forced to depend, for his guidance, on some kind of halter.

With the snaffle, the force derived from the rider's arms is directly taken by the tongue, gums, or corners of the mouth; while with the curb, the mechanical principle of the lever is utilised to increase the power. In it we have the fulcrum or fixed point afforded by the curb chain hooks, the moving power is applied in the direction of the reins, while the resulting pressure falls on the tongue or gums, or on the latter alone, as the case may be.

There are three ways in which the curb can exert pressure on the horse's mouth—1, by the mouthpiece in a direction opposite to which the animal's head is directed; 2, by the curb chain on his lower jaw; 3, by the port, when it presses against his palate. We may readily see that the first method, *viz.*, that of pressure by the mouthpiece on the gums and tongue, is the only legitimate one for restraining the horse. The pressure by the curb chain on his lower jaw is a necessary evil, which we should mitigate as much as possible, while we should altogether obviate the possibility of the port touching the roof of his mouth.

Even if we succeed in getting the animal under control by inflicting pain on him with the curb chain, or port, we will do so, simply by "cowing" him; in other words, we will make him afraid to "go up his bit," which, if he fails to do, he will neither be safe nor efficient, either under saddle or in harness.

That curb chains hurt horses in the manner described, is patent to any one who may have seen how restive and unmanageable curbs render many high spirited animals that will go quietly in a plain snaffle. They "chuck up their heads" in the endeavour to save the lower jaw from the painful pressure of the curb chain; while we will frequently find the part, against which it bears, to be galled and bruised; in fact, not uncommonly, in old standing cases, a bony deposit is formed on the lower jaw, as a result of continued inflammation. More rarely do we find the palate injured by the port.

The habits of chucking up the head, and not going up to the bit, so seriously interfere with the comfort of the rider or driver, and with the usefulness of the animal, that it behoves every owner to avoid, by attending to the proper bitting of his horses, the possibility of their contracting such vices.

The only reason for using curbs at all, is that they

afford far more power than can be obtained with the snaffle.

We will now consider how this increased force may be applied in the best possible manner.

If we examine the under surface of the lower jaw, we will find that the bone at the chin groove (c. Fig. I) is smooth and rounded, while immediately above it, the edges of the branches of the jaw are sharp and sensitive. Hence we may conclude that the curb chain should remain stationary in this chin groove, as it is the only convenient spot on which the chain can press without paining the horse.

FIG. I.

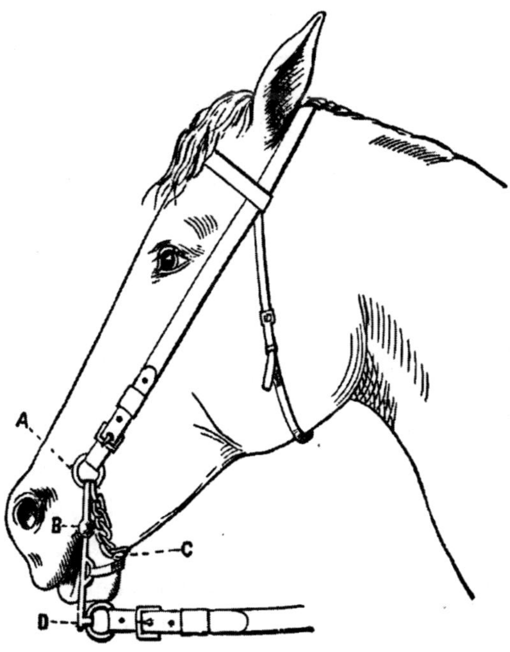

Major Dwyer (*Seats and Saddles*) has pointed out that if the distance A B (length of upper arm of cheek-piece) is greater than B C (see Fig. I) the curb chain will naturally tend to shift upwards on to the sensitive edges of the branches of the lower jaw, whilst if it be less, the chain may fail to act, by reason of the cheeks of the bit tending to come into a straight line with the reins, when they are drawn tight. Hence we may assume that the upper arm of the cheek should be of such a length, that the distance from the centre of the mouthpiece to where the curb hooks act, should be equal to the thickness of the lower jaw at the chin groove. I have found that for, ordinary horses, it is advisable to fix the length of the upper arm of the cheek-piece—measuring from the lower edge of the mouth-piece to the ring on which the curb hook acts—at 2½ inches (see Fig. II).

Major Dwyer also points out that, in order to insure the curb chain remaining in the chin groove, the mouthpiece should lie directly opposite to it (see Fig. I.) The usual rule is that it should be placed an inch above the tushes of horses, and two inches above the corner nippers of mares. This arbitrary method, besides placing the bit too high, does not allow for the differences in the sizes of different mouths, nor for the frequent variation found in the position of the tushes.

Major Dwyer's rule does not provide for the tendency the mouthpiece has to shift upwards, on the reins being drawn tight, for the headstall, by reason of its pull on the eyes of the upper arms of the cheek-pieces of the bit, causes the mouthpiece, and consequently the curb chain, to ascend. Hence, I think, the reader will find it preferable to place the mouthpiece (as directed by Colonel Greenwood in his work *Hints on Horsemanship*), so that it may just clear the tushes of horses, or be about one inch above the corner nippers of mares; in fact, as low as possible without involving the danger of the curb chain slipping over the animal's chin.

Having now fixed the length of the upper arm of the cheek-piece, we may, to obtain increased power, lengthen the lower arm, as we may find convenient, say to 4½ inches.

The width of the mouthpiece should accurately correspond with that of the horse's mouth, so that it may not pinch the lips by being too tight, nor be liable to slip from side to side by being too loose. In the latter case, the horse is apt to acquire the habit of "boring" to one side, which is done by his getting the cheek-piece of one side of the bit close up against his own cheek, which will cause the port to become shifted over to the other side. Owing to the absence of the port, the horse will then be able to relieve the gum of the side, to which he "bores," of pressure, by interposing his tongue between it and the mouthpiece. When the mouthpiece fits accurately, the port will remain in the centre of the mouth, which fact will give an "even feeling" on both sides.

The action of the port is to relieve the tongue of pressure, by transferring it to the gums, which are the more sensitive part of the two.

If we wish to render the bit less severe, we may lower the post, so as to allow the tongue to take some of the pressure.

Keeping in view the principle that the curb chain should on no account hurt the horse's chin, we should select one that will lie flat and even, in preference to one with large and few links. And, further, it may be covered with leather.

With a double bridle, the curb chain should pass outside the bridoon.

For the average sized horse, we may adopt the following measurements with curbs—

FIG. II.

Drawn to ¼ full size.

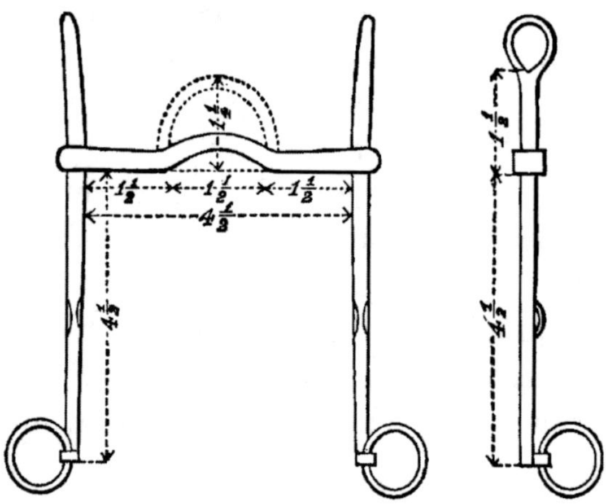

The measurements are given in inches. The maximum height of the port is shewn by dotted lines.

Width of mouthpiece	... ...	4½ to 4¾ inches.
Height of port not to exceed	...	1¼ inches.
Width of port	... ...	1½ ,,
Length of upper arm of cheekpiece, measured from lower edge of mouthpiece to ring	... ...	1½ ,,
Length of lower arm of cheek	...	4½ ,,

If we observe the action of an ordinary curb, we will see that, on the reins being pulled, the forward motion of the end of the upper arm of the cheek is restrained, both by the curb chain and by the headstall of the bridle. The longer the upper arm is, the greater will be this downward pull on the headstall, which will be taken by the poll of the horse, and will therefore tend to draw his head down, a position that will make him "gallop round." We know by experience that curbs have this tendency in a marked manner; hence the advisability of substituting snaffles for them, as much as possible, with horses that are used for fast work. Pelhams are especially objectionable on this score, a fact which appears to be principally owing to the upper arms of the cheeks of these bits being almost always absurdly long.

Pelhams.—The action of the Pelham is very faulty; for when its curb reins are pulled, the cheeks jam against the sides of the mouth, by reason of the working of the joint, which is at the centre of the mouthpiece, whose width, instead of exactly corresponding with that of the horse's mouth, varies at every touch of the rider's hands on the reins.

To obviate the pull on the headstall, Lord Thurlow invented a bit which differed from the ordinary one by having the eyes of the upper arms of the cheeks, formed in the shape of an oval to the rear.

In the Chifney bit this objectionable pull is entirely dispensed with, for its headstall is attached to a short arm, which revolves on the mouthpiece, independently of the cheek of the bit, to which the curb chain is hooked.

The Chifney bit is very severe, and is inapplicable for most horses that are ridden by men with indifferent hands, for its curb chain alone resists the forward action of the upper arm of the cheek of the bit. Thus the whole of the pressure falls on the gums and on the tongue, while none of it is taken by the animal's poll, a part which, I need hardly say, is not sensitive like the other two.

Snaffles.—The following are the most useful varieties of these bits.

1*st.*—The plain, smooth snaffle.

2*nd.*—The twisted snaffle.

3*rd.*—The thin racing snaffle, either twisted or smooth.

4*th.*—The chain snaffle, in which the mouthpiece consists of a chain of 8 or 9 links. For tender-mouthed horses this chain may be covered over with three or four turns of wash leather sewn on.

5*th.*—The double-ringed snaffle which is similar to the ordinary bridoon of a double bridle, except that two rings are placed on the mouthpiece, inside those to which the reins are connected, for attachment to the headstall of the bridle. This bit is in very common use for harness horses in England.

6*th.*—The gag snaffle is used with two reins, one being attached in the ordinary manner, while the other is a continuation of the cheek-pieces of the headstall, which pass downwards through holes in the rings of the snaffle—instead of being buckled to them—and from thence to the rider's hands. When the gag reins are pulled, the bit is forced against the corners of the horse's mouth, which action makes him draw up his head.

This bit is consequently very useful with horses that "bore" their heads down, and with buck-jumpers.

7th.—The double-mouthed snaffle has two mouthpieces, which respectively have joints more to one side than to the other, so that, if the joint of the upper mouthpiece is more to the near side, that of the lower one will be more to the off. It forms a very severe bit. It should not be used with a tight noseband, for, opening out somewhat in the form of a W, it will, then, be apt to hurt the roof to the mouth.

8th.—The Newmarket snaffle has attached to its rings a noseband, whose length can be altered, so as to divide the pressure between the nose and the lower jaw, or to throw it exclusively on one or the other. There are side straps attached to the headstall of the bridle, that prevent the noseband from falling too far down. It forms a very nice bit for a horse with a tender mouth.

The circular mouthpiece for leading horses may be added to the foregoing list. It is an excellent bit for this purpose, as there will be an even pressure on both corners of the mouth, in whichever direction the rein be pulled.

Running reins consist of a pair of long reins which pass through the rings of the snaffle, and buckle on to the Dees of the saddle. This arrangement keeps the horse's head down, and nearly doubles the power of the rider.

Choice of a Bit.—As in all ordinary riding, we require to have perfect command over a horse, the double bridle will be found to be the best for general use.

For horses and ponies that require to be turned sharply, as at pigsticking, and at polo—and for those that bore to one side—a double-ringed snaffle is most efficient, for it gives the pull more directly than an ordinary one. I may mention, in passing, that the Munipuri polo players all use it with their famous ponies. It is a capital bit for harness work.

The gag snaffle, as I have said before, is specially applicable to buck-jumpers, and to those that bore with their heads down. By using both reins, the pressure may be regulated so as to keep the horse's head in a proper position. Stonehenge remarks that "the gag snaffle is particularly well adapted to the double-reined bridle, intended for pulling horses carrying their heads too low, which the curb has a tendency rather to increase than diminish. The combined use of the two, however, corrects this fault, and a pleasant, as well as a safe carriage of the head, may be effected."

For tender-mouthed horses, the chain snaffle, covered with wash leather, or the Newmarket snaffle will generally be found to be the best.

As far as my experience goes, I have never found that a good rider will fail to hold the most determined puller, with a properly made and correctly adjusted curb. But if the curb chain hurts the horse's jaw, and the high port wounds his palate, while the greater part of the pull on the reins is taken by the animal's poll, controlling him will often be a matter of impossibility by even the most powerful horseman.

For a bad star-gazer that does not pull outrageously hard, I know no such efficient arrangement as that which may be obtained by connecting the reins of a snaffle, respectively to the side pieces of a running martingale—after removing the rings of the latter—and then by bringing them through the rings of the snaffle up to the rider's hands. This combines the effects of the martingale and of the running reins.

With a star-gazer that pulls hard, we may use the running martingale on the curb reins.

As far as appearances go, a double bridle, with a noseband, is the best to set off a horse with a plain head; and a Pelham by far the worst. A handsome blood-like head looks best through a snaffle.

Adjustment of the Bridle.—The snaffle should be placed low enough in the mouth to just avoid wrinkling its corners.

Before putting on a double bridle, the bridoon (snaffle) should be placed over the mouthpiece of the curb, which, as I have said before, should be just clear of the tushes of the horse, or an inch above the corner nippers of the mare; in fact, as low as possible without incurring the risk of the curb chain falling over the chin.

The curb chain should pass *outside* of the snaffle, and should be of such a length that it may lie flat and even against the chin groove, with a certain amount of play. The last links, on both sides, should be, first of all, respectively attached to the curb hooks on each side, and then the slack part should be taken up at equal lengths on both hooks, so that the small ring, through which the lipstrap passes, may be equally distant from each of them, and that the shape of the curb chain may be the same on both sides of that part of the jaw against which it presses. The looser the curb chain, the less severe will the bit be.

A lipstrap should always be used with a curb, for, in

its absence, a horse may, at any moment, when galloping, chuck up his head and reverse the position of the cheeks of the bit, thus depriving the rider of proper control over him, until he brings his head down again, when the cheeks of the bit will fall back into their usual position. Besides this, some horses have a trick of catching the cheek, on one side, with their lip, and then boring down to that side, which practice a lipstrap will prevent.

Throat lashes should be put on very loosely.

For preventing a horse, which has that habit, from boring to one side, we may pass a strap through the ring of the snaffle on the other side and through the loop formed by the throat-lash, and then tighten the strap as may be required. The pressure this arrangement puts on the side of the mouth, opposite to which he bores, will generally make him go with an "even feeling" on both reins.

When a horse carries his head too low down in galloping, the snaffle may be fixed higher than usual, so that the bearing on the corners of the mouth may make him hold his head up in a proper position. This arrangement is simply a substitute for the gag snaffle.

The following description of a plan for bridling a buck-jumper may not be out of place here.

Put on a snaffle with double reins, unbuckle one pair at the centre, cross them over the withers, and attach them respectively to the Dees on each side—the near rein going to the off D, and *vice versâ*—so that the horse can by no possibility get his head down. And then ride with the other reins.

Reins.—Having reins thick, thin, broad, or narrow is a matter of taste, which the rider should decide for himself. The question of having them sewn on, or buckled to the bit or snaffle, is also a matter of fancy. The only advantage of the former arrangement is that it dispenses with the necessity of having "stops" on the reins, which pass through the rings of the martingale. It is however inconvenient, as it does not admit of a change of reins. To my mind, a snaffle looks best with plated double buckles.

With a double bridle, I prefer having both reins of equal breadth, instead of having the curb rein narrow, and that on the snaffle broad. A buckle at the centre of the one, which passes through the rings of the martingale, will serve to distinguish it from the other. The "feeling" in the hands, with reins of equal substance, is far pleasanter, than when the contrary is the case. When the reins are properly held, with those of the snaffle on the outside of those of the curb—whether one or both hands be used—there will not be the slightest possibility of the rider becoming confused as to their respective identity.

In order to prevent the reins slipping through the fingers, with a puller, pieces of leather, about a quarter of an inch broad, and as long as the width of the reins, may be sewn across the inside of the latter, at intervals of three or four inches.

If the reins, which pass through the rings of the martingale, be not sewn on to the bit, they should be provided with "stops," so as to prevent the martingale rings getting caught on the buckles of the reins.

If stops be not present, the ends of the straps (billets) of the buckles should be withdrawn out of the keepers, an arrangement which will serve in the place of "stops" (see Fig. III.)

FIG. III.

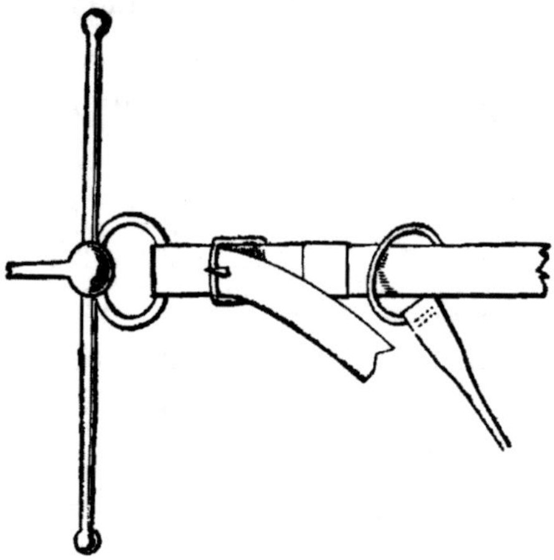

Nosebands.—An ordinary noseband, buckled tight, will considerably increase the power of either curb or snaffle. I cannot offer any satisfactory explanation of this fact.*

The neatest arrangement for the noseband of a snaffle bridle is to give it a separate head piece, similar to the "bridoon head" of a double bridle; it can then be raised or lowered, as may be required.

Martingales.—The uses of the running martingale are—1, to ease the hands and arms in keeping the horse's head down; 2, to increase the power of the rider in "catching hold of the horse's head." With the first object in view, the martingale may be adjusted so as to allow the direction of the pull of the reins to be a little, say three inches, below the top of the withers. But with animals that keep their heads sufficiently low, the martingale should be somewhat longer, so as not to cramp the action of the head. A rider, by an extra expenditure of strength, may keep his hands low enough to be able to dispense with a martingale for holding the horse's head down, but, do what he chooses, he will not have the same command over him. I am here, of course, referring to flippant, free goers, and not to slugs.

I strongly advocate the use of the running martingale.

It being as necessary to keep the horse's head down, and to ride him up to his bridle, with a curb as with a snaffle, the martingale is as equally applicable to the reins of the one, as to those of the other.

A not very efficient substitute for a martingale may be improvised by passing the reins, under the horse's neck, through a single ring, or through two rings attached together by a strap. This arrangement is sometimes called an Irish martingale.

Its disadvantage is, that, with it on, the animal cannot be as readily turned to the right or left, as when the running martingale is employed, because the lateral pull of either rein is not in a straight line, unless, indeed, the other one be let go altogether; an action utterly opposed to good horsemanship.

A standing martingale should be used only with horses that require some such restraint to prevent them throwing their heads up, or for some feats of *manége* riding.

Saddles.—The chief thing to be considered about saddles is that they should be long enough without being too heavy, while their length should, as a rule, be proportionate to that of the rider's thighs. A bad rider may require extra weight in the tree to afford a broad and roomy seat, which a good horseman may well dispense with. Short saddles are most objectionable, both on account of their curtailing the surface over which the weight of the rider is distributed, and also by reason of their tendency, when used, to give horses sore backs (see *Veterinary Notes for Horse Owners*, page 141.)

The saddle between the points of the trees should accurately fit the horse, so that it may not be liable to work backwards or forwards, nor that the gullet plate may hurt the animal's withers.

English saddles are, as a rule, far too wide between the points of the tree for the horses we use in India.

Many people prefer a saddle with a cut back pommel to one with a pommel cut straight down. The idea of the former looking better than the latter is a matter of taste. It probably gives the horse the appearance of having more sloping shoulders, than when a saddle with the other kind of pommel is used. This shape is, however, objectionable on account of its requiring a stronger, and consequently a heavier tree, than one with a straight cut pommel, which, in my opinion, produces a far better fit.

Saddles covered with doeskin, or having the flaps covered with that leather, and the seat with pigskin, afford the rider a very firm grip.

I do not like these cheap machine-made saddles, which, to my mind, are as unmistakable in their appearance as Cawnpore ones, being made from inferior pigskin, with long coarse stitches, and, as a rule, fit the back by reason of extra stuffing in the pannel, and not by the proper shape of the tree. As the substance of each hide varies in its different parts, while the strength, which is applied to each stitch by the machine, remains uniform, the sewing is much inferior to that by hand.

A saddle should have as little stuffing, as possible, compatible with an accurate fit and immunity from the danger of its hurting the horse's back.

The best makers construct saddles now-a-days so admirably, that they leave little, if anything, to be desired.

Saddling the Horse.—The saddle should be placed a little behind the shoulder blade, so that it may not interfere with the play of that part. It may be put further back if the rider wishes to save the horse's fore legs.

The idea that the saddle should be placed in the centre of the back of the horse, regarding him as a sort of four legged table, betrays a strange ignorance of the anatomy of the animal, for the chief office of the fore legs is to support weight, that of the hind to propel it, while the respective methods of attachment of both extremities to the trunk point to the same thing, hence when the attainment of speed is our object, the saddle should be placed as far forward as possible.

Before girthing up, the groom should, if a saddle

cloth be used, bring, with his finger, the front part of it well up into the arch of the gullet plate, in order to prevent it being pressed down on to the withers.

One should avoid tight girthing, and should try to hit off the happy medium between the girths being so loose as to allow of the chance of the saddle slipping, and so tight that it would interfere with the horse's breathing. To lessen the chance of the latter contingency, the girths should be placed well back from under the animal's elbows when the horse is being girthed up. The groom, when he has drawn the girths tight, should run his finger between them and the skin, from the near side to the off, so as to smooth out any wrinkles.

Some horses swell themselves out on being saddled, and consequently require to be walked about for a short time, and the girths taken up, before the rider can mount without incurring the chance of the saddle shifting its position.

For a parade or ordinary saddle, a neat method with the martingale, is to pass the first girth through its loop, and the second one over it, so that it may not hang down.

When a girth is too long, it may be shortened by making a fold of the webbing near one end, passing the tongue of the buckle through this fold, and then attaching the buckle to one of the off girth tugs. This should be only a temporary measure, as it is apt to spoil the webbing.

A stirrup leather looks neatest on a saddle when the loose end is passed to the rear between the flap and the leather, and immediately beneath the spring bar.

Every day after work, stirrup leathers should be detached from the saddle and irons, drawn out flat, and hung up, so as to save them from cracking.

Girths.—Fitzwilliam girths, which consist of one broad girth attached to the saddle by two girth tugs at each side, with an ordinary shaped girth over it, are perhaps the best for every day work. Those made of plaited or twisted raw hide, usually called Australian girths, and ones made on the same pattern, but of cord, answer extremely well. Being made of open material they save the part, over which they pass, from becoming heated, and, consequently, chafed.

A neat arrangement for the drying and stretching of girths, is to have a frame made with two rows of girth tugs, placed vertically, to which the girths may be buckled, after being used.

Saddle Cloths.—The legitimate use of these articles is to save the pannel of the saddle from becoming soiled by perspiration; hence they should be thin in order to avoid giving "play" to the saddle. A thick numdah is but a clumsy make-shift for the prevention of a sore back, and its use should be restricted to cases where it is impossible to have the saddle properly stuffed.

Saddle cloths, made of one thickness of leather, answer their purpose admirably. If constantly worn, they will keep soft and pliable on account of their absorbing the oil which is secreted by the skin on which they rest.

Cleaning Saddlery.—Yellow soap, with a very little water, is the best material for ordinary use. Stains may be removed by the application of some fresh lime juice. A small quantity of sheep's kidney fat, or deer's suet, rubbed in, not oftener than once a month, is all that is required to keep the leather soft. Beeswax, to give a polish, should, on no account be employed, as it makes the surface of the leather sticky to the touch, and soils the clothes if they come in contact with it. Properly cleaned saddlery should be soft and pliable, and should leave no stain on a white handkerchief rubbed over it, while, at the same time, the stitches should be clearly visible, and should be free from grease and dust. A groom should be careful to have the reins and stirrup leathers scrupulously clean. To give the leather a polish, the white of egg, dissolved in spirits of wine or gin, may be lightly brushed over the surface.

CHAPTER IX.

Racing Saddlery.

BRIDLES—MARTINGALES—SADDLES—LEAD CLOTHS—WEIGHT JACKETS—STIRRUP LEATHERS AND WEBS—GIRTHS.

Bridles.—From a racing point of view, there is a great deal of truth in the old remark, that if a horse cannot be held with a snaffle, no other bit will hold him. The disadvantages of a curb are, that it tends to make the horse "gallop round"—by causing him to bend his neck and lower his head too much, and also, that, with it, he will not "go up to his bridle" as freely as he will with a snaffle. However, when every kind of snaffle has been tried, without success, to control a hard puller, the lesser of too evils had better be chosen, and some of his galloping form must accordingly be sacrificed.

The choice of snaffles will generally lie between the ordinary plain, the twisted, the chain, the chain covered with leather, the double-ringed, the gag, the double-mouthed, the New Market—in which the nose-band takes some of the pressure—and the thin racing snaffle. I don't like the last mentioned, as, I think, it tends to make horses pull.

In case of doubt, a double bridle may be used, so that in the event of the rider not being able to hold his horse with the bridoon, he may have the bit reins ready to take up. Horses, that can be held with a snaffle, gallop as a rule, in far better form with it, than with a double bridle, even when the bridoon reins alone are used; the very presence of the bit seeming to deter them from going boldly up to their bridle.

A double bridle is less objectionable for steeple chasing, than for the flat, on account of the greater necessity there is for obtaining command over the horse, in the former, than in the latter business. When it has to be used in a race, the rider, having previously ascertained the exact length of curb chain that suits his mount, should, before going to the starting post, see that the proper number of links, no more, and no less, are taken up.

As Pelhams have a tendency to make horses bore, I cannot advise their employment, except, perhaps, with star gazers.

Martingales.—A running martingle will generally be required; for apart from its use in keeping a star gazer's head down—in which case it will have to be shortened to a proper length—when lengthened out, it is a most powerful aid in steadying a horse in his gallop, in turning him, and in enabling the jockey to catch a firm hold of his head. It is specially useful with young horses that are apt to "yaw" about, and with steeple chasers.

A standing martingale is sometimes used for horses that rear and are restive at the starting post; it has also, with good effect, been employed, in some few instances, for cross country work.

Saddles.—The chief point to be considered about racing saddles—of which Boyce and Rogers of New Market are, probably, the best makers—is that they should be long and roomy, as well as light. A 2½ lb.

or 3 lb. saddle, all complete with irons, webs, girth, and surcingle, ought not to be less than 15 inches in length; while a 6 lb. or 7 lb. training or steeple chase one ought to be more than an inch longer.

For cross country riding, the saddle should fit as close as possible to the horse, without actually pressing on the vertebræ of the back, while all unnecessary stuffing and numdahs should be dispensed with, so as to avoid giving "play" to the saddle.

For a race, the position of the saddle should be such, that it should just escape interfering with the play of the animal's shoulder blade, and no more. But for a training gallop, it should be put further back, so as to lessen the strain on the fore legs, unless, indeed, the horse has a weak spot behind.

Saddles, used for training purposes, generally weigh about 7 lbs. each, all complete.

With a racing saddle, the surcingle alone should pass through the loop of the running martingale, while its buckle should come beneath the stomach of the horse, and should not press against his side, in which position it would hurt him at each inspiration.

A pad, about a foot broad and eight inches long, with about three inches down the centre unstuffed, will be useful, with a light racing saddle, to prevent the gullet plate from pressing on the withers.

Leaded saddles are very useful when dead weight has to be put up; or for trials, when the trainer does not want his jockeys to know more than he can help.

Lead Cloths.—The trainer should have weight cloths capable of containing different amounts, with their own actual weights respectively marked on them. One or two cloths, weighted with leather up to 4 lbs. or 5 lbs., will come in useful; while there should be one, at least, capable of carrying about 21 lbs., so as to obviate the necessity of putting on two small ones, for the saddle will then have less play than it would, were the latter employed.

Each pocket of a weight cloth should be provided with a loop, for a strap—which should be sewn to the rear part of the cloth—to pass through, and thus to secure the leads. The strap should buckle on to the front part of the cloth, beyond the saddle flap. If the buckle be to the rear of the flap, the rider, when using the whip, might hurt his knuckles against it. Or the pockets may be attached to their flaps by buttons. To prevent the weight cloth slipping off during a race, it should be secured by a strap, which is made to pass over the flap of the pannel of the saddle.

The leads should be thin and very pliable, and may be covered with wash-leather, on which it is convenient to mark their respective weights, which will average about ½ lb. There should also be a few light leads to make up exact weight. In order to obtain increased pliability, leads of half the ordinary thickness may be sewn up in pairs.

Covering them with wash leather will make them less liable to slip out of the pockets of the cloth.

In order to save the horse from being hurt, no lead should be put into the pockets over which the girth passes.

A weight cloth should be placed well forward, with

the leads equally divided on both sides. If there be an odd piece, it may be put in one of the off-side pockets, if the race be on a right-handed course, and *vice versâ.*

Weight Jackets.—Instead of a weight cloth, a weight jacket may be used, in case the trainer wants to keep a trial "dark." The jacket should be made to fit tight and should have pockets around the body to contain leads. In this way, a stone or more may be carried. For a race, and particularly so for a steeple chase, a weight cloth is much to be preferred to a weight jacket, as the latter impedes and often hurts the rider.

Stirrup Leathers and Webs.—With racing saddles, the upper part of the eyes of the stirrup irons should be covered with leather, in order to prevent the iron cutting the webs.

For steeple-chasing, stirrup leathers are to be preferred to webs, as they are less liable to break. Besides this, with webs, if the rider loses his stirrup, he will find it more difficult to pick up, than if he had leathers, on account of the former's greater tendency to twist on itself.

With webs, or with light leathers, the part, through which the holes are punched, should be strengthened by an extra thickness of leather, as the fracture, when it takes place, almost always occurs at the hole through which the tongue of the buckle passes.

For cross country riding, it is safest to use none but saddles with locks—and not bars—for the stirrup leathers. These locks should be left open, or, at least, should be well oiled before mounting.

The following is a very useful method for causing a

stirrup iron to remain at right angles to the sides of the horse, in case the rider's foot comes out, so that he may readily pick it up again. With irons thus arranged, the chance of the foot getting caught, in the event of a fall, is greatly lessened. Mr. John Wheal, the well known Indian trainer, was the first to show it to me. He learned it from the celebrated George Stevens. It is as follows:—Twist the stirrup leather in the direction the hands of a clock proceed, if on the off side, till it is pretty well shortened; then pull it hard down by means of the iron, and let it go. On becoming untwisted, the leather will be found to have received a twist which will keep the iron at right angles to the horse's side.

Girths.—Girths, that have never been previously used, should not be put on for a race, as they will stretch considerably, and by doing so, may allow the saddle to shift its position, or even to turn round.

CHAPTER X.

Riding.

HOW TO HOLD THE REINS—POSITION OF THE HANDS—THE SEAT—HOLDING A RUNAWAY—TURNING THE HORSE—STANDING IN THE STIRRUPS—RIDING OVER FENCES—FINISHING—USING THE WHIP—RACE RIDING—STEEPLE CHASE RIDING.

IN the following pages I shall confine myself to the description of the system of riding which is applicable to the ordinary horseman, pigsticker, hunting man, steeple-chase rider and jockey.

How to hold the reins. When using the left hand only, with single reins, draw the near-rein between the third and little fingers, and bring it out between the first finger and thumb. Then place the off-rein over the flat of the same hand, so that the reins may cross on it. Thus—

FIG. IV.

Turn the knuckles down, and the reins will be in the proper position—

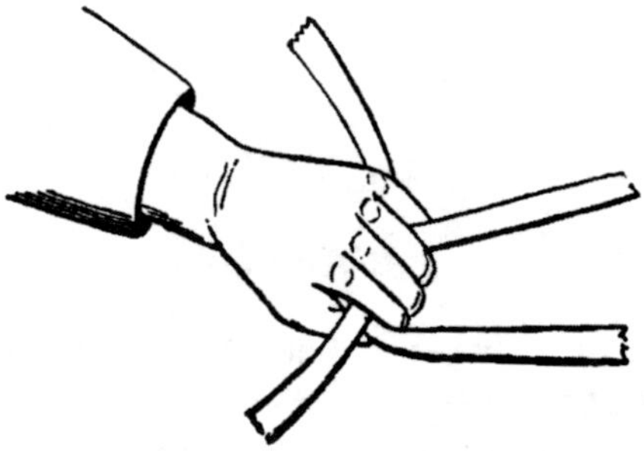

FIG. V.

When both hands are used, the off-rein is taken up between the third and little fingers of the right hand, while the slack of the near rein passes between its first finger and thumb, so that the hold on the reins, by both hands, is perfectly symmetrical, as follows—

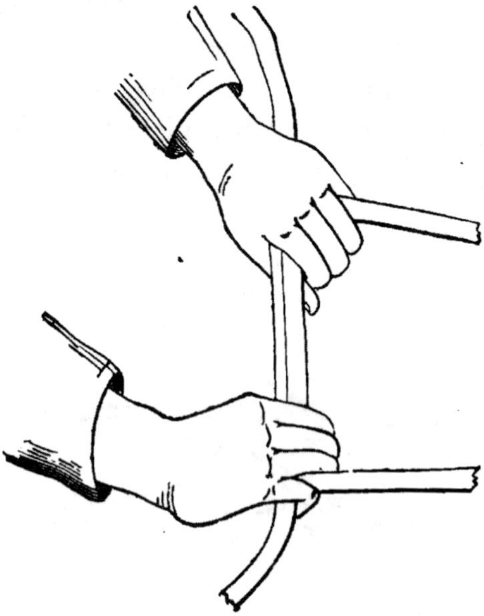

FIG. VI.

The reins can now be shortened or lengthened—without the hands quitting them—by simply drawing the hands apart, and at the same time tightening or relaxing, as the case may be, the hold of the thumb of the right hand on the near rein, and that of the little finger of the left hand on the off-rein. When the reins are shortened in the manner described, the hands are brought together to their proper distance one from another, while the slack of the reins is allowed to slip through the palms of the respective hands.

If the rider wants to shorten his reins quickly, as for instance when the horse "pecks" on landing over a fence and pulls the reins through his hands, his left hand should quit the off-reins and he should slip it forward on the near rein—his right hand, the while, retaining its hold on both—and, having got the proper length, he should catch the off-rein underneath, with the palm of the hand upwards, in the following manner—

FIG. VII.

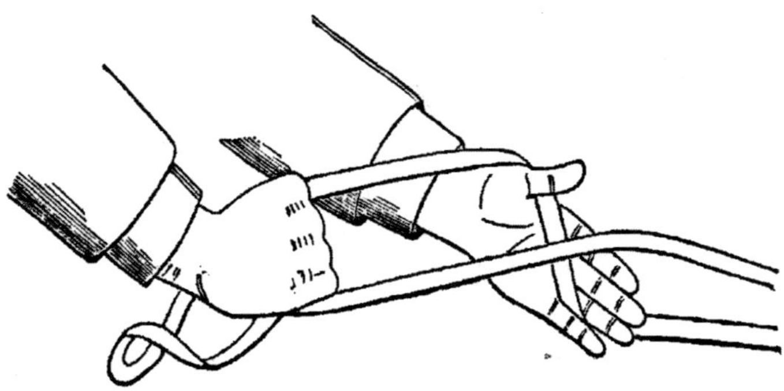

The knuckles of the left hand are now turned down, while the right hand quits its original hold, and takes up the reins as before.

The following two methods of holding double reins may be adopted:

1st.—Take up the rein on which one wants to have the strongest hold—the snaffle rein for instance—with the left-hand, as a single rein, and hook on to the middle finger the other rein, which may be allowed to hang loosely down, or it may be drawn up and passed down between the palm of the hand and the near rein of the other pair of reins.

This is the best way for a lady to hold double reins.

2nd.—Take up the snaffle reins as single reins, except that its near-rein should pass outside the little finger. Bring the near curb rein between the third and little fingers, the off curb rein between the first and middle fingers and cross them, thus—

Fig. VIII.

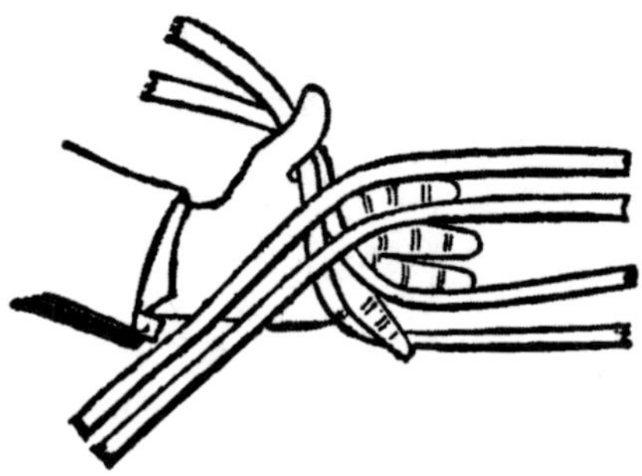

Fig. IX

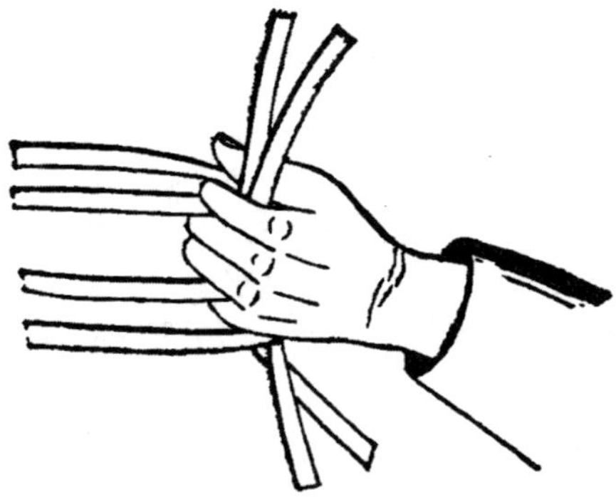

The right hand takes up the reins in a manner similar to that which it did with a single pair of reins—

Fig. X.

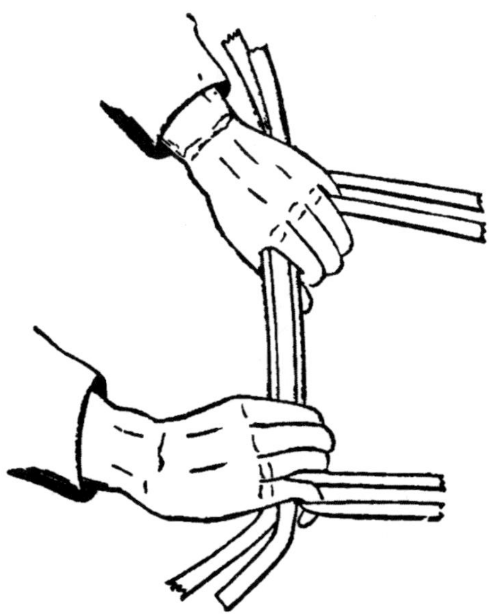

With double reins, when a rider wishes to use only one pair, he may put a *slip-knot* on the other at the desired length, so that he may have it ready to take up in a moment. Ladies, on account of the smallness of their hands, may, with advantage, adopt this method.

When both hands are on the reins, if the rider wishes to use one only—the left for instance—he should quit its hold on the off-rein, for a moment, while he passes it from the right into the left hand.

If a rider who does not *cross* his reins, but holds them in the riding-school manner, wishes to use both hands, he is obliged to lengthen out the off-rein, in order to get an " even feeling" on both reins and, consequently, before the right hand quits them, as when about to use the whip, &c., he will be obliged to draw up the off-rein till it becomes of the same length as the near one. I need hardly point out that doing this necessitates loss of time, quite sufficient for a jockey to lose a race, or a hunting man to fail to prevent a refusal at a fence. But when holding the reins crossed, the left hand picks up the off-rein in an instant, while both reins always remain at the same length.

When riding with the reins crossed, as I have described, the rider has a far firmer hold on them than when they are simply drawn through the fingers.

As a rule, a man should always ride with both hands on the reins.

With a puller, a little powdered rosin, on the hands, will aid in preventing the reins from slipping through them. This precaution is particularly useful when the reins get wet and slippery by rubbing against the neck of an impetuous horse, that "throws his head about."

Position of the Hands.—Whether one or both hands be used, it or they should be allowed to fall loosely from the wrist, with the line of the knuckles forming an angle of about forty-five degrees with the ground. When only one hand is employed, it should work, as nearly as possible, directly over the withers. When both hands are used, they should be kept six or seven inches apart, one on each side of the withers. In all cases—except, at a finish in a race, or when a horse bucks, kicks, or gets his head too low—the hands should be kept down. The reins should never be let loose.

The Seat.—When "sitting down" at the gallop, or canter, or over fences, the rider should get his seat under him, as much as possible, should force his fork well down into the saddle, with the hollow, and not the back of the thighs, against the laps. The knees should be well forward; the legs, from the knee down, should be vertical, or, if anything, somewhat drawn back; while the feet should be parallel to the sides of the horse, with the heels slightly depressed. The feet, except when spurs are used, should be kept quite steady, and should on no account be allowed to work backwards or forwards. The rider will then be in the best position in which to conform to the movements of his animal, and in the most difficult one from which to be dislodged. The shoulders should be kept square to the front, and down. The body and head erect, and the loins braced up, but without any approach to stiffness in the attitude.

The length of the stirrups, with such a seat, will enable the rider to clear the pommel of the saddle easily, when standing in them, and, as a general rule, will cause the lower part of the stirrup irons to reach just below the ankle joints, when the feet are taken out of them, and allowed to hang down. In short, the length of the stirrups should be such as will assist the horseman in assuming a perfect seat, and cannot be determined by any fixed measurement.

If the rider finds that, when on a puller at the gallop, he can get his knees well into the flaps of the saddle, draw his feet back, and in this manner exert his strength to the best advantage, he may rest assured that his stirrups are of the right length.

Men, with round thighs, and small knee joints, will usually require longer stirrups than those of an opposite conformation, for they need a certain amount of grip from the calf of the leg, to aid that of the knee and thigh.

One should ride with the feet home in the stirrups, except perhaps, at the walk, or the trot, when the ball of the foot may rest on the iron.

The muscles of the hands, arms, and shoulders, should be free from all stiffness, so that the rider may give and take with every movement of the horse's head and neck. The elbows should not be stuck out.

When sitting down, in the ordinary manner, at the canter or gallop, the rider should keep his body slightly inclined back, and should yield to the movement of the horse, so that the seat may not quit the saddle for a moment. To avoid bumping up and down, the horseman should get his seat under him, as much as possible, and should draw the feet back, so that the knee-joints may give and take with the motion of the horse.

This method of riding is the one applicable for all ordinary work, while standing in the stirrups—the practice of which is generally confined to the race-course,—being fatiguing to the rider, will only be adopted, occasionally, to relieve the animal.

Holding a run-away.—The rider should sit well down into the saddle, stick his knees into the flaps, draw the feet back, bend the head and shoulders slightly forward, catch the reins rather short, and should take a pull, feeling his knees grip still tighter, and himself jammed still firmer into the saddle, the harder he pulls. If he finds that this does not succeed, he should let the horse have his head again, and should take a shorter hold of the reins, catch his breath for a moment, and take another pull, giving a turn of the wrist to wrench the bit from between the animal's teeth. If this does not do, he may saw the bit, and take a pull the instant he finds the horse's mouth yields.

Many bad riders, when on a puller, thrust their feet forward, hump their shoulders, stick their elbows out, and jam their fists in the pit of their stomach; while others keep their arms straight and throw their whole weight on the stirrups.

Turning the horse.—Before turning a horse to the right, or left, he should be "collected" by the rider tightening both reins, a touch of the spurs being given, if he requires it, to make him bring his hind legs well under his body. The reins of the side, to which the turn is to be made, should then get an extra pull, while the horseman's foot on the other side should be drawn back, and should be pressed hard against the animal's ribs, so as to prevent his quarters from swinging round. The object of these actions is to make the horse turn, as much as possible, on his hind legs, in preference to his fore, as the former are far more powerful than the latter. Besides this, the natural equilibrium of the horse's frame is disturbed by the rider's weight. During the turn, the horseman should incline his body towards the side to which he makes it. These precautions are most necessary to prevent a horse from coming down, when turning at a fast pace. For school purposes, horses are taught to turn on their centre and on their forehand, as well as on their hind quarters.

Standing in the Stirrups.—As the hind legs are virtually the propellers, while the fore-legs are the supporters of the body, horsemen assume the attitude of standing in the stirrups in order to relieve the former of weight, during the gallop or canter.

The body should be slightly bent forwards, and should be free from all stiffness, so that it may conform, to the motion of the horse. The heels should be a trifle depressed, and slightly drawn back. The seat should be somewhat raised from the saddle—not stuck out over the cantle—without any up and down movement. The weight should be on the stirrups, and the balance should be preserved by them, and by the hold the rider has on the reins, while the knees, when the horse is not pulling, should but lightly press against the flaps. By riding in this manner the horse will be taught "to go up to his bridle." The balance should be true and well maintained, so that, in the event of a stumble, swerve, or any unlooked for movement, the horseman may be ready to throw his shoulders back, grip the saddle with his knees, and "catch the horse by the head" in a moment.

The harder the animal pulls, the tighter should the grip of the knees become, so that the correct position may always be preserved. If the rider, when trying to hold his horse, uses the stirrups alone as a *point d'appui*, his feet must come forward, while his seat will be carried over the cantle; a position that will throw the weight back towards the loins, and will cause the body to bump up and down; proceedings which will materially interfere with the motion of the animal.

A horse should be controlled alone by the give and take action of the muscles of the arms and hands; hence, with a puller, the body should remain as steady as possible by means of the grip of the knees. If, on the contrary, the stirrups be used as a fulcrum, the feet must be thrust forward, and the seat thrown back over the cantle; actions that will necessitate, in order that the balance be maintained, a dead pull on the reins, which, I need hardly say, is quite incompatible with good riding.

As a rule, the hands should be kept down by the sides of the withers, with the knuckles at about an angle of forty-five degrees to the ground. The wrists, elbows, and shoulders should be kept as loose and pliable as possible.

Riding over Fences.—The art of riding well across country chiefly consists in making as little as possible of the jumps. The fact of the rider treating fences and level ground with equal indifference inspires his horse with confidence to take things in the same spirit.

When riding across country, the horseman should have both hands on the reins, and when taking a fence, should sit down and lean back, so as to reduce the jar on the fore-legs, and to be able to catch hold of the horse's head in case he tries to refuse at the last moment, or makes a mistake.

When taking off, the rider should interfere with the horse's head as little as possible, but, as he leans back in the saddle, he should feel the reins, so as to prevent him from landing "all abroad." A touch of the spurs, or cut of the whip—close behind the girths—may be required to make the horse extend himself or jump big enough.

Over fences, a man should always keep his hands down, and should on no account chuck them up, for this would raise the head, an action that would prevent the horse from using the muscles of his loins and hind quarters, to the best advantage, on landing and in getting into his stride again, or in the event of making a mistake.

When the rider can take his own time over jumping, the old axiom of riding a horse slow at timber, *i. e.*, any high obstacle, and fast at water, *i. e.*, any broad place, holds good; but in steeple chasing, a great deal has to be left to the honor of the horse, while the jockey does his part by sitting still and keeping a good hold of his animal's head.

Over post and rails, the horseman should always ride at the former, in preference to the latter, as it is by far the easier of the two for the horse to see. When racing over small fences, there is no need to sit down.

Finishing.—When the jockey sits down at the finish, he grasps the flaps of the saddle tightly with his knees, and as the feet of the horse, at each stride, come to the ground, he jerks his weight forward, giving the impetus to his body at the same moment as the horse makes his stroke, so that the animal is actually relieved of a certain portion of his rider's weight. The jockey should catch a good hold of his horse's head, so as to collect him at each stride; should draw his feet well back, so that weight may not fall on the stirrups in a forward direction, which would cause it, by re-action, to be projected to the rear; and should keep his head erect, shoulders back, and his seat, as much as possible, under him, so that he may be able, effectively, to impel his weight forward at each stroke of the horse. He should give a forward motion to his hands, at each stride, yielding to the extension of the animal's neck, but without slackening the reins in the slightest. This action is extremely fatiguing; hence the great difference that may be observed among jockeys, according as they are strong or weak riders. The popular idea about a man, that is good at a finish, is that he "lifts his horse" at every stride, "throws him on to the post;" or "takes it out of him," to some extraordinary extent with whip and spur!

When we speak of a jockey "lifting" a horse, at a finish, we use the expression to describe the forward impulse, at each stride, the animal gets, which it is impossible that he can receive from the rider's hands, as their action is confined to the reins, which may serve to "collect" the horse, or to retard his movements, but cannot afford him any onward impulse exterior to himself. As the legs of the rider are the only other parts that connect him to the horse, the "lift" must proceed from them, and is the result of the rider's weight, more or less, being taken off the animal's back, at each instant, as his feet touch the ground.

As the action of finishing can be maintained only for but a very short time, a jockey, as a rule, does not begin "to ride his horse out," before he comes to the distance post.

The art of finishing—so as to aid the horse, and not to impede him in his stroke by rolling about in the saddle—is so difficult of attainment, and its action is so fatiguing, that the ordinary amateur would be wise to "sit still," instead of trying to finish, until he is quite sure that he can do it properly. The paramount necessity of being in good training for race riding is particularly observable at a finish. How many cases do we know of races being lost by the rider having been more tired than his horse, in the run home.

Using the Whip.—Unless when correcting the horse, preventing him from swerving, &c., the rider should, in my opinion, never hit him on any other part than that just behind the girth. If a cutting whip be used, as in race riding, the side away from the whip will, if any thing, be more hurt than the other, so that the horse, when the whip is used in this manner, will not nearly be so liable to swerve, as he would be, were he hit on the shoulder, or on the flank. Striking a horse on the former part is most apt to make him change his leg, while punishing him about the sheath—as duffers who get up to ride races are particularly fond of doing—is barbarous in practice, and tends to throw the horse out of his stride.

In race riding, the whip, as a rule, should only be used in the last few strides. During a race, it should be held lash down, for if it be kept up, the horse will often watch it, expecting a cut every moment, and thereby his attention will be distracted from his work. When the moment comes to use it, the whip should be quickly "picked up," by turning it in the hand, lash uppermost, the reins are firmly grasped in the other hand, the knees grip the saddle as tight as possible, the shoulders are kept square, and the body steady, so that no sway from it may jar on the motion of the horse, when the cuts, which should rarely exceed two or three, are given. They should be timed, so that the horse may be hit just as his feet come to the ground.

A novice should not use a whip, for none but a good rider can sit still, hold his horse together with one hand, and flog at the same time. Though spurs do not present these difficulties, they are much less efficient than a whip is in the hands of a "workman."

Race Riding.—As a rule, a jockey should not make the running in a race, if he can get any other rider to do it for him; in which case he should wait on him, instead of racing against him, for horses, generally, go better, and settle down in their gallop sooner, with a lead, than without one. This is especially true with young animals, who are very apt to sprawl about, and go on with all sorts of "calfish" tricks, when they are in front during the first part of a race. Some horses, however, will never run kindly, unless they are leading.

With orders to force the running, the jockey should accurately judge the pace, so that his mount will have just enough left in him to make an effort at the finish, in the event of being collared.

When a jockey finds that his horse can go no faster than he is galloping at the time being, he should, almost invariably, take a pull at him, if only for half a dozen strides, in order to give the animal a chance of "coming again," which he could not do, were he not eased off for a moment. Exceptions to this would be, when the jockey is quite near home, has the lead and finds he can keep it; and, when the horse is one of the jady sort that will not stand his mouth being touched.

As a rule, light weights ought to make the running, especially if the ground be heavy, for then, weight tells far more than on a light course.

The longer the distance the more will weight tell.

Horses with high action act best on a hill; while those with upright pasterns are unsuited to go down one.

Horses with oblique pasterns generally go well on hard ground, which is most trying to those with upright ones on account of the greater jar. A horse with weak hocks is most unsuited to face a hill.

Horses with large, broad feet will generally act best through "dirt" or sand, from the mechanical advantage they have over those with small feet.

The generality of hard determined pullers are done

running, when they stop pulling, and the moment this occurs, they are left without the power of making an effort; for this reason a jockey ought to be particularly careful "to keep a bit in hand" with a horse of this sort.

That hard pullers often fail to stay is frequently the fault of their riders. I quite agree with Hiram Woodruff, the celebrated American trainer, when he remarks that, "it is often said that a horse cannot pull hard, and last; and this is contrary to the facts I am about to mention. Trustee lasted; and he was a hard puller. Captain McGowan lasted; and he is the hardest pulling horse in America, I suppose. Dexter pulls a pound or two. I can assure you; and he has shewn his capacity to go on. The truth is, that the pulling-horses last well enough, but the riders do not last so long. It is just so with the runners."

The advantage of making a waiting race, for even a part of the journey, is that one can then see how the other horses are running, and having ascertained this, can remain where one is, or go in front. But if the jockey forces the pace from the start, he runs a risk of "choking" his horse in the beginning of the race, while if it turns out that the tactics of making the running were injudicious, he will find this out only after the race is lost.

Many horses are so impetuous, that they cannot be kept behind without it taking more out of them, than the severity of the pace itself. If such an one be not a particularly good stayer, his jockey should "wait in front" with him; in other words, he should merely keep in front without forcing the running on his own account, and should simply conform to the pace of those immediately behind him, whether it be fast or slow, till the moment arrives for him to make his effort. A horse, however, should never be kept back to an extent which will cause him to fight in his gallop: far better let him go at a speed just beyond that at which he would expend his strength in the air.

When a jockey, who has waiting orders, finds that all the others have similar instructions, he should avoid "getting the slip" from one of the others; which is done by a jockey, seeing his opportunity while they are all going slow, catches his horse by the head, and sends him, sometimes, five or six lengths in advance, before the others know where they are. If this happens, half a mile or nearer from home, these lost lengths will be very hard to pick up again. When there are several horses in a race, the chance of slipping one's field will very rarely occur, for some one will be almost certain to cut out the running.

If the orders be to wait, they should not be carried out, as is done, by losing the start, or by pulling the horse out of his stride in order to get him behind at all hazards, for whatever distance is lost at the start, or during the race, will, generally, have to be made up when the other horses are going fast. But the rider should always get away as well as possible, and should settle down, as soon as he can, into a steady uniform pace, a trifle slower than that of those that are making the running, and should then wait till they "come back to him," or until he arrives at the spot from which he sees it most judicious to make his effort, judging by the way the horses he has most to fear are going, and by the distance they are from him; he should then sit down in the saddle, catch hold of his horse's head, and trust to speed to make up lost ground and win the race.

When giving orders to wait, it is always risky to lay down too precise directions for one's jockey, such as to keep a certain number of lengths behind the leading horse, who may be sent from the start to cut out the running for another, at a pace which will cause himself to collapse before half the distance be gone; or to wait on some particular horse, a proceeding which has been the cause of many a mistake, for the dreaded one may turn out a rank duffer that is unable to go fast, so that the jockey, by waiting on him, may have, in the meantime, allowed the others to get so far a-head, that there may be no catching them before it is too late. As a rule, it is far better to ride a race, so as to suit the capabilities of one's own horse (with which one ought to be fully acquainted), than to devote one's entire attention to the weak points of the supposed dangerous horse or horses, which must naturally be problematical; for this reason, I would never hamper a jockey's judgment by laying out the programme cut and dry, but would simply tell him my horse's peculiarities, and what kind of running would most likely bring him quickest home. For instance, with a speedy horse in a 1½ mile race, instead of telling him to wait so many lengths behind, I might say "get off well and keep at about three-quarter speed to the ¾ mile post, gradually get up within a couple of lengths of the leaders at the distance post, take a pull at your horse for a few strides if you find him distressed, and make your effort the moment you think you can get home." And then if the animal gets beaten, the probability is that the winner was the better horse of the two, at the weights and distance run, a fact which owners of beaten horses often overlook.

It sometimes happens that the riders of the two best horses mutually wait too long on each other, and allow their field a start that cannot be recovered in time.

Inexperienced riders are often deluded into waiting, when they ought to keep going on, by a jockey pretending to flog, when in reality he is but whipping his boot. This dodge is, of course, only tried on by the rider of the speedier horse of the two, in the hope of inducing the man on the stayer to slacken speed, on the supposition that he has the race in hand and that there is no use hurrying. I need hardly say that, if a man perceives his opponent trying on these tactics, he should at once increase his speed, supposing of course that there were no other horse formidable in the race.

As a rule, in a match, if one's opponent be on a "cur," one should try to jump off with the lead, and cut out the running at once, whatever sort of a horse one may be on, provided he be but game; for nothing makes a "rogue" shut up so soon, as being collared. A jockey on such a horse should do all he can to persuade him that he is running away, and, generally, the more the man on him pulls, the faster will he go. Many horses have to be ridden in this fashion.

Giving half a bottle of port or sherry, or their equivalent in spirits and water before a race, is a well known plan for making rogues run kindly. A stimulant is often advisable, after a race, when the horse has to run a second time on the same day.

Some horses won't extend themselves unless spurs are on; others will "shut up" if they get the slightest prick. The same can be said of the whip. At almost every meeting we see races lost by inattention to horses' peculiarities, so it behoves the trainer and jockey to find out those of their animals. If a horse will not stand spurs, or runs unkindly when they are used, the rider, after taking them off, may, with advantage, in the preliminary canter, give his horse a couple of kicks in the ribs, just to show him that he need not fear the Latchfords.

Old horses, which are somewhat stiff on their legs, should have a steady preliminary canter for half mile or more, to warm them up before starting.

During a race, as a rule, one ought to avoid horses directly alongside, especially when on an impetuous animal.

A jockey should allow a horse, that is at all shifty, to make his own running and effort while interfering with him as little as possible. All horses very quickly learn what a race means, and I believe that better results would be obtained, than we get, by trusting to their judgment, oftener than we do, concerning how races should be run. I have seen several instances of success having been secured by acting thus.

When coming up the "straight run in," if one finds that the leader has the race easy, one should get directly behind him, on the chance that he may slacken speed to look round, or at his boots, or at the Stand, and then with a rush, on the side from which the other's head is turned, he may manage to beat him on the post, before he can set his horse going again.

Many a race has been lost by over-confidence of the rider of the leading horse, when winning easily, by trying to make a race of it for the "gallery," or by being cajoled into slackening his pace by one of the riders in rear, and then being unable to make an effort in time to stall off the other's rush.

At a finish, it is always best to be on the whip hand of one's most dangerous opponent, who might close in, either intentionally, or by his horse swerving, which would prevent the whip being used with the right hand.

If a jockey be behind two horses—the leading one close on the inside and the other away from it, but in rear of the leader—he should never attempt to get through on the inside, for all that the rear jockey will have to do in order to shut him out, will be to close on the leader and then the pair of them can keep him there. This is a common trap, and many, who ought to have known better, have been caught in it. This is not foul riding according to racing law.

It is always dangerous to try to get through on the inside, for *all* men won't give way, and it is anything but pleasant to be shoved up against a post, or against the railings.

The straight run in on the Dehra Doon Race Course is about one-third of a mile up a stiff hill, with about the last 200 yards level. On this course, when riding a close race, one should always endeavour to take a pull at one's horse, even for a second, immediately on reaching the crest of the hill, in order to allow him to catch his wind for the final struggle, and to settle down in his stride on the level ground.

As a last piece of advice, I would advise the tyro never to be too anxious to "get home," and never to "draw it too fine."

Steeple-chase Riding.—A friend of mine, who has been, for many years, one of the best cross-country riders we have ever had in India, has kindly placed, at my disposal, the following hints on this subject:

Before riding a chase, the jockey should walk a couple of times round the course, if it be strange to him, in order to select the best spots at which to take the fences, and to observe the nature of the ground, so that he may know when to go fast, where the "going" is good, or to take a pull at his horse, where it is heavy. He would also see where it might be advisable to make a slight detour from the straight line.

The rider should endeavour, if possible, to get away in front for the first couple of fences, for if he does so, he will then, generally, be able, more or less, to take his time, as tailing, usually, commences early. After that, three quarter speed will, as a rule, enable him to keep close up with the leaders.

Above all things, the rider should make up his mind to go straight, and should never allow his horse the chance of even *trying* to refuse, for the latter will always be the first to find out whether or no the former funks.

The jockey should stand in his stirrups, between the fences, but should sit down when he approaches them, steadying his horse about twenty lengths away from each jump, and then letting him freshen his pace going up to it.

Unless the pace be very hot, the horse should not be taken at height, faster than three quarter speed, but at water, the pace should be somewhat better, care being taken that the horse's hind legs are well under him.

The rider should avoid hitting the horse with the whip when jumping, for the sight of it is apt to distract his attention, making him, probably, blunder over the fence, in the attempt to escape punishment. If a stimulus be required, spurs should be used. He should encourage him with his voice throughout the chase.

The horse's head should never be let loose, while an extra pull should be taken, when going through heavy ground, so as to make him shorten his stride.

It is quite as necessary for the rider to be in good condition, as it is for the horse.

Stirrup leathers, for riding across country, should be a hole or two shorter, than for the flat.

I may add that when riding a horse, which is apt to refuse in a steeple-chase, the jockey would be wise to manage, as often as he can, to keep on the side—away from which his horse usually refuses—of any of the others when nearing a fence, for having a horse on the side to which he is inclined to swerve, will often keep him straight. As a rule, horses refuse to one particular side, that being the left in most cases, the cause being, perhaps, an injudicious use of the whip on some previous occasion. Besides this, horses are led, handled, and mounted from the near (left) side, which naturally makes them turn more readily to it, than to the right side.

Many chase courses in India are very dusty, so it is often, on that account, advisable to get away in front, if possible, at the start, so as to be able to take one's own line and not have to ride in a cloud of dust behind other horses.

The remarks I have made on race riding, also apply, within certain limits, to chasing.

CHAPTER XI.

Management of Horses on Board Ship.

As my experience extends only to the transport of single horses on boardship, and not to that of large numbers, I shall confine my remarks to the former.

The frogs and soles of a horse's feet, before he is embarked, should be hard, strong, and as fully developed as possible. Hence it is advisable to let him go bare foot for a couple of months beforehand, or to shoe him *à la Charlier*, or with tips, while the crust and heels are kept low, and to forbid all paring of the soles and frogs with the drawing knife, or stopping with cowdung, &c. If thrush be present, the animal's feet should be treated for it without delay. (See *Veterinary Notes for Horse Owners.*) Shortly before being put on board, the shoes (if they be used) should be taken off, and the heels and walls of the hoofs should again be lowered, so as to obtain frog and sole pressure as much as possible.

The foregoing precautions are most necessary in order to lessen the possibility of the animal getting inflammation of the feet (*laminitis*) from long standing. I believe that I am not incorrect in saying that fully half of the horses, which come from England to India, suffer more or less from this most serious disease.

For ten days or so before sailing, the horse should be put on laxative food, if he be at all gross, so that his system may be as little prone as possible to the attacks of any kind of inflammation. With this object in view, I would advise a bran mash every night, and carrots and green fodder, with very little corn.

The amount of food to be laid in for a voyage can be calculated on the following allowance—

Amount of forage per day.

Hay	18 lbs.
Oats	4 „
Bran	5 „
Linseed	3 oz.
Salt	2 „
Water	6 gallons.
Straw	5 lbs.

The linseed may be given as a mash, from time to time.

Besides this, a bag and a half of sand per week should be allowed for the animal to stand on.

The following articles of clothing, &c., will be necessary—

A suit of warm clothing complete.
A couple of horse rugs.
A waterproof sheet.
A pair of knee-caps.
Head collar and side reins.
Watering bridle.
Brush and curry comb.
Hoof pricker.
Half-a-dozen cotton rubbers.
A sponge.
A large pot for boiling linseed, &c.
Slings.

The rugs may, with advantage, be covered with canvas.

It is advisable to lay in a few medicines, &c., as follows :—

Six physic balls (containing 4½ drachms of aloes).

Nitrate of potash (nitre)	4 oz.
Sweet spirits of nitre	1 pint.
Tincture of opium	12 oz.
Carbonate of ammonia	2 ,,
Oil of turpentine	12 ,,
Camphor	2 ,,
Alum	1 lb.
Linseed oil	½ gal.
Tincture of myrrh and aloes (for abrasions)	6 oz.
Sulphate of iron	2 ,,
Lunar caustic	1 ,,
Fleming's tincture of aconite ...	¼ ,,
Bicarbonate of soda	1 lb.

A rasp.

A searcher.

A pair of leather shoes for fomenting the feet.

A horse should be provided with a box in which to live. Its dimensions may be as follows :—

Internal length	6 feet	3 inches.
,, breadth	2 ,,	8 ,,
,, height	5 ,,	
Height of door	3 ,,	9 ,,

It should be provided with doors at both ends, so that the horse may walk into it whichever way it is turned.

The framework of the box may be composed of beams of the following dimensions—

Two beams (for the bottom)	... 7′ × 7″ × 3″
Two cross beams ...	... 3′ 2″ × 7″ × 3″
Ten uprights (for the sides) ...	... 5′ × 4″ × 3″
Two side beams to connect the uprights together ...	... 7′ × 4″ × 3″

At the side of each doorway, a strong wrought iron support should pass underneath the box, and come half way up the upright beams to which it should be securely rivetted, and should, at its extremities, be provided with massive iron rings to enable the box to be hoisted over the side by means of the crane. Two additional iron supports, passing under the box, should be attached to the next two uprights, in order to give increased strength. The two doors should be very strong, and should be made to take off readily.

The inside of the box should be thoroughly well padded through its entire extent. Straw padding, covered with canvas, is very ineffective, for it soon gets hard and works downwards, leaving the upper portions of the woodwork unprotected. I would strongly advise the use of large pieces of felt, to be secured by being laced through holes bored in the planking, so that the employment of nails of any sort, next the horse, should be dispensed with.

Five semi-circular iron bars, to put on and take off, should be placed over the top of the box to give it stability and to afford support to tarpaulins, during wet weather, or to a canvas shade, during fine.

On the floor of the box, a foot from each door, a strong batten $1\frac{1}{2}'' \times 3''$ may be placed. I don't see any necessity for them. Beyond both doorways, an arrangement should be made for placing a manger, out of which the animal may feed. It should be at least a foot away from the door.

The floor of the box should be laid down with about three inches of sand, which will afford firm footing. On no account should straw be put under the horse during rough weather, as it is very slippery. A little may be shaken, a couple of times a day, under the animal, for him to stale on, so that his legs may not become wet. Straw may also be used for preventing the horse from knocking himself about.

The box should be placed on the deck as much "*amid ships*" as possible, and "*athwart ships*," not "*fore and aft.*" Strong iron rings should be let into the deck to enable the box to be securely lashed down.

On long tacks, the horse should face to windward, the box being turned round if necessary.

Steamers, with flush decks and little "shear," are by far the worst on which to convey horses. Those furnished with high bulwarks are the best.

In placing the box, advantage should be taken of any cover that may afford protection from seas breaking over the vessel.

The box should be opened morning and evening to enable the attendant to clean it out, on all other occasions it should be kept closed.

During fine weather, slings should be placed, under the animal, so loose as not to press against his belly, when he stands up, but tight enough to enable him to rest his weight on them if he chooses. If it gets at all rough, the slings should be at once removed.

If the horse be quiet, he may be taken out, from time to time, when the sea is very smooth. On no account should he be allowed to walk on the deck, if it be at all wet or greasy.

There is no need to groom the horse beyond sponging out his eyes, nostrils, dock, &c., and picking out his feet, except when the weather is so fine that he can be taken out on deck, for accidents are most liable to occur.

The horse's head should be secured by means of side ropes attached to the head collar.

During hot weather, the horse should be kept principally on bran and hay, with very little corn. A stock of carrots should if possible be laid in.

After a horse has been on board three weeks, his heels and the walls of his hoofs should again be lowered.

An owner should make arrangements with the captain of the ship, for help to be given by some of the crew, in the event of its being required, during bad weather. "Paying one's footing" on the forecastle, with liberality, will have a good effect.

CHAPTER XII.

Servants.

SYCES—GRASS-CUTTERS—SHOEING SMITHS—RIDING LADS.

Syces.—Although remarks on the management of native servants hardly come within the scope of this work, still the subject so nearly concerns the welfare of the noble animal of whom I am writing, that I cannot refrain from offering the following hints for the use of inexperienced horse owners.

Endeavour to give orders concerning the horses as clearly as possible, so that there may be no chance of their being misunderstood.

Pay the servants liberally and regularly.

Insist on the practice of the syce, in case anything goes wrong with his horse, instantly reporting the matter.

On no account allow a syce, on his own responsibility to treat any ailment his horse may get, such as cracked heels, cuts, &c.; to have any voice in the shoeing of the animal; nor to make any arrangement about getting corn from the *bunnyah* (grain seller).

Avoid abusing or striking the native servants. If any of them be not amenable to kind treatment, dismiss them at once; for a master, that is known to be good to his syces, will never be in want of a choice of applicants for employment.

Never keep a discontented syce.

Make certain that the syce can live on his pay, for if he cannot do so, he will assuredly steal his horse's grain.

Never fine a syce.

Before the cold weather comes on, supply each syce and grass-cutter with warm clothing and a blanket, so that they may not be induced to take off the horse's rugs at night, to use as bedding for themselves.

In racing stables, syces are generally given a month's pay for each race their horses win.

It is the custom to allow each syce a bottle of oil and a pound of country soap, for their respective horses, every month.

If an owner suspects that his syce steals the horse's gram, he may have it sprinkled, by a sweeper, with water before it is given, for then he will regard it as polluted and will not eat it.

The old adage about the master's eye making the horse fat, applies particularly well to India.

A native shoeing-smith usually gives a syce four annas for each time his horse is shod.

It is usual in large stables to make the steadiest syce headman over the others, and to have him responsible in case anything goes wrong. He is called a jemadar syce, and gets an increase of one or two rupees a month.

Grass-cutters.—When a grass-cutter goes out to cut grass, he should bring back a double supply, say 28 lbs, so that half the number of these servants may remain present to help the syces.

Grass-cutters are sometimes expected to provide bedding for the horses. I would advise that, instead of this being done, the owner should allow a rupee a month per horse for straw, requiring in return that the grass-cutter should assist in grooming.

When marching horses by road, each grass-cutter should accompany his horse, and should carry a feed or two of corn, four or five pounds of grass, a brush and currycomb, a hoof-picker, a rubber, picketing ropes, and any odds and ends required, so that the horses may not be inconvenienced by the carts, which carry the corn, gear, &c., being delayed on the road. One bucket between two or three horses will be sufficient.

Shoeing-smiths. — Native shoeing-smiths generally charge from Rs. 1-4 to Rs. 1-8 for shoeing, and 12 annas for removing.

With a large stable, it is a good plan to employ a shoeing-smith on a fixed salary. As a rule, they are neat workmen, and will readily learn if properly taught. Their pay will vary from Rs. 10 to Rs. 16 ; for this they will shoe and plate their master's horses, and, if attached to a racing stable, will accompany them from one meeting to another. They expect permission to shoe during spare hours on their own account.

Riding Lads.—Having got horses to train, the next thing is to find some one to ride them in their gallops, for owners are hardly ever light enough to do this ; besides that, a man can generally train better by superintending work, than by riding gallops himself. If possible, no one over 8 st. 7 lbs. at the very outside should be put up, for any more weight will certainly tend to shorten the stride of a horse, especially that of small ones like

Arabs. On the other hand, too light a lad, say one of 7 stone, may not be strong enough to hold a big horse together, and it is always better to put up a little extra weight in the shape of muscle, than to allow a horse, and particularly a young one, to sprawl all over the place. When a horse has once learned to gallop, unless he be a determined puller, an 8-stone lad will generally be able to do all that is wanted, and with such an one up—if he be at all a "workman"—a horse's legs will stand far longer than under a heavier weight, while the owner need not fear fast work in the same degree, as he should do with the other. One may sometimes chance on an English jockey that is light, does not drink, and is a good race rider. Such a man is indeed a treasure, and will be cheap at Rs. 150 a month, five gold mohurs for a winning, and Rs. 50 for a losing, mount, if an owner keeps four or five horses. But anything short of the genuine article should be shunned, for one of the nondescript lot would take more looking after than a stable of twenty horses. In default of a regular English jockey, an owner's only safety is in employing quiet native lads. Probably he will have to make a selection from his syces and grass-cutters, or from their sons, and be obliged to teach them himself to ride. As the British nondescript is to be avoided, so is the genuine "coachwan," who delights in gold laced caps, and in sticking out his toes in front of his horse's nose. The best native riding lads I have met have been syces' sons, whom their masters taught, and succeeded in keeping in order. From Rs. 6 to Rs. 10—the "coachwan" will require Rs. 30 a month—will be quite enough for such boys, with a small present, say Rs. 5, when any of the horses win. The master should be most careful in keeping them in their place, and should always insist on their helping the syces when grooming. Treat them fairly, and a little liberally at times, but never "give them their heads," nor allow them to gallop a horse, or take one out of the stable without being present one's self. The three great faults of native boys are, that they ride with too long stirrups, stick their toes out too much in front, and don't "ride a horse up to his bridle;" this latter failing is most marked in race riding. Besides this, when silk is donned, they almost all lose their heads when it comes to a finish with English jockeys.

After a native boy has been taught to ride with a fair seat and good hands, the next thing is to give him some idea of pace, which is usually taught by employing the "anna system." As there are sixteen annas in a rupee, a four-anna gallop is made to stand for quarter, eight annas for half, twelve annas for three quarters, and sixteen annas for full speed.

Each quarter of a mile being clearly marked by a post or pillar on the course where horses are galloped, the trainer, when instructing native boys, should tell them, before each gallop is given, how many annas' speed he wants, and then may accurately time each quarter of a mile with his stop watch, so that, after the gallop, he may be able to correct the boy, and point out where the latter went too fast, or too slow, as the case may be. The eye alone is not sufficient to detect slight variations of pace; besides that, if the master holds the watch, the boy will more readily believe that he is being told correctly. If the lad be willing and intelligent under this system, and be given instructions as to holding the hands, keeping the proper position of the leg and foot, judging the right length of stirrup, &c., he ought to learn to ride a training gallop fairly, in say three months. The trainer may teach the lad the rates of speed by a conventional standard (*vide* Chapter on Training); or by the exact division of time; as take for instance that the length of the race course is 1½ miles, that the horse in question can do this, with the boy up, at full speed in 2 m. 50 s., and that the order for the training gallop is "once round at eight annas;" then the time the horse should take would be 5 m. 40 s. This I know is slower than the accepted idea of what half speed should be; but if a faster pace be required, it is just as easy, and perhaps tends less to confuse the lad, to increase the number of annas ordered. Here I take for granted that the race course is level, like almost all our Indian ones. At Dehra Doon, for instance—which is nearly flat for the first half mile, down-hill for nearly 5 furlongs, pretty level for a quarter of a mile, and then up-hill for about the last half mile from home—further directions would be requisite to teach the lad to slightly vary the pace, as the nature of the ground would require.

CHAPTER XIII.

Shoeing.

FORM OF THE NATURAL HOOF—PREPARATION OF THE FOOT—THE SHOE—NAIL-HOLES—PUTTING ON THE SHOE—NECESSITY OF FROG-PRESSURE—PREVENTION OF KNUCKLING OVER AND TRIPPING—PREVENTION OF SPEEDY CUTTING AND BRUSHING—PLATES—CUTTING DOWN.

Form of the Natural Hoof.—The natural shape of the healthy foot of the horse is as follows:

1*st.*—The frog is large, and comes well down on the ground, so as to act as a buffer in diminishing the effects of concussion, and also to prevent the animal from slipping.

2*nd.*—The sole is thick and well protected from injury.

3*rd.*—On hard, level ground, the bearing surface of the foot is composed of the frog, wall of the hoof, and a considerable portion of the sole within the wall.

4*th.*—The slope of the fore-foot, viewed in profile, will, as a rule, be about 50°, while that of the hind feet will be about 55°. This difference in obliquity is due to the fact that the hind feet are chiefly used in propelling the animal, while the fore-feet are principally employed in supporting the weight of his body, hence the wear of the former, at the toes, is greater than that of the latter.

Owing to the manner of attachment of the back tendons and suspensory ligaments (see *Veterinary Notes for*

Horse Owners, pages 9, 10, and 11) the more the toe is raised, while the heel remains on the ground, the tighter will these structures be drawn; hence, the more oblique the foot, the greater danger will there be of sprain.

The more upright the foot, the more direct will the effect of concussion be on the sensitive *laminæ* (the membrane that secretes the inner layer of the horn of the wall), on the pedal bone, and on the coronet; hence, the greater the susceptibility to inflammation of the feet or of the coronet.

As the unprotected hoof readily wears down by friction with the ground, it assumes, when the animal is in a natural state, the slope best fitted to equalise the risk of injury from concussion on the one hand, and strain to tendon and ligament on the other.

The horn of the sole and frog, when it becomes too thick, exfoliates or flakes off, while that of the wall of hoof will grow to an indefinite length, unless it be subjected to friction with the ground, or to some mechanical means for keeping it short.

"If we place a fresh hoof that has never been shod—I mean one that has not been trimmed and dressed by the farrier, and that belonged to an animal with no hereditary defect in this respect—on a table, we will find that the crust, bars, and a considerable portion of the posterior part of the frog are on the same plane and must have sustained wear together. The outer surface of the crust looks shining, tough, and solid; the sole is wonderfully thick, and the horn beneath the flakes, if there are any, is moist, flexible, and easily cut; while the frog, if it be a fore-foot, extends well towards the toe, and is full, round, and solid, with perhaps a few loose shreds in process of exfoliation, and the cleft extending to a very slight depth. In consistence it resembles a piece of India-rubber, if in a moist condition; but if dry, then it is harder and less vulnerable. This is the condition in which the hoof should be studied by every horseman and every farrier: as it is the condition in which it should and can be maintained by careful management and shoeing." (Fleming.)

As the frog and sole form a pedestal for the support of the column of the bones of the foot, they should, naturally, have a firm basis on which to rest.

Young horses require to be shod, or their shoes removed, oftener than older animals, as the horn of their feet grows faster. A three or four year old should, generally, have his shoes taken off every three weeks, while an aged horse may go a week longer.

The clenches of the nails of the old shoe ought to be cut off by the buffer, without the use of the rasp.

As the shoe is used simply as a protection against wear, it should be applied in a manner that it will interfere, as little as possible, with the natural shape and functions of the foot; hence we may adopt the following rules for preparing the foot, before putting on the shoe.

Preparation of the foot.—The horn of the hoof grows equally fast all round, but when the animal is shod, the shoe, being immoveable at the toe, protects it from wear, while the heels are constantly being shortened by the effect of friction with the iron at that part; hence, when the shoe has been on some time, the horn under the toe—in order that the proper slope of the hoof (about 50° or 55°) may be obtained,—will require to be reduced by the rasp or drawing knife, while the heels will seldom need being lowered.

The slope of the foot may be readily measured by a six-inch protractor, furnished with a small plumb line.

The heels should be brought down to a level with the frog, or, if the latter happens to have been cut away, or to be smaller than natural, with the point it would have reached down to, had it been fully developed. When the heels are abnormally low, allowance for the fact should be made by the use of thick-heeled shoes.

The foot should be kept short, not alone to utilise the frog as a buffer, but also to prevent it from becoming diseased, which it will do unless the parts, that secrete it, be constantly stimulated, by pressure, to healthy action.

The horn under the toes and quarters should be lowered, so that the entire breadth of the shoe, on its foot surface, may lie perfectly flat on the sole, as well as on the wall of the hoof; while, at the same time, the proper slope of the foot should be obtained. "It must ever be borne in mind that, if the wall does not stand beyond the level of the sole, it does not require reducing." (Fleming.)

The foot should be of equal height both at the inner and outer heels and quarters.

In this reduction of horn, the rasp only should be used.

"When the circumference of the hoof has at length been brought to a condition to receive the shoe, the rasp must finish its task by removing the sharp edge, and rounding it so as to leave a thick strong border not likely to chip. The unshod hoof nearly always exhibits this provision against fracture of the wall-fibres." (Fleming.)

All loose portions of the frog should be removed by the drawing knife, in order to prevent the lodgment of moisture, which would tend to produce thrush.

In order to prevent the occurrence of corns, the "seat of corn" (see *Veterinary Notes for Horse Owners*) may be slightly eased off with the drawing knife, before applying the shoe.

Thinning the sole, cutting away the "bars," and "opening out the heels," should on no account be permitted.

When a horse goes bare-foot, the lower margin of the walls of the hoof should be rasped round, so as to prevent the fibres of the horn from splitting.

The Shoe.—The following considerations should determine the shape of the shoe:

1*st.*—The foot surface of the shoe should be perfectly flat, so that the sole may aid the wall of the hoof in supporting the weight of the animal.

2*nd.*—The shoe should be as thin as possible—consistent with its standing wear, and retaining its shape—so that pressure may be put on the frog.

3*rd.*—The shoe should be of a uniform thickness at the toes, quarters, and heels, so that the proper bearing of the foot be not disturbed.

4*th.*—The ground surface of the shoe should be bevelled, in order to increase the foot-hold of the horse, and also to lessen the weight of metal employed.

I would strongly advise the adoption of Mr. Fleming's shoe, as described in his work *Practical Horse-shoeing*, to which I beg to refer my readers.

The narrow heeled shoe advocated by Mr. Thacker and Professor Williams, on account of its accurately conforming to the shape of the ground surface of the crust, is not applicable to use in India, because it requires very careful fitting, unattainable when horses are shod cold, moreover the iron used in India is so soft that there is always danger of the heels of the shoe getting shifted in position during wear. Such an eventuality would cause the heels of the foot to become knocked to pieces by the edge of the heels of the shoe. Hence it is advisable to have the shoe moderately broad at the heel, so as to allow for a possible change of position. In this case the "seat of corn" should be eased off before shoeing.

For ordinary saddle horses, shoes, weighing ½ lb. each, will be quite heavy enough.

For fast road-work, I would advise that moderately thick shoes be used, so as to diminish the effects of concussion, for on metalled roads it is almost impossible, with the ordinary system of shoeing, to obtain sufficient bearing on the frog to make that part adequately perform its office as a buffer.

The inside edge of the ground surface of hind shoes should be rounded off, so that the horse may injure himself as little as possible, in case he happens to over-reach.

Fore shoes may have clips in front. Hind shoes should have side clips, while the toes should be square—

leaving an overlapping rim of crust at the toe, which should be rounded off with the rasp—so in order to lessen the chance of over-reaching.

The shoes should be made to project slightly beyond the ends of the heels, though, of course, not to an extent that would render them liable to the risk of being caught—if on the fore-feet—by the hind, so that advantage be taken of the hard heels of the foot to support pressure. If the shoes be set slightly within the heels, it will be found, when the time for removing comes round, that, owing to the growth of the foot, the heels of the shoe will have become imbedded into the softer horn in front, so that it will be impossible to keep the profile of the foot at its proper slope.

Native shoeing-smiths, to save themselves trouble, will, almost always, if ordered to supply thick heeled shoes, bring ordinary ones, whose heels they have thickened by simply reducing the breadth of the web by hammering, instead of getting shoes made expressly for the purpose required. As they manufacture neither shoes nor nails, but get them ready made from the *mistree* (blacksmith), there is usually some difficulty in inducing them to adopt any new ideas concerning the shape of shoes.

I cannot too strongly condemn the practice, that is carried on in some forges, of always applying thick heeled shoes. To such an extent is this observed, that I have often seen the heels of sound strong feet cut down, in order to fit these shoes. Their habitual use is never necessary, except in the case of disease, or when the foot has been mutilated; even then they should be used only as a temporary measure. The practice of applying shoes considerably thinner at the heels than at the toes—with the view of obtaining increased frog pressure—is now almost obsolete. They cause an abnormal amount of strain to be thrown on the suspensory ligaments and back tendons.

When the ground is slippery, calkins may be used on the hind feet. For ordinary saddle work, they should not be more than one-third of an inch high. They should never be put on the fore-feet.

A set of shoes of good iron will generally bear two removings.

A bar shoe for a fore-foot—to be used when the horse is at work—should not be made circular, but heart-shaped, so that it may not get caught by the hind shoe.

Nail-holes.—Shoes should not be fullered, but the nail holes should be punched square and to narrow downwards. "The square cavity, wide at the top, and tapering to the bottom, gives a secure and solid lodgment to the nail-head, which of course should be of the same shape; it does not weaken the shoe, is easily made, can be placed nearer the outer or inner margin as required, and when filled with the nail is as capable of resisting wear as any other part." (Fleming.)

Except for road work, the nail-heads, after the nails are driven, should not be filed level with the shoe.

Shoeing-smiths, in India, almost always make the mistake of punching the nail holes too near the outside edge, which necessitates the baneful practice of fixing the shoe within the circumference of the wall. Were the outside edge of the shoe, with nail-holes punched thus, to fit exactly with the outside of the wall, as it ought to do, the hold, the nails would then have, would be too slight to retain the shoe in its position for any time. By setting the shoe within the circumference of the sole, in order to obtain more hold for the nails, there is a rim of horn left round the shoe, which has to be rasped round to prevent it from breaking and splitting irregularly; this accounts for the univeral use of the rasp, on the lower part of the crust of the hoof, among ignorant shoeing-smiths. Having accepted a false system of punching the nail-holes, they are forced, in order to keep the shoe on, to fix it in a manner that necessitates the use of the rasp on the outside of the horn. If a horse owner makes one of them fit such a shoe exactly to the circumference of the foot, and if it, from insufficient hold, comes off in a few days, the fact of its doing so will be a convincing proof to the shoeing-smith of the excellence of his own views on the subject, and the absurdity of our new fangled ideas.

For a foot with a full amount of horn, $\frac{3}{10}$ths of an inch will be about the proper distance that the nail-holes should be from the outside edge of the shoe on its foot surface; a little more towards the toes, and a little less towards the heels.

The nail-holes should not be punched before the foot is ready for the shoe to be applied to it, so that the smith may avoid the parts of the hoof, which may have been pierced by the old nails, or which may have become chipped or split.

Several years ago, Mr. W. Thacker invented a shoe in which the nail-holes were punched in the centre of the web, inclining outwards, so that the nails took a very firm hold and came out low down, extending upwards not more than $\frac{3}{4}$ inch, thereby diminishing the risk of pricking the horse. The bevel of the ground surface of the shoe protected the nail-heads. This is an admirable system with feet that have plenty of horn.

Fitting the Shoe to the Foot.—As the old adage expresses it, "the shoe should be made to fit the foot, and not the foot to fit the shoe."

If practicable, the shoe should be fitted on at a red heat and never cold. The advantages of the former over the latter practice are as follows:

1*st.*—The shoe is more readily brought into the required shape.

2*nd.*—Exact juxtaposition between the iron and the hoof is obtained, with consequent increased security.

3*rd.*—The bearing surface of the hoof is rendered impervious to the injurious action of water, by the fact of its having been charred.

4*th.*—The heat renders the horn less liable to split on the nails being driven.

Putting on the Shoe.—The nails should take a short thick hold of the crust, and should not come higher up on the crust than one inch from the lower margin.

After the nails are driven, the rasp should not touch the crust, except to file a little of the thin horn from underneath the ends of the nails, so that the clenches, when they are turned down, may be properly supported.

Unless a horse is inclined to brush, the clenches

should not be filed down, and then, only those on the inside quarter.

Necessity of Frog-pressure.—If the crust and heels of a horse's foot be allowed to grow too long, the frog will contract, shrivel up, and become diseased, owing to the absence of the pressure which is essential to its healthy development. In such a case, the means to be adopted for curing the complaint should be the opposite to that which induced it, namely, allowing the frog to get as much pressure as possible, by lowering the heels and crust as far as is compatible with the horse being able to walk bare-foot without tenderness. No shoes should be applied until the frogs have recovered their natural size, while the animal, in the mean time, should get plenty of walking exercise on soft ground. If the feet be brittle, tips may be used.

Prevention of Knuckling over and Tripping.—Horses often knuckle over with the hind feet, as well as trip with the fore, on account of the profile of the foot not being upright enough. Rasping down the toes, or raising the heels will be the proper preventive means. In harness especially, horses frequently knuckle over behind, from not being sufficiently held together. In draught, an animal is more " by his forehand," than when in saddle.

Prevention of Speedy Cutting and Brushing.—By proper shoeing we can generally prevent speedy cutting, which is the act of a horse striking the inside of one foreleg, close below the knee, with the inside edge of the shoe of the opposite fore-foot. Horses that turn out their toes ("dish"), are very liable to this accident. It is impossible to see the exact manner speedy cutting occurs, for, as it happens in the fast gallop, the eye cannot follow the action of the horse; it can only occur, however, at a moment when the hit leg is on the ground, while the other is in the air; for were it otherwise, no system of shoeing could diminish the liability of a horse to speedy cutting; because the method of shoeing can only affect the position of the leg when it is actually on the ground, for the moment it is raised, the effect of the shoeing, in lessening its liability to be struck by other leg, must be inert. This is evident when we consider that, by keeping the inside quarter of the hoof higher than the outside, we can generally prevent a horse, that turns his toes out, from getting cut on that leg, as the direct action of this arrangement is to counteract the "dish" of the pastern, and thereby to remove the knee from the line of the stroke of the other leg. If the hoof will allow of it, is always better to alter the level by rasping down the crust and sole on which the outside half of the shoe will rest, than by using a shoe of which the inside half is thicker than the outside half.

This system of shoeing horses, that turn out their toes, will also, generally, prevent them from "brushing."

If we carefully observe the action of the forelegs of the horse in the canter, we will see that the leg, which is not leading, comes first on the ground in advance of the other, and immediately afterwards the hoof of the latter passes by the cannon bone of the non-leading leg (which at that moment is on the ground) in front of whose hoof it is placed, though of course in its own line of progression. It is evident that, if speedy cutting occurs, it must happen at the very moment when the hoof of the leading leg passes close below the knee of the non-leading one, and consequently the latter's liability to be struck can be lessened, or altogether obviated by removing its knee and cannon bone out of the line of the stroke of the leading leg. Mr. Spooner remarks—"Many horses strike from weakness, and cease to do so when they regain strength and condition. This is more particularly observable with young horses." I have also known a horse, that was a most determined puller, speedy cut only when he tired in his gallop. The shoeing of such horses should not be interfered with, but boots should be used for prevention.

Plates—Are simply very light shoes, which are intended to last for only one or two races. They are generally fixed on the morning of the day before the race, and the horse is then sent for a short gallop to see that all is right, which constitutes that day's work. A light plate for an Arab will weigh about 2¾ oz. and be about half an inch broad. But as most horses, out here, have to run at different meetings, that follow each other in quick succession, I much prefer using a stouter plate, in fact a compromise between the plate and shoe used in training. Such an one for an Arab will weigh about 3½ oz. and ought to last through three weeks' work, and may be made five-eighths of an inch broad all round. Plates and light shoes may have a clip in front for the fore-feet, to give them additional hold. Nails for plates should be much lighter than those for ordinary shoes.

Mr. Darvill recommends, "if a horse's feet are weak

and low, and he has to run on hard ground, it would be advisable to let him run in his shoes."

Cutting down.—To get ponies, galloways, and horses for "give-and-take" races down to a height lower than nature ever intended them to be, owners have often used the most ingenious expedients. Shoeing *à la Charlier*—with a quarter of an inch allowed for plates—will, of course, be a direct gain of a quarter of an inch. Again a horse will measure lower after a hard gallop than at any other time, especially if he be allowed to stand, after the exercise, long enough to get chilled. But the real art lies in teaching a horse to measure low. A horse's height will only be affected by cutting down the heels, for the length of the toes makes no difference. Better, indeed, never run a horse at all than to be obliged to resort to such expedients. Teaching a horse to measure low is simply the art of making a fool of the person appointed at a race meeting to determine horses' heights, and to accomplish this, the owner has previously to train his animal to stand quiet in the most advantageous position. Some horses measure lowest with their heads down, others with them up, and all with their fore legs wide apart as viewed in front. The latter dodge often passes muster, though of course no one would fail to see, if a horse's fore legs were stretched out as viewed in profile.

When an animal is well within the *limit* of height, it is the most foolish policy to try to gain a small allowance of weight, by even very slight paring down, if such cutting bring the foot out of its natural slope, or be liable to make the horse go tender; for a quarter of an inch off a horse's heels, more than ought to be taken off, will often endanger the suspensory ligaments by the strain entailed upon them from the abnormal slope of the profile of the foot. To lessen this strain, the toe also should be cut down as far as practicable. By the C. T. C. Rules, 4 lbs. is allowed for each ½ inch in galloway and pony races, while an official measurement once made holds good for the meeting.

TRAINING AND RACING.

PART II.

TRAINING AND RACING.

CHAPTER I.

Racing in India.

ACING MEN AND HORSES—ON FORMING A USEFUL STABLE—THE STYLE OF RACE-HORSE SUITED TO INDIA—THE DIFFERENT CLASSES AND THEIR RESPECTIVE FORM—TIMING.

In England, racing is almost entirely confined to professionals, and to a few monied men, who can afford to run horses for amusement, just as others go in for yachting, hunting or shooting, caring little for the cost, as long as they get sufficient excitement out of the particular sport they may pursue. There, racing is such a complete business, and its attendant expenses are so heavy, that a man of moderate means cannot, with any safety, follow it, unless he adopts it as his profession. In India, the small amount of public money and limited speculation render the turf too precarious a means of living, except in the case of jockeys and trainers, while few of the latter find training pays, unless they be light enough to earn their winning and losing mounts on the horses of which they have charge.

There are few representatives of the monied section

of the racing public in India, which is, above all others, the country for a comparatively poor man to do a little racing in, without it costing him much, provided he knows *something* about horses; for stable expenses are very moderate (say forty rupees a month for each horse including every thing), while none but first class animals cost any extravagant sums. But the fact which enables men of small means to race in India, is the system that divides the majority of races among different classes of horses. These events serve both to fill up prospectuses, and to accommodate owners. It is, in most places, difficult to collect sufficient money to attract first class animals, even were there more of them in this country; the fact being that, except at the few centres of racing, it is impossible to get a field of such horses, while handicaps have to be resorted to in order to bring the one or two of them, that ever appear at a small meeting, together with the second raters. On this account, stewards of race meetings, in order to get fields together, are obliged to add to handicaps, "all horses,' and selling races, those for Arabs, country-breds, galloways, ponies, and for maidens of the different classes, not to mention still more minute division. Thus an owner would have bad luck indeed, were he not to find some event or the other suitable to his horses, even if he had nothing better than a country-bred pony, a half miler, and a jumping nag of sorts, although their united value might not exceed a thousand rupees. It may be objected that this is not *racing*, which it certainly is not in the English sense of the word, but for all that, a man, who is sufficiently fond of horses to look after and manage them himself, can get good sport with a few moderate ones. Personally I'd take more interest in training an inferior horse and by skill and work, winning races with him in moderate company, than in owning (as many do at home) first class horses, which might be entirely in the hands of a trainer, on whom I would have to be solely dependent for information as to their form and pretensions.

Six or seven horses will be found a large enough string for up-country meetings, if the owner intends to look after them himself, and expects them to win enough to cover their expenses. To accomplish this, one should have horses of an useful class, that would be certain to find races to run for, at the different meetings to which they might go, with a fair chance of pulling off an event now and then. Keeping horses too good for one's line of country, is hardly more paying than owning horses too bad for it. The presence of first class horses (if their form be known) deters owners from entering against them, the races do not fill, and even if they do so on an odd occasion, there is either no lottery, or the horses get bid up so high, that it is simply "buying money" to touch them. While in handicaps, a good horse, among moderate ones, gets so much weight piled on, that the odds are, it either breaks him down, or spoils his action.

A first class steeple chaser does not come under this objection, for "between the flags" one's money being "in the air," men will always enter on the outside chance of a fall or refusal. Besides this, the added money alone is generally worth running for, even without dipping into the lotteries, which, by-the-bye, usually fill well on a "lep race."

One or two good second class Walers, which can stay up to a mile and a half, a couple of Arabs—especially if one or both be galloways, and are at the same time good enough to run among the big ones—like what Chieftain, Caliph, and Abdool Rayman were—a fast 13-2 Arab, or 13-hand country-bred pony, a half miler for selling races, and a good chaser would form the beau ideal of an useful stable for up-country meetings.

A good maiden is a real Eldorado, whether Waler, Arab, or chaser; but they are particularly hard to get, and uncertain to back, unless one has first-rate trying tackle with which to test their powers. I may here remark that maidens in India take, to some extent, the place which two and three year olds occupy in England, for many of the most important races are confined to horses that have never won during any previous season, irrespective of their age, though, of course, allowance of weight for it is always given.

Though Arabs and country-breds get three and two stone respectively from Walers for class allowance, this difference does not bring the best of them together with even second rate Colonials.

In late years, except Echo and Merryman, we have had no Cape horses that could hold their own against Walers, while the C. T. C. scale of weights, by which they get an allowance of a stone from the latter, show clearly how cheaply their powers are held among racing men.

There is a sort of fatality about English horses in

India, for few indeed out of the many that are imported, prove, either as racers, or as ordinary riding horses, to be worth their passage-money out to this country. Their feet and legs generally go to pieces on our hard ground.

The style of race horse which will pay out here, is one that is particularly sound, can stay a distance, carry weight, and be at the same time pretty fast—qualifications that will ensure a long figure for their possessor in any country.

The majority of Indian race courses are so hard that they tend to make horses, which are trained on them, go short, and "stilty;" while even when the track happens to be soft, the "going" is simply heavy without any elasticity, so that the horse is taught to "dwell on his stride." We hardly ever obtain the happy medium afforded by the light springy turf in England. Good legs and feet are the first considerations, and then comes the power of carrying weight and being able to stay. An English horse should be able to race under 11 stone, and a Waler under 7 lbs. less, and with these weights up, should be able to travel 1½ miles. If a sound game horse can do all this, his being a little "troubled with the slows," will not prevent him from paying his way. A flashy thorough-bred, that can stagger home in extraordinary good time over 5 furlongs with 6 stone up, would be utterly out of place in India, and would only be fit for selling races.

Race horses cost so much in England, that I strongly suspect, since the time of Morning Star, there has been hardly a single horse sent out here with even third class pretensions. Bridesmaid is the best we have had for some years, and the way this mare—which at home was only up to about fifty-pound selling form—made our best Walers gallop, goes far to prove that the only reason English horses get beaten by Walers in India, is that those sent out are but the very dregs of English racing stables. Perhaps the greater soundness of the Waler may have something to say to his success. I believe that blood stock are bred in the Colonies more with a view to obtain stoutness, than they are at home; besides this, Australia has more or less a tropical climate. We have yet to see how even a second class English race horse—not a selling plater, but one worth say £1,000—would fare with our Walers. Possibly one as good or better could be imported from Australia for a similar sum. There is hardly scope enough in India to make such a large investment in one horse pay, which few out here could afford to do, even if so inclined. At the prices which are given in India—£500 or £600—for a Kingcraft or a Satellite, and a couple of thousand rupees for a second rater, more value for one's money can be got by investing in Walers, and consequently they are the only horses, with an occasional exile from England, that are kept for races for "all horses."

When the Waler colt Kingcraft, 3 years, 5 st. 13 lbs., won the Governor-General's Cup (January, 1873), 2 miles in 3 m. 41 s., almost everyone said that he was the best horse ever imported, while some few wondered at his owner not sending him to run in England. To estimate approximately the chance he might have had there, even in Handicaps over his own best distance, let us take the only "line" at our disposal, namely "time." Chivalrous,

4 years, 7 st., won the Great Ebor Handicap (August, 1874) 2 miles, in 3 m. 31 s. Both Chivalrous and Kingcraft respectively won these races with great ease.

In hack selling races—winner to be sold for from Rs. 200 to 500—when not beyond ¾ mile, country-breds sometimes hold their own; those that do so having almost always a strong dash of English blood, from which they generally derive their turn of speed, as well as some of their inherited infirmities, which doom them to running for such minor events. A useful horse for such races—winner to be sold for Rs. 500 or Rs. 600—ought to be able to do with 10 st. up, ½ mile, in 53 to 53½ s., or ¾ mile in 1 m. 21 s., or 1 m. 22 s. on an ordinary race course.

Since the time of Meg Merrilis,—which won the Governor-General's Cup in 1858, and again in the following year—Shamrock, the black mare Gypsy, Deception, and M. T. late Mermaid, late Jessie, have been nearly the only country-breds that could stay as well as gallop. Gypsy beat the Earl and Silvertail, who were both quite first class Arabs, at the Calcutta Meeting of 1871, doing the mile in 1 m. 52 s., carrying 8 st. 8 lbs., but by maiden allowances and penalties, the Arab's were actually giving her 8 lbs. At weight for age and class the Arabs might probably have beaten her, and would certainly have done so under these conditions, for two miles.

As a rule Arabs will always beat country-breds for any distance from a mile and a quarter upwards, at their class allowance, though the latter have the legs of the former for shorter races.

For galloway and pony races, Arabs are undoubtedly

the best, though now and then a Waler may be found good enough to run in these classes, but a country-bred never. The *multum in parvo* style, which is here wanted, is the very thing that is found almost impossible to breed in India. The chesnut 13-2 Kattywar Robin was the best country-bred pony or galloway I have seen, but even he was never within a stone of his stable companion King David, the Arab pony, though they were exactly the same height. Robin looked quite three-quarters Arab, as did that little wonder Orion.

Though there are many instances of 13-2 ponies running successfully among galloways (14 hands and under) at the usual allowances of 4 lbs. the half inch, it is rare indeed to meet with a pony lower than that which can do so.

At most meetings, the following classes are those for which races are generally made, with the distances usually run:—

1	All horses	1 to 2 miles.
2	Arabs	1¼ to 2 „
3	Arabs and country-breds ...	1 to 2 „
4	Country-breds	½ to 1 mile.
5	Galloways (14 hands and under) ...	½ to 1 „
6	Ponies (13-2 and under)	½ „
7	Ponies (13 hands and under) ...	¼ to ½ „
8	Selling Race horses	½ to 1 „

In discussing the "form" of horses, I have been obliged to bring in the subject of timing, as it is so universally used and regarded out here. I am quite aware how fallible a test it is, and how much it varies according to the state of the course and the way in which a race is run. The great majority of Indian courses are so level, and the "going" so very much the same on all, that there cannot be the same objection to timing in this country as in England, where every course varies in severity, while rain may fall at any time and make the track heavy. Nevertheless, in races where several horses start, and in which the running is certain to be cut out by some of them, the timing of similar horses is singularly close, on the same courses, considering how variable the English climate is. For instance, take that of the great three-year old races, from year to year.

We find timing is a perfectly reliable test in pedestrianism, and can pronounce with certainty that a man, who can do his 100 yards under 10 seconds, or his mile under 4 m. 20 s. on level ground, is undoubtedly a first class runner; and so would be a horse which could, with weight for age and class, do his mile in 1 m. 44 s., or two miles in 3 m. 42 s., on the Calcutta Course for instance, *if he'll but try* in public; for herein lies the source of nine-tenths of the disappointments timing leads to. The "going" on most Indian race courses, except at Bangalore, Secunderabad, Poonah, and Dehra Doon, is very similar, being almost quite level, and pretty hard. As it is impossible to get all horses to run the same in public as in private, I would strongly advise the young turfite, to limit the use of the stop watch to public performances, and to regulating the pace of training gallops. If one wishes to test the powers of a young one, it should be done, not by "putting him against the watch," but by trying him with some horse that has recently run well in public, and is at the time of the trial in racing condition. Then, if the young one beats the trial horse, and does the distance in really good time, it is all the more to his credit. No exact information as to a horse's form can be obtained by timing his gallops when he takes them alone: for not one horse in ten will run the same by himself, as in company, and it would only lead to disappointment to allow for an error that, for all the owner knows, may be either for, or against his horse's powers.

I believe that, even with the greatest care and under the most favourable circumstances, the time test alone cannot be relied upon, with a smaller margin for error than 10 lbs. in 1 mile, which, allowing for difference in horses, and for the different way races are run, we may assume would be equivalent to from 20 to 30 yards in that distance, or from 1¼ to 2 seconds, which doesn't say very much for timing, beyond affording an approximate idea of a horse's powers.

On a heavy course a horse will take, to do a mile, 4 or 5 seconds longer than on a light one.

Another thing to be considered is, that we must allow at least half a second for the timer's own individual error: while there is still more to be allowed for the way horses get off whether from a flying start, or from a walk.

It does not at all follow that because a horse cannot be got to do good time in private, he is, on that account, a moderate animal; for many—and particularly stayers—require the stimulus of company to make them extend themselves.

When timing in private, the trainer should be most careful to observe how his horses finish, for one who finishes strong, will always—provided he runs honest—beat another that can do even slightly better time, but is "all out" on nearing the winning post.

We will now glance at some instances of first class timing, done by horses of the different classes which I have specified.

At Calcutta, 1869, the Viceroy's Cup, 2 miles, was won by the Waler mare Favourite, 9 st. 5 lbs., in 3 m. 42 s.

At Calcutta, January, 1873, the br. w., 3-year old colt Kingcraft, 5 st. 13 lbs., won the Governor General's Cup, 2 miles, in 2 m. 41 s.

At Sonepore, 1873, Satellite, 10 st. 8 lbs., and the 5-year old mare Phillipine, 8 st. 9 lbs., went out the 1st mile in the race for the Ticcaree Cup in 1 m. 44 s.; and the mare won in 2 m. 57 s., the distance of the race being 1 mile 5 furlongs.

At Calcutta, December, 1877, the b. w. g. Fisherboy won the Merchants' Cup, 1 m. 6 f. 132 yds., in 3 m. 19¾ s., doing the last 1¾ miles in 3 m. 11 s. The br. w. h. Kingcraft, 10 st. 11 lbs., running third, was beaten by four lengths.

Now for Arab timing.

At Calcutta, December, 1869, Akbar, 9 st. 4 lbs., won the 1 mile Handicap with ease in 1 m. 52 s.

At Bombay, March, 1871, Growler, 9 st. 5 lbs., beat The Earl in the 1½ miles Handicap in 2 m. 52 s.

At Sonepore, in 1871, Silvertail, 9 st. 10 lbs., won the Desert Stakes, 2 miles, in 3 m. 54 s.

At Madras, February, 1874, g. a. h. Lucifer, 10 st. 5 lbs., with a flying start, won the 1 mile Arab Handicap in 1 m. 52 s.

At Calcutta, December, 1877, g. a. h. Saracen, 9 st, won the Little Albert Cup, 1 mile, in 1 m. 50½ s.

The chesnut Cape horse Echo, 9 st., at Calcutta, December, 1871, won the Stand Plate, 1 mile, in 1 m. 48 s.

The b. c. b. g. Shamrock, 8 st. 13 lbs., at Calcutta, 1870, ran a mile in 1 m. 52 s., which is the same time that we have seen Gypsy do that distance with 8 st. 8 lbs. up.

Both Lurline at Sonepore, and M. T. at Mozufferpore, have done ¾ mile in 1 m. 24 s. with 10 st. 7 lbs. up.

At Meerut, November, 1877, the c. c. b. m. Clemence, 9 st. 1 lb., won the Haupper Stakes, ¾ miles, in 1 m. 21 s.

At Sonepore, 1871, the 13-2 King David, 8 st. 9 lbs., did ½ mile in 54 s.

The 13-2 Arab Abdool Rayman (Little Hercules), 8 st. 10 lbs., won the 1½ mile Handicap, in 1871, up the trying Poonah hill, in 2 m. 55 s. In the same year he won the Maiden Galloway Plate, 1¼ mile, at Bombay, with 8 st. 6 lbs. up, in 2 m. 23 s.

The 13-hand c. b. p. Orion, with a feather, was able to do in his best days ½ mile in 55 s.

In giving these times, I have, as much as possible, considered only the performances of aged platers, in order to simplify comparison between the different classes; and for the same reason have given even distances.

It is hard to define what second class form is, as it principally depends on where one is racing; for, of course, what would be second class at first class meetings, would become first class at minor ones. At the large fixtures, second class time, for Walers at weight for age for a mile, would be about 1 m. 50 s.; for 1¼ mile, 2 m. 20 s. A second class Arab, that would be useful for up-country meetings, ought to do a mile in 1 m. 57 s. and 1½ mile in 2 m. 55 s. carrying weight for age.

The following are a few instances of the best Arab timing in former days:—

At Calcutta.

1845-46, b. a. h. Selim	...	9st. 5lbs.	3 miles in	5m. 54s.
1846-47, b. a. h. Child of the Islands	...	7st. 8lbs.	1½ „ „	2m. 48s.
„ „ „	...	8st. 13lbs.	2 „ „	3m. 50s.
„ „ „	...		1 „ „	1m. 51s.
1847-48, „ „	...	8st. 7lbs.	¾ „ „	1m. 21s.
„ g. a. h. Honeysuckle	...	8st.	2 „ „	3m. 48s.
„ b. a. h. Minuet	...	8st. 7lbs.	2¼ „ „	4m. 19s.

An idea of first class Indian time may be gained from the following extract from the *Oriental Sporting Magazine*:—

"We subjoin our notion of good timing for the distances given by, of course, first class horses, and on a course equal to that of Calcutta."—Editor, *O. S. M.*

Timing for Walers.			Timing for Arabs.		
Weight.	Distance.	Time.	Weight.	Distance.	Time.
10 stone.	½ mile ...	0m. 52s.	9 stone.	½ mile ...	0m. 54s.
„	¾ „ ...	1 18	„	¾ „ ...	1 21
„	1 „ ...	1 49	„	1 „ ...	1 54
„	1¼ „ ...	2 20	„	1¼ „ ...	2 24
„	1½ „ ...	2 49	„	1½ „ ..	2 52
„	1¾ „ ...	3 19	„	1¾ „ ...	3 26
„	2 miles ...	3 44	„	2 miles ...	3 54

The following are two instances of first class Australian time made at the Hawkesbury Race Club, Spring Meeting, August, 1875.

Hawkesbury Grand Handicap, 2 miles, won by ch. m. Calumny, 6 years, 8 st. 4 lbs., in 3 m. 35 s.

The Turf Club Handicap, 1½-miles, won by br. h. King of the West, 5 years, 7 st., in 2 m. 41 s.

The quality of the Walers imported is improving every year, while that of the Arabs appears to be deteriorating.

CHAPTER II.

Food.

As the subject of food has been fully discussed in Part I on Horse Management, I shall treat on it here, only as far as it relates to training. If oats can be procured heavy enough, they are by far the best grain on which to train. In England, old horses, whose powers of assimilation are somewhat impaired, are often allowed, with good results, a small proportion of beans, or half beans and half peas, with their corn, in order to increase the nutrient value of the food, as the measure of a horse's appetite is by bulk, and not by weight. With our light Indian oats, one part of gram to three of corn will be found to be a good general division. The same proportion of *kúlthee* and oats may be used. Boiled *úrud* may be substituted for *kúlthee.* If oats be not procurable, parched barley and gram may be given.

I may here remark that beans, peas, gram, *kúlthee,* and *úrud* are very similar in their composition, while barley closely resembles oats. These grains differ, however, in their action on the digestive organs, beans having a constipating tendency, while both gram and barley have the opposite effect.

The dung of a healthy horse should be fairly formed, brittle, friable, and devoid of any adherent mucus. As health is, above all others, the one essential condition, without which it is impossible to get a horse fit, the trainer should so regulate the food that the dung should present a normal appearance, which is comparatively easy to do in England, where sound, heavy oats are procurable; but in India, where gram or barley often have to be used, the task is much more difficult, always considering the large amount of hard food that is requisite for the utmost development of a horse's powers. In cases where the digestion begins to become upset by too highly stimulating a diet, the trainer should diminish the quantity, and should further use means to restore the functions to a healthy condition. With this object in view, he may mix chopped hay through the corn, or use, instead of it, from 1 to 2 lbs. of dry bran daily; or give a few bran or bran and linseed mashes.

As a rule, as soon as a horse gets gradually into strong work, he ought to have as much corn as he can eat, provided the chief part of it be oats. Ten lbs. will be enough to commence on with a Waler, which quantity may gradually be increased by 1 lb. a week. A full average amount would be gram 4 lbs., oats 14 lbs.; or gram 6 lbs., parched barley 10 lbs., together with 1 lb. of *suttoo.*

An Arab will eat from 2 lbs. to 4 lbs. less corn than a Waler.

Oats, gram, and barley should always be given quite dry, the first should be bruised, and the other two broken.

I found the following food suited an old Arab, that I trained very successfully, better than any other :—

Oats ...	...	...	... 6 lbs.
Gram	...	...	... 4 „
Bran ...	...	...	... 2 „
Linseed	...	...	... 1 „

At night, the two latter—the linseed having been previously kept boiling for two or three hours—were given mixed with 1 lb. of corn.

My experience is, that even with Indian oats, a horse can be got at least 7 lbs. better, than when any other grain is substituted for it.

Horses in training should get a bran, or bran and linseed mash once, and in some cases twice, a week, as they may seem to require it. Saturday and Wednesday nights are generally the most convenient times at which to give it.

Through the cold weather, a couple of pounds of carrots may be allowed, with great advantage, to each horse; in case they be not available, some other green food may be substituted. The roots, or green fodder, may be stopped a week or ten days before running.

Linseed or hay tea may be given from time to time.

It is impossible to train a horse properly without good grass, on the quality of which, quite as much, if not more, depends than on that of the corn. For this purpose only the best picked *doob* grass (Madrassee *hurry-alee*) should be used, after being dried in the sun for a day. As a rule, the horse should be allowed as much of it as he will eat; unless, indeed, he be a very gross feeder; the time of his preparation be limited; or he be fat, while his legs are infirm. A horse on a full allowance of corn will eat far less hay than what is commonly supposed. Colonel Fitzwygram states, that "practically it will be found that horses, which are not limited in regard to oats, will not usually consume above six pounds of hay per diem."

In concluding this subject, I may remark that the trainner, while supplying the horse with food suitable for the requirements of his system, when undergoing severe work, should never lose sight of the fact that the proper assimilation of such food, can only be ensured as long as the functions of digestion are in a healthy condition. To maintain which, he should study the general question of diet, the various peculiarities of each individual horse; should preserve a sufficient variety in the food, so that the animal be not disgusted by a never-ending monotony, and should supplement the hard fare, from time to time, with a handful of carrots or turnips; a bunch of lucern, of freshly picked green grass, or of young oats or wheat; a piece of sugar-cane; a linseed mash; anything, in fact, to keep their appetites from palling on corn, which is, after all, the chief source from which to obtain muscle.

CHAPTER III.

Daily Routine.

DURING the training months, the syces should be up nearly an hour before day-light, and should give each of the horses a little water, say half a gallon, and from one, to one and-a-half pounds of corn, which quantity may be increased to two pounds, if the animals are to be kept out longer than three hours. When this is eaten, the clothing worn at night should be taken off, the horses' coats should be wisped over, and smoothened down with a towel, their manes and tails set straight, their eyes, muzzles, and docks sponged out, and fresh clothing put on according to the weather. They are now taken to the exercising ground and are kept walking for fully an hour, so that they may empty themselves, and then they get their work, fast or slow, as the case may be.

When a horse has finished his exercise, he is trotted to the rubbing-down shed, or to the lee of any favourable cover. The girths should now be slackened, and if he be worked in clothing, his hood should be quickly removed, and if there be any sweat visible on his neck, it should be scraped off with the copper scrapers that are made for that purpose. Above all things, the hollow between his jaws should be carefully dried with a towel, for neglect of this precaution has often been the cause of subsequent cough, or sore-throat. His bridle should now be changed for a common watering one, as horses are apt to spoil the reins by biting them whilst being groomed. If the animal be restive, a man may stand in front with a rein in each hand, and hold his head up, while one or two syces, at each side, rub him down with a wisp of dry straw, or of *sun* (unprepared hemp). The wisps should be rubbed well into the coat, and should not be used as fans. If he be inclined to bite, the syce who holds the reins may keep a stick in one hand pointing across the horse's face, so as to keep him in order, or a muzzle may be put on. His breast-piece is next removed, the base of his neck and chest scraped and dried, and lastly, his body clothing is taken off, and his barrel, loins, and quarters finished. Dry, light clothing is put on, and he should get half a bucket of water—say about a gallon. This rubbing down should not take more than five or six minutes, and after it, the animal should be started home at a walk, without further delay.

Though the horse, on leaving his stable, should be ridden at a walk before his work commences, he had better be led home, for then he will return cooler, and will not be so liable to break out into a sweat again, as he would be, were he ridden back. Having arrived at his stable, he may get half a bucket of water, with or without *suttoo,* as the trainer sees fit; and then he is tied up, his clothing removed, and the grooming begun.

I may here remark that, if a horse's coat is long, a considerable amount of hair can be got off by hand-rubbing him completely over, immediately after his gallop, in place of wisping him down. For this, the help of four men is imperative, lest any one part of his body be allowed to cool faster than another. While handrubbing, the syces should keep their hands damp with water, so as to get more hair off.

The grooming being finished, the horse gets the remainder of his water—as much as he will drink—or water and *suttoo*, as the case may be. He may have a handful of dried *doob* grass to amuse himself with until he gets his feed. The syce now tidies up the stable, lays down the bedding, prepares and gives the corn. He should not spend more than a quarter of an hour over these preparations.

I strongly advocate the practice of putting dried grass before the horse at the same time that he gets his corn. A supply of fresh water may, with advantage, be always left in the stall.

The stables are now closed till twelve or half past, and the horses are allowed to rest undisturbed.

At noon, the animal is lightly groomed, fed, and is left again to himself till four or half past, at which time he is watered, groomed, and gets half a feed. After that, he is taken out for an hour, to an hour and-a-half's walk; on returning, he is fed, clothed for the night, the bedding, &c., is put in order, and he is then left to enjoy his well-earned repose.

When a horse is galloped in the evening instead of the morning, the same routine should be observed, except that the afternoon's grooming should be commenced half an hour earlier, while only a few go-downs of water should be given before it. Here, instead of being watered in the afternoon, he should be watered at mid-day, and then should have no more water, except the few go-downs already mentioned, till after work. When taken out, he should have, at the very least, an hour's walking exercise before his gallop, and after that he should get half a bucket of water, with a full allowance on his return to his stable. He is then groomed, fed, and bedded down for the night.

Supposing that a horse in training gets 16 lbs. of corn a day, they may be divided into feeds in the following manner:—

Early morning feed	...	1lb.
Morning "	...	4lbs.
Mid-day "	...	4lbs.
Afternoon "	...	2lbs.
Evening "	...	5lbs.

CHAPTER IV.

Treatment during the hot weather.

In India, the hot weather stops racing in the same manner as the winter does in England. During the months of April, May, and June, in fact until the rains commence, the trainer—if he be in the plains—should not think of working his horses, beyond giving them healthy exercise, for the climate itself will produce a considerable strain on their systems.

Through these slack months, any injuries that the horses' feet and legs may have sustained during the previous season should be carefully treated. On this subject it is sufficient to remark, that *time* and *rest* are the only true means to obtain repair of injured structures; and I would earnestly advise my readers to avoid heroic methods of treatment, such as blistering, firing, bleeding, and giving strong purgatives.

During the hot weather, horses should get a less quantity of food than when in training, though they should on no account be kept low, for if they be not liberally fed, their systems will be unable to resist the debilitating effects of the climate. It is not from theory, but from what I have seen in practice, that I speak positively on this subject. An Arab may get eight, and a Waler ten pounds of corn—three parts oats, one part gram—with a couple of pounds of bran; and twice a week, at night, a bran and linseed mash; or, every second night, a feed of boiled barley mixed with a pound of bran.

The chief point to be considered is that the dung should be properly formed—though that of some, which have been trained a good deal, always remains abnormally loose—brittle, devoid of all stickiness, and bad odour, and should be of a healthy yellow colour. When oats are used, the fæces are much more yellow than with any other grain.

During the hot weather, the horses should have an hour-and-a-half's walking exercise in the morning, and a little less in the evening. It is preferable to have horses ridden at walking exercise than led. Almost every syce can ride well enough for this. Horses should be made to walk smartly, while nothing looks slacker, or causes a horse to walk in a more slovenly manner, than the way syces often lead horses, with a long rein or rope over their shoulder, while they hobble along in front, at about two miles an hour.

CHAPTER V.

On the Theory of Training.

TRAINING—DEVELOPMENT OF MUSCLE—EXERCISE—NATURE OF EXERCISE—STRAIN OF THE SUSPENSORY LIGAMENT—EFFECTS OF HARD AND SOFT GROUND—LOSS OF SPEED—FOOD—HEALTH—SWEATING—STALENESS—REDUCTION OF FAT—ARTIFICIAL SWEATING—PHYSIC—SIGNS OF CONDITION.

TRAINING is the art of preparing a horse to gallop a certain distance at the greatest possible speed.

In order to accomplish this, the following conditions are necessary:—

1st.—That the muscles, used in galloping, be developed to the highest extent for the object in view.

2nd.—That the whole system, both nervous, muscular, and functional, be in a healthy state.

3rd.—That the organs of breathing be in the best possible condition to sustain the system in its required effort.

4th.—That the muscles be accustomed to the nature of the action they will be called upon to perform.

5th.—That there be a minimum of fat in the system—compatible with the performance of its healthy functions—so that the animal be not retarded by its weight, nor his muscles be impeded by its presence.

Development of Muscle.—On this subject Dr. Carpenter (*Human Physiology*) remarks that "the frequently renewed exercise of muscles, by producing a determination of blood towards them, occasions an increase in the nutrition; so that a large amount of new tissue is developed, and the muscles augment in size and vigour. This is true, not only of the whole muscular system when equally exercised, but also of any particular set of muscles which is more used than another. Of the former, we have an example in those who practise a system of gymnastics adapted to call the various muscles alike into play; and of the latter, in the limbs of individuals who follow any calling that habitually requires the exertion of either pair, to the partial exclusion of the other, as the arms of the smith, or the legs of the opera-dancer. But this increased nutrition cannot take place unless an adequate supply of food be afforded; and if the amount of nutritive material be insufficient, the result will be a progressive diminution in the size and power of the muscles, which will manifest itself the more rapidly as the amount of exertion, and consequently the degree of *waste* is greater. Nor can it be effected if the exercise be incessant, for it is during the intervals of repose that the reparation of the muscular tissue occurs; and the muscular system, like the nervous, may be worn out by incessant use. The more violent the action, the longer will be the period of subsequent repose required for the reparation of the tissue."

From this we see that while giving the horse the exercise necessary to develop those muscles which are used in galloping, we should attend to his due nutrition; should afford him the rest indispensable for the repair of tissue, and should preserve around him the conditions that are most conducive to health.

Exercise.—The various tissues of the body have but a limited time for existence, which period is directly influenced by the amount of exercise taken by the animal. Apart from the necessity there is for exercise to develop muscle, to reduce fat, and to maintain health, experience also teaches us that tissue, which is formed under conditions of rapid waste and repair, is stronger and of better quality than that subjected to more gradual change; while anatomical investigation proves that the former, from being more vascular, is redder and healthier looking than the latter. Hence, to improve the *quality* of the muscular and nervous tissues, we should give as much exercise as is compatible with the individual capabilities of the animal trained.

Exercise purifies the blood, by quickening the action of the lungs, by which means an increased supply of oxygen is absorbed into the vital fluid for the oxidization of effete matters contained in it.

By quickening the circulation, it stimulates the processes of nutrition for the building up of new tissue, and of excretion for the removal of effete and deleterious substances.

It also strengthens the action of the heart and lungs.

Nature of Exercise.—We may conclude that this should gradually conform to that of the race for which the animal is being trained, so that—within certain limits —only the muscles which are used in galloping may be specially developed, for were other muscles also called into abnormal play, their extra nutrition would but tend to deprive the muscles used in galloping of material for repair, and would add unnecessary weight to be carried.

No amount of trotting or walking can prove an efficient substitute for galloping, of which exercise the trainer should endeavour to give his horses as much as possible, under certain reservations, to which we shall presently allude.

In order that fast work may be given with safety, the horse should be gradually accustomed to it. The golden rule here being, that the length of a horse's gallop should never exceed the distance which he can go—at the time being—without his muscles becoming fatigued, or—which is the same thing—without his becoming "blown," for neither man nor horse are ever so "beat," as when they are "out of wind." In fast work the suspensory ligaments are particularly liable to sprain, as I have remarked in *Veterinary Notes for Horse Owners.*—"When the horse is fresh and untired, the muscles, to which the perforans and perforatus tendons are attached, contract with such precision that the foot is 'picked up' (flexed) before undue strain can fall on the suspensory ligament; in fact, these tendons act as assistant braces to it. But if the pace be continued, the horse will 'dwell' mor eand more in his stride, and as the two muscles which move the tendons become gradually fatigued, they also become unable to contract with sufficient quickness to save the suspensory ligament from undue strain; besides this, the muscles get tired, while the ligament does not experience the sensation of fatigue; hence the horse throws weight on the latter to save the former. We may easily imagine how great this strain must be, in the case of a race-horse struggling home during a desperate finish. When the muscles which flex the fore-legs become tired, almost the whole weight of the horse and his rider, which is propelled forward by the hind, has to be borne by the suspensory ligaments of the fore-legs. No wonder then that race-horses, as a rule, break down within the 'distance,' especially if the ligament has been previously injured. We also may readily see why they are more apt to break down when out of work, than when in condition."

Fast work should be very sparingly given on hard ground, owing to the great danger there is of horses exercised on it spraining their suspensory ligaments. "Soft ground gives more time for the muscles attached to the perforans and perforatus tendons to contract; and thus to save the ligament; while on hard ground the whole strain falls on that part with extreme rapidity; hence the danger of inducing sprain of the suspensory ligaments by galloping on such soil." (*Veterinary Notes for Horse Owners.*)

Besides the risk of accidents, and the undue strain on the system, there is another most important consideration that tends to limit the amount of fast work which we may give in training, namely, the fact that the practice of constantly extending a horse tends to make him slow. Horses vary so much in the manner they stand fast work that it is impossible to lay down any detailed rules for guidance on the subject. Sluggish horses are, as a rule, far better in this respect than are impetuous ones, and thorough breds than "cocktails." Men stand more training than horses, and will often bear being extended day after day without losing their "turn of speed." This fact is probably to be accounted for by the higher development of their nervous system. When a horse is restricted for some time to slow gallops, his style, however good it may have been originally, will gradually accommodate itself to this pace, and will, in course of time, become permanently altered, or take a long period to recover. The reason for this is that the muscles which are called into play, obeying a beneficent law of nature, gradually acquire the style of action which will enable them to perform their accustomed task with the least possible exertion to themselves. Thus, when they have become habituated to a slow gallop, they will be unable to act at a fast pace to the best advantage, simply because they are unused to it.

This law is well proved by the fact that training horses for long distances has a very prejudicial effect on their speed for short races.

Most men, who have sparred much, know how slow the use of dumb-bells makes them.

Galloping on heavy ground, and carrying heavy weights, naturally follow the same law as slow work does in spoiling the speed of a horse.

We have a very instructive instance of the same thing afforded us by the use of heavy clothing in galloping work, whether for ordinary exercise, or for sweating horses.

We may safely conclude that a horse should very rarely be fully "extended" over a distance equal to that of the race for which he is being trained, and only then towards the latter end of his preparation. "Getting the distance into them" is too often synonymous with "taking the speed and life out of them."

Repeated fast work, for comparatively short distances, with intervals of rest between, will be found to be accompanied by less risk of accident, and less danger of making a horse slow, than long fast gallops.

I am purposely neglecting the question of a horse's "wind," in favour of avoiding risk of accident and danger of spoiling speed, for I think that the last two considerations demand far more attention than the first, for if a horse be thoroughly fit and well, has had lots of work, and has been sent a few fast gallops for nearly the length of the race for which he is going to run, he will, in nineteen cases out of twenty, stay the distance, unless indeed it be beyond that of which he is naturally capable.

From the foregoing remarks we may see that in order "to bring a horse fit to the post," we must give him a large amount of exercise, which should not be at a long slow gallop. Hence the remainder of the exercise, that we are unable to give at a fast pace, should be at one which will be as little prejudicial to his speed as possible, such as the walk, trot, and canter, which are totally different in their action to the gallop.

Food. — The older writers on training were accustomed to lay considerable stress on the necessity of "hard" food, and a restricted allowance of water, in order to reduce the size of a horse's stomach and intestines, and to harden his muscles. At first sight, the former consideration seems to be a most important one, because if these organs be distended by the bulky nature of the food, the diaphragm will be impeded in its effort to afford room for the action of the lungs. The question of food, however, is one entirely dependant on conditions of health and nutrition, while the trainer may rest assured that if they be duly maintained, the animal's organs will accommodate themselves, in the best possible manner, to the work which he is called upon to perform.

When a horse's powers are fully taxed, we may safely rely on his appetite as the best guide for determining the amount of his hay, corn, and water, for he will instinctively choose the proportion best calculated to furnish material for the repair of tissue; always supposing that he shews no signs of ill-health.

Health. — As the due nutrition of the system is dependant on the state of the general health, we should endeavour to secure the former by maintaining the latter in the best possible condition, thus avoiding the too common error of neglecting the cause for the effect. Hence, if the slightest symptom of indisposition can be traced to the effects of the food, its nature or amount, as the case may be, should be at once changed. The usual symptoms of derangement, caused by errors in diet, are feverishness with quickened pulse, hot dry skin, &c.; looseness or constipation of the bowels; the presence of flakes of mucous mixed with the dung, indicating irritation of the intestines; sour smell from the mouth, grinding of the teeth, licking white-washed walls, &c., shewing acidity of the stomach; dark coloured urine, evincing that the animal is fed on food of a too highly nitrogenous nature; yellowness of the gums and lining membrane of the eyelids, pointing to derangement of the liver; a disordered state of the skin; abnormal appetite, &c.

Sweating.—The result of my own observations—through a long experience in several branches of training—on drawing either man or horse "fine," is that it is entirely a question of the state of the nerves of the individual trained; as Stonehenge justly remarks, "the nervous system cannot respond to the calls of its great centre without having a due supply of fatty matter." Horses, like men, vary, one with another, in regard to the amount of fat which their systems can lose without their becoming "stale." Most men who have trained hard for pedestrianism, rowing, race riding, &c., will practically understand the meaning of staleness; while we may safely infer that its causes are the same both in men and horses. When a man gets much below his ordinary healthy weight, whether by excessive exercise, physic, sweating, or Banting, and continues hard work, he will, as a rule, soon become nervous and shaky; a state which can be cured only by rest, and by discontinuing the means taken to get thin; and then as his weight rises, so will his nerves regain their tone.

I do not, for a moment, mean to say that the disturbance of the equilibrium of the system, due to an abnormal loss of fat, is the sole cause of a horse becoming stale, for I know well that the effects of over-work and the feverishness induced by excitement and high feeding, also tend to bring about that condition. But I wish, simply, to impress on my readers the fact that a certain amount of fat, in the body of the horse, is indispensable to the continued healthy action of his nervous system, on which is dependant the exhibition of all muscular force. Hence we should avoid the mistake of drawing a horse fine too soon, and should endeavour to apportion his work in such a manner that he will be "trained to the hour," knowing well that it is impossible to keep him "wound up to concert pitch," beyond a very few days.

When a horse, under ordinary conditions, is well fed and little worked, there is not alone a quantity of adipose tissue deposited in his system, but also a certain amount of *infiltration* of fat, in the form of distinct drops, takes place in the cells of the different tissues, and particularly in those of the liver. This fat, by distending the cells, renders the muscles, liver, and other involved structures, unfit to bear the strain of violent and continued exertion. The object of training is not alone to get rid of the retarding weight of a quantity of useless fat, but also to eliminate the infiltrated fat from tissues that are called into action during work; hence, when we sweat a horse, we do so in order to remove from his system a certain amount of fat, some of which is broken up by the oxidation of its carbon by the agency of respiration, while the greater part of the remainder is carried out, in the form of oily matter, along with the perspiration, which fluid is directly abstracted from the blood. For the maintenance of health, the blood must contain a certain proportion of water, which varies, under special conditions, such as violent exercise, purging, deprivation of water, excessive perspiration, &c., from 700 to 800 parts in a thousand. If, in case of loss, the normal proportion of water be not speedily restored, the animal's health will suffer. Thus we may see that the proper object of sweating a horse is to reduce the amount of fat, and not the amount of water there is in his system; and that as soon as we fail to find that oily matter is given off, to any appreciable extent, with his perspiration, so soon should we stop giving him any more sweats. I need hardly point out how opposed to common sense and to physiological teaching, is the practice of stinting a horse of water after sweating him. In fact, want of a due supply of water interferes with the whole process of nutrition. "The activity of absorption by the blood-vessels depends upon the due fluidity of the materials to be absorbed, for it is well known that no fluids quickly penetrate the vessels, but such as are of lesser density than the blood." (Williams.)

From the foregoing remarks we may draw the practical conclusion, that we may take, during training, the state of the perspiration as a guide by which to judge of the amount of fat in the horse's system, and that we should regulate his work, so that the sweat, after his gallops, may not completely lose its greasy feel, until within a few days of the race for which he is being trained. This is, of course, supposing that he is one of the sort that will stand being "drawn fine."

Artificial Sweating.—By this term I mean any process of sweating which is accomplished without the aid of exercise, such as that by the Turkish bath, or by clothing the horse very heavily in a warm, closed up stable, &c. Such sweating, I think, is most objectionable, unless indeed the state of the animal's limbs precludes exertion. When perspiration is thus artificially induced, the increased excretory action is confined to the pores of the skin, so that the blood rapidly becomes charged with effete matter which the lungs fail to eliminate with due promptness, as the respiration is not accelerated by exertion. Hence the lungs become gorged with insufficiently ærated blood, which causes the breathing to become laboured, while the action of the heart is tumultuous. These abnormal conditions cause general distress, and tend to injure the healthy working of the heart; results that speedily—if oft repeated—upset the nervous system, and render the animal stale and incapable of prolonged and vigorous exertion.

Physic.—Before commencing training, it is generally advisable to give a moderate dose of physic, in order to eliminate from the system an excess of the products resulting from the waste of tissue, which are not excreted with sufficient rapidity for the new state of hard exercise, and to get rid of the superabundant nutritive material absorbed from the chyle. The diseases known as *azoturia* and *lymphagitis* are respectively brought on, when these two conditions exist to a highly injurious extent. In both, a purgative is most advisable. Although we may not have either complaint developed, still feverishness, "filled" legs, dark coloured urine, &c., often result from similar causes, when the precaution of giving a horse a dose of physic is not observed before putting him into training.

Signs of Condition.—When a horse is in perfect condition, his coat will be soft and glossy like satin; his eye bright, but tranquil; his sweat scanty, will dry readily, and will be free from oily matters ; his legs and feet cool; his muscles hard, prominent, and distinct from each other; those extending along each side of the vertebræ of his back will be full and massive, while those over his quarters will swell up to a certain convexity. The ribs will be clearly visible, and the "quarter mark"—division between the *biceps rotator tibialis* and *triceps abductor femoris* muscles—well defined; the space round his anus should be prominent and well filled; his thighs should be so developed that they should meet for a considerable way down; his crest should be full and hard; and the *caput* muscles—which lie just above his forearm—should come out in a distinct lump. "Who can fail to see in a well-trained race-horse the muscles standing, as it were, prominently one from another about the quarters and thighs, 'hard as iron' to the touch, and giving the animal an appearance of being thin and poor. The appearance of thinness is the result of the great prominence of each individual muscle, of increase in their volume and weight, and an extraordinary healthy tonicity." (Williams.)

CHAPTER VI.

Practical Training.

REMARKS ON RACE HORSES IN INDIA—TRAINING QUARTERS—GENERAL RULES FOR WORK DURING TRAINING—DETAIL OF WORK—SWEATING—TRAINING BY SHORT REPEATED GALLOPS—TRIALS—TRAINING PONIES — SETTING — TREATMENT AFTER RUNNING — RACE HORSES TRAVELLING BY RAIL.

It is an old and true turf maxim, that the better bred a horse is, the more training will he stand. In this country, blood is but an uncertain guide to the trainer, for almost all our horses, with but few exceptions, are "cocktails" in the strict English sense of the word. A few of our best Walers are thorough bred in the loose colonial acceptation of the term. At the same time, I must admit that the type of horse Australia sends us, is improving yearly in quality and breeding, and that cases of giving "salt water pedigrees" are becoming of rare occurrence.

The subject of pure blood and high caste in the Arab is one on which I have never been able to gain any exact information, nor do I think that any distinct rules, as to external appearance, can be laid down, that would not equally apply to any other breed of horses intended to gallop fast, and "stay," with a fair weight up. Many Arabs, which are most unlikely shaped, to our eyes, often turn out the best. These horses take a long time to mature, while their powers rarely become fully developed before they are eight or nine years old, and until they have been raced for two or three seasons. On this account, one should not lose heart because a likely looking son of the Desert does not answer one's expectations at an early date. Arabs can stand more work in India than any other class. Their *forte* is undoubtedly distance.

A young Waler—say a four-year old—appears to be—allowing for the difference between the dates from which they respectively take their age—nearly a year, a Country bred a year and a half, and an Arab two years, more backward than an English horse of the same age.

Young Arabs especially, and indeed all young horses, may, with great advantage, be trained and taught to gallop, without being brought to the post, the season before they are actually run. We generally find a horse, that has been raced the first year he has been trained, to become in the next season from 10lbs. to 1 st. better than he was during the preceding one. In India, horses are often run the first year they are put to work, and even receiving as maidens from 7lbs. to 1 st. they can rarely successfully contend with platers, simply because they have not had time to learn their business. We seldom see maidens that have been run thus, come out in anything like their subsequent form, until perhaps towards the end of the season, say for Lucknow, or for some of the other spring meetings; and then, when they are at their best, it is a pity to lose their maiden,—if they have not won previously,—when the most important maiden races are over. In England, a young one can be kept at work for six months before he runs for the first two or three year old events, but out here, the hot weather allows but little more than three months, during which to prepare a maiden, without suffering many of the best stakes, which are reserved for his class, to pass by uncontended for. We should not lose sight of the fact, that it often takes more time to teach a horse to gallop than to get him into condition.

I have seen it remarked in the "Field," that it takes at least two years' conditioning to enable a horse to live among the first flight in "the Shires." This being the case, it certainly would require no shorter period to bring a young one—probably fresh off the ship—fit to race over a distance in India.

Small, compact horses mature earlier than those of a larger and looser frame, and consequently may be run at an earlier age.

Sluggish horses can almost always both stand work better and stay longer than impetuous ones.

Old horses require usually less work to get into galloping condition than young ones do, though they require more *time* to put up muscle.

In India, horses are rarely trained specially—as in England—for one particular race, as there are few events worth doing this for. The usual practice is to give horses, within certain limits, more of a general than of a particular preparation. However, one should never sacrifice the speed of a flyer by giving him long work, when it has been proved that, fit and well, he is unable to stay a distance.

Ponies, 13 hands and under, had best be trained for

from a quarter to half a mile. Although there have been many instances — take Chieftain — of Arab galloways being able to hold their own, at even weights, with Arabs of all sizes, still, in ninety-nine cases out of a hundred, allowance for height—4 lb the ½ inch—will not bring a 13 and 13-2 pony together, nor the latter with one of 14 hands, provided the galloway has any pretensions to racing form; but if an owner happens to possess such a rarity, like what Abdool Raymon was, he had better train him for distances at which he will meet the class bigger than himself; for if the animal can succeed with them, he will have little difficulty in beating those of his own size, even in races shorter than those for which he was prepared.

For "all Arabs," 1½ miles will be a fair average distance over which to train them; while ¼ mile less will usually answer for Walers and English horses.

Quite as much, if not more, depends on a horse's stable management, as on the work he gets, in bringing him fit to the starting post. Many horses have been got into good condition, and have won important races, by being simply hacked, with, now and then perhaps, a canter on a soft bit of turf; or even by doing nothing more than trotting work in a very light trap, when their legs have been particularly infirm. But I doubt whether a horse has ever been brought within a stone of his proper form, when he has been but indifferently looked after in the stable.

Training Quarters.—The worst of the hot weather being over by the beginning of July, the horses may be put into slow work from that date. Before this, the owner should have made up his mind as to what he intends doing with them during the ensuing season; whether, if he be in the Bengal Presidency, to run them early in October at Dehra Doon, to wait for some particular meeting later on, or to commence at Dehra, with his animals partly fit, and gradually gallop them into condition, as they work down country from one meeting to another. The latter is the usual plan adopted, as the different meetings are fixed to suit this arrangement, while, by the time Calcutta is reached in due course, the horses will have had nearly six months' work, and ought, by that time, to be as fit as possible. The racing season on this side of India commences with the Dehra Doon meeting in the beginning of October; immediately after that the Umballa one comes off, then those of Meerut, Sonepore (which is a moveable fixture), and Calcutta at the end of December. After that come Lucknow, Meerut, and Umballa spring meetings. This is the usual programme, while the smaller ones, such as Dacca, Mozufferpore, &c, are fixed so as to suit the larger ones.

The race-course at Dehra Doon is a hilly one, and it takes time to "get the hill into a horse," as all frequenters of that lovely valley know well. An instance of this was strikingly shown by the moderate Malabar, who trained on that course for two seasons, won the Dehra Derby very easily with a good field behind him. The Doon has the great advantage of a good climate, in which to train horses during the beginning of the training season, but the race-course is a dangerous one for animals with not the best of forelegs, as it is often very slippery going down the hill on the far side. However, if an owner intends running his horses at Dehra, he ought to give them at least a month's work there.

The course suits horses with high action, which enables them to climb the hill far easier than those that go lower. Another point to be considered is that, a horse must have good hocks to go up a hill well.

Perhaps, the best thing to do with valuable horses is to send them at the close of the racing season (the end of March) to Dehra Doon, where, after a month or six weeks' rest, they may be hacked about with a light weight up, and got into good working order, before being put into regular training. In this way they may be healthier and fresher than had they remained in the plains. In point of fact, horses can be galloped much earlier in the plains than at Dehra, for the course there becomes very hard in the hot weather, while during the rains it is anything but safe going, until after August, and even then is very dangerous for youngsters that are apt to sprawl about.

I think the practice of sending horses, which have spent the hot weather and rains in the plains, as late in the year as September, to Dehra, is accompanied by some risk, as the nights there are then getting cold—especially towards the end of that month—and horses, whose livers are more or less deranged by the effects of the preceding hot weather, are very liable to get congestion of that organ from the sudden change of climate. (see *Veterinary Notes for Horse Owners*, page 249.) If an owner intends sending his horses to Dehra,

I would advise him to do so before the hot weather commences.

It appears that the worst kind of climate for a horse to live in, is a damp hot one, like that of Bengal, for instance. A damp, cold climate, like that of Scotland, is not incompatible with the breeding of good cattle, provided they be treated more or less as exotics. But the best of all is a dry warm one. During the excessive heat of several hot weathers at Meean Meer and at Cawnpore, both of which places possess a very dry climate, I have never found that the horses I kept suffered in any way from the great heat, as long as they were well protected from the direct rays of the sun, and had a free circulation of air through their stables. Although I do not say that horses will thrive quite as well during the hot weather and rains in the plains, as in cooler climates, such as Dehra and Bangalore, still I do not think that the balance is very much in favour of the latter, specially when we take the cases of horses that it would be injudicious to train on a hilly course. In making these remarks, I again except all hot, damp climates in which it would be most unwise to keep valuable horses during the trying months of the year.

Mozufferpore, possessing, as it does, a race-course covered with soft and elastic turf, offers many advantages, but I question much if its climate is not too damp, in which to summer horses. The same objection may, with still greater force, be urged against the Sonthal Hills.

General Rules for Work during Training.—Before a horse be put into training, he should, if possible, be in a sound state of health, and his muscles should be well developed by quiet, slow work and hacking.

If practicable, gallop only in the morning, and get the horses back early to their stables, not later, during the cold weather, than eight o'clock. Apart from the fact that evening work, by exciting a horse, is apt to prevent him from having a good night's rest, we should remember that the ground, on account of the presence of the dew, is softest in the early mornings.

I think, however, it is a mistake, as some do, to gallop horses too early in the morning when it is all but dark, for, by this practice, accidents are liable to occur, especially from horses putting their feet into holes, that are made by rats, which rodents burrow very rapidly on many of our Indian courses. Besides this, too early rising deprives horses of a part of their valuable night's rest. I am rather inclined to think that this practice is apt to make horses "go higher" in their gallop, than they would do, were they worked at a time when they could clearly see where they were going.

Never work horses twice in a day—here we do not take into account their evening walk—however backward their condition may be.

Do not gallop them until they have walked for at least an hour, and cleared themselves out.

When training for a Monsoon Meeting, it is often desirable to gallop one's horses in the evening instead of the morning, for flies, which are fearfully annoying during the rains, are much less so in the former than in the latter time. Besides this, if the course be far from the stable, the horses can rarely return before the morning sun is well up. A sweat, however, should never be given in the evening, if it can possibly be avoided.

Before sending a horse a gallop, always look at his legs and feet, and if there be anything wrong, or the slightest heat present, send him back to his stable. As a rule, unless a horse, that is suffering from some injury, goes actually lame, a syce will rarely inform his master of the accident.

Give a horse always a preliminary canter before sending him a sharp gallop.

The heavier topped a horse is, especially if he have a thick neck and coarse shoulders, the more careful should the trainer be about giving him fast work, particularly down any incline, such as there is at Dehra on the far side of the course.

Do not keep horses too long on hard food, and never be afraid of giving them a bunch of lucern, or a few carrots.

If a horse, in strong work, begins to leave much of his corn untouched, say, anything over half a pound at each feed, the chances are that he is getting too much work, which should be lessened, or altogether stopped, as the case may require, and he should have two or three bran mashes at successive feeding hours, some green meat, or even an alterative ball, if he be at all "over-marked." The time a horse takes to eat his allowance of corn may be used as a measure of his appetite. Thus, say that a certain horse, who after work usually consumes his morning feed of 4lbs. in 25 minutes, takes on a particular day half an hour to get through the same amount, the owner may reasonably conclude that he is a little off his feed. By observing such indications, in time, the chances of overworking a horse will be materially lessened.

Never fully extend a horse earlier than a fortnight before the day on which he has to run, for if this be done, he will be apt to get slow; yet, for all that, he should be sent along pretty fast, occasionally, during the latter part of his training, in order to vary the monotony of the work, "and to get the pace into him."

Avoid trying your horses against each other, or against the watch.

"When a horse gets to know his speed in his exercise, it is seldom he can afterwards be got to struggle well in a severe contested race." (Darvill.)

On finishing a gallop, always turn round towards the inside of the curve on which you are galloping, but if the direction be in a straight line, turn in preference to the right about, as you would on a right-handed course. This practice will tend to prevent horses learning to bolt off the course, for when they do so, they almost invariably go off towards the outside and not to the inside of it.

If on a race-course, finish the gallop a couple of hundred yards beyond the winning post, and then gradually pull up.

Have the rubbing-down shed placed beyond the winning post, and on the inside of the course.

Avoid galloping horses in clothing, as it cramps their action, while the extra weight tends to shorten their stride, and strain their legs.

I cannot help condemning the practice, many adopt,

of having their horses galloped constantly in heavy clothing. An English jockey, whose lowest riding weight is say 8 st., will, when not wasting, and when wearing warm clothes on a cold morning, weigh close upon, if not quite, 9 st.; to this add 7 or 8lbs for the saddle, 2 to 3lbs for the bridle and martingale, and from 14 to 21lbs for the clothing, and we will have the animal carrying about 11 st., which is a truly preposterous weight for a training gallop; and then men, who allow this, will, when their horses go lame or get slow, wonder how in the world it occurred! If a trainer wants to get the fat off a horse, by all means let him put clothing on, and give the animal his sweat, a little later than usual in the morning, at a trot, or at alternate trots and canters, so that he may not spoil his action, or risk his legs. When the horse is pulled up, let him be well covered over with rugs till the sweat trickles down his pasterns; and repeat, every week or ten days, this process, which will take the "beef" off the grossest horse quite quick enough. A trainer should consider the feelings of his horses, for it is only reasonable to suppose that an animal which is constantly galloped in heavy clothing, must feel his movements cramped both by the weight he carries, and by the presence of the rugs, and that he will consequently lose heart for want of the exhilaration of spirits produced by a free and untramelled gallop. The mind of the horse has undoubtedly a great deal to say to the quick, elastic stride, and the lightning dash of speed at the finish, exhibited by a well trained race-horse.

Admiral Rous, in his book on "Horse-racing," states

that "generally speaking, race-horses ought to be galloped stripped all the year round, but comfortably clothed indoors suitable to the temperature."

Have as light riding boys, as possible, compatible with their being able to hold their horses together. Even with a screw, it is generally better to put up a stone or so extra, than to be obliged to employ a curb instead of a snaffle for his mouth, in order to enable a light lad to hold him.

If a horse can be held with a snaffle, never use any other bit for him.

Never use whip or spur in a training gallop, unless with a very sluggish horse, with one that is apt to bolt off the course, or with young animals that go awkwardly and require a deal of collecting.

Never extend a horse over a longer distance than he has to run, as it will tend to make him slow.

The longer distance a horse has to go, the finer should he be drawn.

As a rule, do not have a less interval than ten days between each sweat.

Rarely sweat later than ten days before a race, for a horse should have just enough time before running, to be eased off, so as to get a little "above himself;" sufficient, in fact, to allow his nerves to regain their tone.

A horse should never scrape quite clean and watery sooner than the last ten days of his final preparation, for if he does so, he is almost certain to become stale.

Assuming that a horse, in training, continues in good health and spirits, with his legs cool and fine, that he is never off his feed, and that his dung is in good order, we may safely be guided by the way he scrapes, after his morning gallop, in judging of the manner in which his condition is progressing, and whether he requires a sweat, or more or less work, so that his sweat may be gradually reduced down to the desired consistency. When a horse is gross, his sweat is thick and greasy to the touch; but when he is in perfect condition, it is generally scanty, comes off as clear as water, and dries almost as soon as the scrapers have passed over the surface of the skin. He will then have the smallest amount of fat in his system, compatible with his nerves remaining for *but a very few days* in good order. Of course, he should be wound up to this concert pitch, only just before his race.

Here I am, naturally, supposing that the animal is of the sort which bears being drawn fine.

When a horse, after slight exertion, breaks out into a watery and copious sweat, and dries slowly, we may be pretty certain that he does so through weakness, and that he is in a most unfit state in which to continue training. In fact, what such an animal would require in this case, would, as a rule, be a few linseed and bran mashes, some green food, and several days' rest.

Many excitable horses, when in the most perfect condition, will break out into a copious sweat if brought on to a race-course. This should not be confounded with sweating from weakness, or grossness.

The great thing to avoid is getting a horse fit too soon. Condition is only relative, for a horse may be in perfect training, although showing little muscle; but what we want is quantity, as well as quality of muscle, with clean "pipes," and the "faculty of going" thoroughly developed. This desired state can only be obtained by work, which cannot be *continued*, if the horse be prematurely brought too fine, for the consequent strain on his nervous system will be more than it can bear, and he will, consequently, soon become stale.

"It is well known to horsemen who are close observers, that, though a horse cannot make a great race when decidedly off the feed, some of the finest efforts that ever were made, and some of the greatest successes that ever were won, came just as the horse was beginning to get dainty, and to pick and nibble at the oats." (Hiram Woodruff.)

I think experience will bear me out in saying that Country-breds, during training, can very rarely stand being galloped oftener than every second day.

Horses differ so much in the way they stand work, that it is impossible to lay down fixed rules on this subject; while a writer on training can only give illustrative work and general rules, just as a whist authority may point out the proper leads, and how to play certain hands. In both cases, the inferences to be drawn, and lessons to be learned, will be only for general application.

In the following pages I shall consider the training of the average style of Waler we have in India, taking for granted that he continues sound and in good health. If a horse in training has a soft constitution, or has infirm legs, I must leave the trainer to exercise his own common sense, to provide for the varying circumstances under which the uncertainty of horse-flesh may place him.

Detail of Work.—To proceed to the routine of training, one should first consider what length of time the horse has to get fit in before running. If there be five or six months, they may be divided into three periods; namely, preparatory work, and first and second preparations, each lasting from seven weeks to two months.

Before commencing any work, the horse may get the following alterative ball:—

Barbadoes aloes	...	...	... $1\frac{1}{2}$ to 2 drachms.
Nitre	...	...	... 3 "
Tartar emetic	...	...	... 1 drachm.

Treacle enough to make a ball.

But if he be gross, or with not the best of forelegs to stand the work necessary to reduce his system, a physic ball (of four drachms of aloes and two of ginger) should be given. Before administering the medicine, the corn should be stopped, and bran mashes substituted, for a couple of days.

I think the morning, say about 9 o'clock, is the safest time to give a ball to a horse, and that there is then little chance of his becoming over-purged during the night, when help cannot be readily obtained.

The first month's exercise may consist of walking for a longer distance than the horse has done during the summer, say eight miles in the morning and four in the evening, varied every second day or so by a couple of miles trotting, or a slow canter for half a mile now and then. In fact, the work should not exceed gentle hacking. On commencing the second month, the trotting may be stopped, and slow cantering, up to one mile, substituted. This work ought only to take place in the morning, and should be gradually lengthened. The speed of the canter ought only to be just sufficient to keep the horse out of a trot, or perhaps a very little more. During this month no clothing should be put on at exercise, for the weather will be still very warm, and on no account should a horse do more work than, in the morning, a slow canter after an hour's walking, and in the evening, nothing more than a four or five-mile walk. The morning work should be completed, and the horse back in his stable, before the sun is well up.

On finishing the canter, the horse should be pulled up very gradually, so as not to strain his forelegs or hocks, and not until he has gone a couple of hundred yards beyond the winning post—if on a race-course—he should then be turned round towards the *inside*, and trotted to the rubbing-down shed, where he is scraped and rubbed down, as I have before described.

These canters may be given two or three times a week, while, on two other days, the monotony of the work may be broken, by taking the horse out in the country, and then trot, canter, and walk him by turns for eight or nine miles. This will keep him fresh and in good spirits, for he appreciates an "outing" and change of scene, just as much as we do ourselves.

After these two months of preparatory work, the horse's muscles and sinews will have begun to harden, and he may now be put to regular galloping.

Want of preparatory work, before giving horses

regular gallops, is but the too frequent cause of strains and breakdowns.

The work we shall now consider, is that which I think suitable for an ordinary Waler. An Arab's gallop should be quite a quarter as long again. With him one may leave out the short "spurts;" while long slow gallops for two and-a-half or three miles may be substituted in their place. In timing, allowance should be made for the fact of the Arab's comparative slowness. Thus, for instance, a second class Arab that could do at weight for age a mile in 1m. 57s., *i.e.*, say 7s. worse than a second class Waler, ought in a gallop, at conventional half speed over that distance, to take about 12s. longer, than would the Waler under similar conditions: for, of course, the difference of time between the two, at half speed, would be nearly double that between them when fully extended, the distance being the same in both cases.

It is not without considerable hesitation that I give illustrative timing, for I know well what a large margin must be allowed under varying conditions dependant on the style of horse, the weight he carries, and the state of the galloping track; and I crave the indulgence of the reader in the attempt, which I make, to furnish, to the best of my ability, inexperienced amateur trainers, who are unable to obtain practical assistance, with a sound *general* idea of the nature of the work required to bring an ordinary race-horse in India fit to the starting post.

The first preparation of two months should commence with slow canters, which may gradually be improved towards its close, up to a little better than half speed. An ordinary Waler, unless, indeed, he be wanted for some particular distance, may commence at half a mile every morning and increase it up to one mile and a quarter by the end of the first preparation; further than this may make him slow.

But if he is to be trained for races of only one certain length, then half of that may be begun with, and he should gradually go up to nearly the full distance. This may be varied once a week by a half mile spin, somewhat quicker than the usual pace, in order to keep up the horse's "faculty of going," while an off-day's hacking in the country will be of great service, as well as a slow gallop once a week for a couple of miles. For instance, the week's work might be divided in the following way, after the horse has been in regular training for a month and a half:—

Monday ...	... ¾ to 1 mile, half speed.
Tuesday ...	... hacking in the country.
Wednesday ...	... ½ mile, three-quarter speed.
Thursday ...	... ¾ to 1 mile, half speed or rest.
Friday ...	... ¾ to 1 mile, half speed.
Saturday ...	... 1½ to 2 miles, slow.
Sunday ...	... rest.

Besides this rest on Sundays, I would advise the trainer to give the ordinary Arab or Waler an extra day's rest once a fortnight in the middle of the week; and a bran, or linseed and bran mash may be substituted for the usual feed of corn on the evening of the preceding day, just as if it were a Saturday. Horses that are at all shy feeders, or are easily upset by work, should have this extra day's rest every week.

What we call half speed is considerably faster than if the distance were done in twice as long a time as the horse could do it at full speed; while the same remark applies to three-quarter and quarter speed. The latter is in reality about seven annas, half speed somewhat better than ten annas, and three-quarter speed about fourteen annas (adopting the custom of counting pace by annas.) Thus, for a horse that can do his mile in 1m. 50s., the time that he would take to do that distance at the different rates, would be about as follows :—

Quarter speed	4	mins.		
Half speed	2	„	50	secs.
Three-quarter speed...	2	„	10	„
Full speed	1	min	50	„

As a rule, a uniform pace should be maintained during each gallop, for nothing upsets a horse's style of going, and temper, more than "putting on the steam" the moment he enters the straight run in. Horses accustomed to this practice often refuse to extend themselves, until their "heads are turned home," and then, either bolt, or run away. This, of course, would be fatal in a race.

The speed and distance of the weekly work that I have detailed, should be gradually increased as the preparation proceeds. Thus, a second-class Waler, say, one who could do his mile with weight for age up in 1m. 50s., might commence doing his half mile gallops in 1m. 50s., and towards the close of this preparation do the mile in 2m. 40s.

During regular training, a horse should travel *about* twelve miles a day, including every kind of exercise. For instance, four miles before the morning gallop, which might be for one and-a-half mile, a one and-a-half mile walk back to stable, and a five mile walk in evening; this amount should be rarely exceeded, for long continued walking makes horses stale and leg-weary. On days of rest, a five-mile walk in the morning, and a four-mile one in the evening will generally be enough. If a horse be gross, and have at the same time doubtful legs, I would prefer to trust to a mild dose of physic, say, once a month, and a sweat, say once a week, given at a trot and at a walk, alternately, late in the morning, than to long continued walking exercise.

I have previously pointed out, that the trainer must be guided by the manner a horse scrapes, in deciding as to the advisability of giving him a sweat, for in this preparation, he will not be sent quick enough to try his lungs so as to judge by their condition. During this time, the sweat will gradually lose its greasy feel, though it will still come off pretty thick. On this subject it is impossible to give minute advice, and I must leave the tyro to be guided by his own common sense, and by the general principles on which I have touched.

Sweating.—Before describing the process of sweating a horse, I would beg my readers to remember that the grosser and more unfit a horse is, the slower the pace of the sweat, and the less violent should it be.

If time be limited, a stout, lusty horse will probably require a sweat once a fortnight, while I would advise it to be given at a much slower pace than is the custom in England. And that English blankets, and not country ones, be used, as the texture of the former is much closer and softer than that of the latter. The clothes and distance may be arranged as follows :—

Put a thick rug over the horse's back in the ordinary manner, then take a long blanket, fold it lengthwise in two or three folds, so that it may not be too broad, pass one end under the horse's belly to a man on the off side, make him draw it towards himself till it be properly divided, and pass the ends one above the other over the horse's back, so that the rug and blanket may be tightly wrapped round his body. A long blanket, folded like a shawl, is passed in front of the horse's chest, and well up his neck,—so that it may not interfere with the action of his forelegs—the ends are now crossed over his neck, chest, and withers, and are brought down on each side, under the place where the saddle will come, which is now put on, and will keep his chest wrapt in its place. A couple of hoods— the underneath one having the ears cut off—complete the clothing. The horse may now be sent on his journey, the length of which, as well as the amount of clothing, will depend on the style of the animal and on the heat of the weather. If the sweat be given in September, October, February, or March, it will be quite enough to send a stout, hardy, well bred horse two miles at a trot, or very slow canter, and another two miles at half speed, which would be about 6m. 20s. for the latter distance (taking into consideration the extra weight of the sweaters), while the pace may be slightly improved for the last half mile. After this, he is trotted to his rubbing down shed, the girths of his saddle are slackened, and he is covered over with more clothing for about 10 minutes, or until the sweat begins to trickle freely down his legs, and drop from his fetlocks; but if the trainer perceives by his laboured breathing that the horse is much distressed, he should lose no time in relieving the horse of the clothing, the hoods being first removed and the neck well scraped, wisped down, and dried. Particular care being taken to dry the space between the jaws.

The saddle and blanket across the chest are taken off, and after that the body clothing. Each part on being uncovered is scraped and dried in succession. The horse should now get about a gallon of water to drink, and a suit of dry clothing, rather light than heavy and suitable to the weather, being put on, he should be walked about for a few minutes, so that the trainer may see whether he will "break out" again or not. If this occurs, he should be stripped, dried, saddled, and ridden quietly about, in the direction of his stable, till he has cooled down. But if the animal shews no signs of breaking out, he should be led home to his stable without further delay.

During the colder months—November, December, and January—the distance may be increased.

With the clothing I have described, a five or six-mile trot, or alternate trots and canters, will be sufficient for ordinary horses possessed of no remarkable gameness or stoutness.

Light carcassed horses will not require sweating at all, as a four-mile gallop at half speed without clothing, or with only a hood, or one light suit, once a fortnight, will be all that is generally required.

If, after a sweat, a horse refuses his corn, he should get some green food, such as carrots or lucern, during the day, a bran mash at night, and no work next day beyond walking: his regular gallops should not be commenced again, until he has recovered his appetite and spirits. As a general rule, a horse should have no work on the day following a sweat, and for that reason, it is usually given on a Saturday.

In the case of a lusty horse with doubtful forelegs, it would be dangerous to trust alone to exercise to get him fine enough, or even to sweating in the ordinary way, which, from the extra weight carried, would try his legs too much. Such an one will probably require physic once a month, and a sweat once a fortnight, which may be given at a trot, or by trotting and walking alternately, and later than usual in the morning, so that the heat of the sun may aid the wasting process without entailing extra work on the legs. Gross horses with infirm forelegs are always the most difficult to bring out, for the heavier they are above, the worse chance will their legs stand; for this reason, before the trainer can venture to send them fast, he must get off some of the weight.

It is a matter of importance to have a light weight up, when giving a horse a sweat; while, in order to obtain proper control, there is no objection to the use of a curb, instead of a snaffle. If a lad much over 8st. rides, the pace should not exceed that of a trot.

If, at the end of this first preparation, the horse appears at all feverish, or his legs inclined to inflammation from work and high feeding, he should be thrown out of work for a week, bran mashed for the first two or three days, have some green meat given, and an alterative ball administered. For three or four days after this, his corn should be diminished by one-half, and only walking exercise allowed.

Through the first month of the second preparation, the horse, if a Waler, may at first be sent a mile at about half speed, say in 2m. 50s., the time and distance being gradually improved until he does 1¼ miles in, say, 2m. 40s., which would be about conventional three-quarter speed. The short spin once a week may now be gradually increased to ¾ mile. During the last month of the training, the spin may be discontinued and a long gallop substituted, or an extra day's rest, in the middle of the week, according as the horse is found to stand his work. The speed of the regular 1¼ mile gallops may be gradually increased, up to the beginning of the last fortnight, to within 7 or 8 seconds of full speed, while no sweat should be given later than this. During the last fortnight, the trainer should be most careful not to overwork his horse, though he ought to wait till then before fully extending him. Two Sundays' rest, another day's extra rest between the fast work, with perhaps a day's hacking, two long slow gallops, six or seven fast ones, to be run at nearly, if not quite, full speed, and gradually working up to the distance that has to be run; a slow canter for ¾ mile, on the day before the race; and the race day itself will be a judicious division of the last fortnight. The fast gallops should not be given by racing horses against each other, for a very little of that kind of work will go a long way.

I have endeavoured, by using approximate times for the gallops, to give a general idea of what would be advisable with a sound, stout, second class Waler, which with 9st. 7lbs. up could do, on a level course, his mile in 1m. 50s., or $1\frac{1}{4}$ mile in about 2m. 21s. But there is such infinite variety in the way different horses stand training, that it would be fruitless to give more than a general outline of the system to be pursued, with some hints and general directions which I hope may prove useful. All the same, however well up a man without personal experience may be in book lore on training, the chances are that he will ruin a horse or two in his first essay; but as soon as he gets some practical experience, he will quickly learn how to apply his book knowledge.

Training by short repeated gallops.—There are many horses whose legs would not stand the preparation I have described. With such animals, the trainer may adopt, with advantage, the system of short repeated gallops, instead of that of the ordinary long ones. For instance, in place of sending the horse a mile gallop, he might tell the riding lad to walk him round the course to the half mile-post, and gallop him in at the speed ordered, then walk him round to the same place, and gallop him as before. In this case, the muscles will have performed the same work as they would have done, had the distance been one mile, while the suspensory ligaments would not have run a tithe of the danger of being sprained, for the time that these structures are peculiarly liable to injury, is after the horse has begun to tire in his gallop (see *Veterinary Notes for Horse Owners*, page 13). At other times, accidents rarely occur, except when a horse puts his foot on uneven ground, or hits himself.

These repeated gallops may be commenced at a quarter of a mile, and be increased by degrees, say, in six weeks' time, up to three-quarters of a mile. At the shorter distances they may be given three times in a morning, and at the longer twice; while the pace should be gradually improved, as the horse's system becomes braced and strengthened by exercise.

For a horse that can stand them, I think long single gallops are, as a rule, best in India, taking into consideration the peculiarities of the climate, and the difficulty there exists in getting a sufficient number of riding lads.

One should never forget that many horses run best untrained; these are generally light carcassed, impetuous ones, which a sight of a race-course would upset for a fortnight; they should be well looked after in their stable, get lots of walking exercise and quiet hacking, and have a gallop only once in a way—say every ten days—and that away from a course.

Rogues or bolters should never be trained on a race-course, but should get their work hacking, pig-sticking, or with the hounds. One can often get a long stretch of soft ground by the roadside or in the jungle, on which to extend a horse without letting him suspect that "business" is meant: horses are extremely sharp in this respect, and know a great deal more about racing than we give them credit for.

At the risk of being laughed at, I positively assert that many horses know when they lose or win a race, and show this knowledge often most markedly by the way they look and carry themselves after running. I have frequently remarked that, the well-known Arab galloway Caliph very seldom on the day of a race required a setting muzzle, for he would, of his own accord, neither touch his hay, nor his bedding, and only just wet his lips in the morning, though he would take his allowance of corn all right. I believe the Arab Sunbeam had the same peculiarity. It may be asked how they knew they had to run on some particular day? Very easily, I should say, from the fixed routine they had been accustomed to at previous meetings—such as being plated, having their manes plaited, having a slack day on the previous one after several days of fast work, &c.—while the appearance of the race-course showed plain enough, that races were about to come off.

Most platers, on coming on the track of a race-course for the first time, will plainly show that they recognise it as such. Then again, how many old race-horses know when to make their effort on nearing the winning post, though some of them would probably shut up were they called upon earlier by their jockeys. How well a horse knows whether his rider has spurs on or not. Some will be as sluggish as a cow if they are absent, though were the Latchfords on, they would be all life, even without being touched. Others will refuse to try if they get the slightest prick, and, even when the jockey is without spurs, they will require a few kicks in the ribs, just to show no punishment is meant, before they will consent to go kindly.

There is always a difficulty about riding boys in this country. In England, stable lads can either ride, or are capable of being taught, but among natives it is not the *custom*, and, as it is most difficult to get lads, one is frequently forced to send horses alone, or at most in pairs. I am aware of the difficulty of finding a boy who has even a little idea of pace, and in default of having such an one, I strongly recommend the amateur trainer to time every gallop, as well as each quarter of a mile of it, so that he may be able to correct the lad as occasion may require. To do this, one will require a good stop watch. I prefer a chronograph in which a needle point passes vertically down the extremity of the second hand through a small reservoir of ink there, and marks on the dial the different distances noted, without the holder of the watch having to stop it.

Young horses should generally have a horse to lead them in their gallops, and should occasionally be allowed to draw level and pass the other on nearing the winning post. In doing this, the pace of the leader should be checked, so as to allow the change of position to be made without an effort on the part of the youngster, who, in this way, will gradually learn his business, and, towards the end of his training, will be accustomed either to wait or to lead.

When horses are to be trained for short distance races, as for ½ or ¾ mile, they may be run much bigger than were they intended for longer ones, while the trainer should avoid ever sending them long gallops, except at a canter now and then, which will be less detrimental to their pace than gallops at, say, three-quarter speed for a mile, or a mile and a quarter. They should have lots of walking and hacking. Three gallops a week over the short distance they will have to race will usually be enough. Another point is that, for short races, horses should never be galloped on a heavy course, as it teaches them to dwell in their stride, and to lose the quick stroke in the gallop which is essential to speed. They should be also taught to start well and get quickly on their legs. To do this the rider must have hands good enough to catch his horse by the head, and send him "into his bridle" in a moment.

Trials.—In order to obtain a satisfactory trial, horses should only be tried when they are quite fit, which ought to be but a few days before the actual race comes off, unless the owner trains his horse specially for a trial, to see, for instance, if he be worth keeping for another season. The trial horse should be in every case equally well trained, and be one whose *present* (not past) public form is thoroughly well known to the trainer. Equally good jockeys should be put up, or, in default, equally bad, and the trial should be ridden out, as in a regular race, without favour or affection. Even with every precaution, trials are not always to be relied on, and a margin of 10lbs. for mistakes would be little enough in the generality of cases, for so many horses perform differently in public from what they do in private. Besides, with a lot of horses in a race, one can never tell how it will be run, or what accidents may happen.

If an owner tries a lot of fresh horses, and finds but little difference between them, or, at least, between the best three or four, he may be almost certain that there is not a race-horse among them. According to Admiral Rous there is an average of about three remarkable runners in 2,000. There being so many failures among even English thorough bred stock, it would be unwise for Indian owners of small strings to be over sanguine respecting the subsequent career of their likely, though untried, maiden Walers, Arabs, or Country-breds. Trials between untrained horses are worth very little, because training makes such a vast difference between animals of different stamps, for light carcassed, impetuous non-stayers, who would probably never be fit for anything but selling races, would, perhaps, in a trial for a short distance, beat with ease a race-horse equally untrained, who might require months of galloping to get fit. Really valuable horses, which can race and stay, are the very kind that require a long time, and an enormous amount of work to develop their powers to the utmost; while impetuous non-stayers, that are often hardly worth their keep, will always be more or less in condition by dancing about, and fretting, whenever they are taken out of the stable.

I am very averse to trials, as a general rule, for they are liable to upset a horse in his work and to cause accidents, while, with the best arrangements, they are often most misleading as to the idea they give of actual form.

We have considered the work a horse may get, if there be five or six months to prepare him in before he runs; but if the time be limited to only two or three, a dose of physic on commencing will be generally required, for one must hurry on the work, which, with high feeding, if physic be not given, is apt to upset a horse's system and make him feverish, thereby rendering his legs prone to inflammation. Pursuing the system I have already described, the horse will be put, without loss of time, into slow work, which may be increased up to a little beyond half speed by the time half the period allowed for training has elapsed. If the horse is well, and his legs fine and cool, no more medicine need be given, and the work can be continued as I have shown in the second preparation. But if the horse's system appear at all out of sorts, or his legs inclined to fill, an alterative or physic ball—as the case may require—should be given; and three or four days after the medicine has "set," work may be re-commenced.

It will be a great assistance to an amateur unaccustomed to training to keep a diary in which to enter the distance and speed of the work done, and the amount of corn eaten, every day by each horse, with any remarks on their condition, &c., he may wish to note.

I have already gone fully into the subject of food, so shall not again notice it further than by saying that, in training, a horse's corn should be gradually increased up to the last two months, during which time he should have his full allowance, namely, as much as he can eat. If a horse's digestion gets upset by too much corn, it should be diminished, while a bran mash may be given for a couple of nights, and some green meat, such as carrots or lucern, substituted for a part of the corn.

The amateur trainer will do well to study the marks of good condition in the horse, and until by practice he is able to recognise them, he need not hope for much success in his efforts; for to train well one must have an educated eye to detect the minute gradations of condition, and having acquired it, one will see at a glance what each horse lacks.

The most unerring sign of condition in an athlete is the fact of his being able to go through hard work without becoming thirsty; so will the trainer also find that as a horse gets fit, the avidity with which he takes his water after his morning gallops will decrease; while staleness is almost always accompanied by more or less thirst.

Training Ponies.—Ponies should be galloped neither as long, nor as fast—I mean as regards comparative speed—nor as often as big horses, though high caste Arabs sometimes form an exception to this rule.

For ordinary country-bred ponies, six weeks' training will generally be quite long enough, provided they commence in hard working condition. As a rule, they should not be galloped oftener than twice a week, nor farther than half a mile, except when the distance they have got to run is much longer, in which case they may be sent on an extra bit. Sweating and long slow gallops should be avoided, while I would advise that the pace of the work should be kept pretty brisk.

In some parts of India—as in Cachar—only ponies are used for racing, and are often asked to go long distances, frequently over a mile. Let us suppose a country-bred pony to be trained for a race of that length, and that he has six weeks in which to get fit; for him I would advise something like the following preparation:—

First fortnight.—A gallop at ½ speed, on Mondays and Thursdays, for ¼ mile, twice on the same morning, with a walk for a mile between the spins.

Second fortnight.—Single gallops on the same mornings, commencing at $\frac{1}{2}$ mile, and going up to $\frac{3}{4}$ mile, improving the pace up to $\frac{3}{4}$ speed.

Last fortnight.—Four gallops, a little better than $\frac{3}{4}$ speed, for something under a mile.

If an owner has a real "glutton" for work, he may take liberties with him, but ponies usually are not that sort.

On off days the pony should have a fair amount of exercise, hacking, &c., which I think should not exceed 9 or 10 miles a day.

Setting.—The degree of "setting," which term is used to express the routine employed in stinting a horse of his food and water before a race, will depend on the distance to be run, the time of day at which the horse is to come to the post, and on the condition and constitutional peculiarities of the animal itself. The longer the race is, the sharper should he be set. If it is to come off in the morning and the horse be gross, he should get, on the previous day, only about three pounds of hay or dried grass, given in quantities of one pound each after his morning, midday and evening feeds, the muzzle being put on to prevent him eating his bedding. The evening feed may be slightly decreased, while the early morning feed of one pound should be given three hours before the race comes off. In this case, no change in the system of watering on the day preceding the race is needed.

Water is very rapidly absorbed into the blood, and on that account, when taken in moderation, a couple of hours or so before a race, it does not act as a mechanical obstruction to the organs exerted in violent exercise, nor does it occupy the functions of the digestive apparatus in its assimilation, for a considerable time, as corn would do: for these reasons one need not stint a horse so sharply in the matter of water, as in that of food.

If the races be held in the evening—as they almost always are up-country—the setting need not be so strict, and an allowance of, say, 6lbs of dried grass may be given the day before. The trainer will now be guided by the style of horse, whether to put on the muzzle the night before the race, or to wait till the next morning; in most cases I think it better to adopt the latter method, for if the muzzle be applied over-night, there is a great probability of the horse getting fidgetted by it, and thereby being prevented from having a good night's rest. Anyhow, on the morning of the race, he is given his usual one-pound feed and is taken out for an hour and a half's walk, or he may get a very slow canter for three-quarters of a mile, and be sent the next quarter at nearly full speed just to open his pipes and to give him the idea that his day's work is finished. After that he may get about half his allowance of water, and nearly his full feed of corn with a small handful of dried grass. The muzzle is now put on, and at noon he may get a couple of pounds of corn. If the race comes off about 4 o'clock, he should get nothing more; but if at a later hour, a double handful of corn may be given three hours, or three hours and a half, before the saddling bell rings.

If a muzzle does not irritate a horse, it is better to use one than to take up the bedding, without which horses will not lie down during the day, while many will abstain from staling much longer than they ought to do. On the day of the race, the grooming should be got over quickly, for the horse should be disturbed and excited as little as possible: for this reason I would never plait the mane of an excitable horse.

The use of plaiting the mane is to prevent the hair flying about and getting entangled with the fingers of the rider, while he is holding the reins, especially when he wants to shorten his grip on them.

Having arrived at the race-course, the horse should be kept walking in the shade, if possible, while the saddling should be done quietly, and without any fuss; I think it is advisable for the owner to look after this operation himself, and to see that the weights, girths, stirrup leathers, etc., are all right. The horse gets now, from a leather-covered soda water bottle, just enough water to rinse his mouth out, the jockey is given a leg up, the syce dusts his boots down, and off they start for the post, where a syce should always go in case of accidents, and if he takes a spare stirrup leather and girth, they are not much weight and may come in useful, for such things often break at false starts. Besides this, the jockey may have to dismount in order to arrange some part of the gear, and will require the syce to hold his horse, or to lead him up to the starting post in case he be fractious.

Treatment after running.—A horse should be watered immediately after a race, while, if he be much distressed, he may get 1½ oz. sweet spirits of nitre in a drench, or 2 drs. carbonate of ammonia in a ball. If he has not to run for five or six days, he may get a bran mash or two. But if a fortnight or more is to elapse before his next race, he may have an alterative ball, and be kept on green food for a couple of days or more. His legs and feet may, with advantage, be fomented after running.

Race-horses travelling by rail.—It may not be out of place for me here to remark that when race-horses are taken by rail, during the cold weather, their tails (when they are in the horse-boxes) should be pointed towards the engine, so as to obviate, as much as possible, the chance of their catching cold.

CHAPTER VII.

Race-Courses.

ON KEEPING A GALLOPING TRACK IN ORDER—EFFECT OF GROUND ON HORSES—MEASURING COURSES—LENGTHS OF DIFFERENT COURSES IN INDIA.

THE climate and the hardness of the ground are the two great difficulties which a trainer has to contend against in India. When a race-course is on the ordinary soil we meet with in this Presidency, having generally a substratum of *kunkur,* nothing but constant manuring and picking up can keep it in order. This costs so much, that the Clerk of the Course (unless the Race Fund be particularly rich) may be well contented if he can keep a galloping track, even if only four yards broad, in good going order all the year round. Just before the close of the rains, he should take advantage of the softness of the ground to plough it up. It will cost about Rs. 30 a mile to plough and harrow a course 40 feet broad. If the ploughing be delayed, nothing but the pick-axe will touch hard soil. When arranging coolies for picking up ground, it is a good plan to have two men to each pick-axe, or hoe (*phurwa*), so that one may relieve the other, who will then pulverise the clods with a wooden batten (*mungurree* or *tapee*). The cost of labour may be calculated as follows :

On the hardest *kunkur* soil, a coolie, using a pick-axe (*gyntee*), can pick up and pulverise about 30 square yards, 4 to 6 inches deep, a day; or, with a hoe, he can do about 40 square yards of ordinary hard, sun-baked soil; or 60 square yards of easy soil. The clods should be pulverised as the picking up proceeds, for if left for a few days exposed to the sun, they will become almost as hard as so many stones. The best pick-axes for this work are those supplied by Government to regiments among their entrenching tools. Litter or tan should now be put down without delay. It is no use applying them before the ground be thoroughly loosened, for, until it becomes so, manure would have as little chance of working into and amalgamating with it, as it would on a metalled road. On a track four yards broad, such as I have described, it would take 2,000 maunds of tan, or 1,500 maunds of litter, to lay down a mile properly. The cartage of this will come to about Rs. 3 a hundred maunds, when brought from a distance of three miles. The spreading of the litter or tan will come to about eight annas a hundred maunds. Litter can sometimes be got, for the mere carting of it away, from artillery, cavalry, or elephant lines; but when it is sold, its price will not usually exceed eight annas a cart-load of about 20 maunds. Old and thoroughly decomposed litter is the best. New litter always contains a large quantity of particles of undigested grain that have passed through in the dung of the horses, while the presence of these particles will generally attract numerous field rats that burrow all over the course, and thus give a great deal of trouble before they can be exterminated, which is best done by filling the holes with water, and killing the rats as they come to the surface.

The Indian sun bakes the earth hard, and seems to burn up in a very short time whatever kind of manure is put on it; so that nothing but constant picking up and laying down litter, sand, or tan, at least twice a year, will keep a galloping track in anything like good order.

A track, 5 feet broad, will be found to be quite wide enough on which to work single horses.

By constant manuring, a thin layer of good soil will in time be formed; but if the course be neglected for but a couple of years, it will become as hard as a turnpike road.

The beau ideal of a galloping track is an elastic one, that will neither jar the joints and suspensory ligaments by its hardness, strain the back tendons, or cause a horse to hit himself by its stickiness, like on soft clay, nor shorten the stride and make it dwelling by deadness, like on sand.

A heavy course is particularly trying to a horse with oblique, and a hard course to one with upright pasterns.

Irregularities on the surface of the ground are a frequent cause of sprain to tendons and ligaments.

A galloping track such as I have mentioned, and 1¾ miles round, will cost about Rs. 400 a year to keep in good going order.

The length of a race-course, for big horses, should not be less than 1¼ miles. One of 5 furlongs will do for ponies.

A *distance* is 240 yards.

On the race-course, where the horses are trained, one should erect a rubbing-down shed beyond the winning-post and on the inside of the course. These sheds are made of split bamboo and dry thatching grass (Hind. *phoos*). A couple of stalls, roofed over in case of rain, with a small enclosure in front to keep off people troubled with curiosity, will cost about Rs. 16. *Ghuramee* (thatcher) is the name given to the labourers who do this *chhuppur* work.

When a course is intended for racing in the evening, the stand should face to the east, and *vice versâ.*

There should be, near each stand, a piece of ground carefully flagged and made level, on which to measure horses.

Race-courses are supposed to be measured on a line 5 feet from the inner edge all round; but practically the best plan is to measure close to the inside and then add to the length obtained 10½ yards, under the assumption that the course is a circle, which is near enough for all practical purposes. This mathematical problem I leave to my readers to work out for themselves.

If the inside of a course be closed, and horses are obliged to be galloped on the outside, the increased distance, once round, which might require to be done, in the event of a trial, may be readily calculated. For instance, say that the gallop is to be taken 25 feet from the inside, *i. e.*, 20 feet outside the line on which the course was measured; then the increased distance would be four times 10½ yards, *viz.*, 42 yards. In fact, we add 10½ yards to the length of the course, for every 5 feet the galloping track is outside the line on which the course was measured.

A surveyor's large perambulator is more correct and expeditious than the ordinary chain.

As a rule, courses in the morning give about a couple of seconds slower time for a mile, than they do in the evening.

I believe that the Bangalore course, for 1½ miles, is about 6 seconds slower than that of Madras.

The 1½ miles at Dehra Doon is very little slower than that on an ordinary flat track, while the mile is quite 2 seconds slower.

Races over ¾ mile at Lucknow, generally give bad timing, owing to the slight hill, for about half a mile, that leads up to that post.

Three quarters of a mile races at Umballa, are generally run in good time, but distances over that, in slow time.

The Calcutta, Sonepore, and Meerut courses are very fast, while that at Allahabad is quite 3 or 4 seconds in a mile slower than they are.

LENGTHS OF RACE-COURSES.

	Miles	Fur.	Yds.
s Agra *r* ...	1	4	0
Ahmedabad ...	1	4	55
p Ahmednuggur *r*	1	3	0
s Allahabad *r* ...	1	2	75
s Allygurh *l* ...	1	0	0
s Assensole *r* ...	0	6	217
s Bangalore *r* ...	1	2	0
s Bareilly *r* ...	1	6	45
Baroda ...	1	4	10
p Barrackpore *r*	1	4	37
Belgaum ...	1	2	63
p Berhampore ...	1	6	0
p Bhawulpore ...	2	0	0
Bolarum ...	1	3	160
s Bowenpilly *r* (3 miles from Secunderabad, monsoon race-course) *r*	1	1	204
Burdwan ...	1	3	95
p Byculla *r* ...	1	4	67
s Cachar *r* ...	0	5	0
s Calcutta *r* ...	1	6	21
s Calcutta St. Leger *r*	1	6	132
s Cawnpore *l* ...	1	5	148
s Chudderghat *r* (8 miles from Secunderabad)	0	7	107
p Chupra *r* ...	1	4	146

LENGTHS OF RACE-COURSES.—(*Contd.*)

Course	Miles	Fur.	Yds.
Cuttack ...	1	5	83
s Dacca *r* ...	1	3	140
Debrogurh ...	1	4	0
p Dehra *r* ...	1	4	192
s Dharwar *l* ...	1	1	58
p Dinagepore ...	0	7	0
s Dum-Dum ...	1	0	200
s Do. Steeplechase	2	1	80
p Ferozepore *r* ...	1	6	0
Fyzabad *r* ...	0	7	187
Goruckpore ...	1	3	99
Hyderabad (Sind)	1	4	7
s Jacobabad ...	1	6	25
s Jamalpore ...	1	0	0
Jessore ...	1	4	11
s Jhelum ...	1	2	0
Jorehaut ...	1	1	125
s Joudhpore ...	1	4	200
s Jubbulpore *r* ...	1	0	126
Jullundur *r* ...	1	3	5
s Kamptee *r* ...	1	4	92
Kurrachee ...	1	3	45
s Lahore *l* ...	1	6	20
s Lucknow *l* ...	1	6	0
Madras *r* ...	1	4	0
s Meerut *r* ...	1	5	46
p Mhow *r* ...	1	4	89
s Mooltan ...	0	6	134
s Moradabad *r* ...	1	4	118
s Morar ...	1	4	10
s Mowl Alee *r* (4½ miles from Secunderabad; Hyderabad races held there) ...	1	4	60
s Mozufferpore *r*	1	3	202
Muttra ...	1	4	0
Mysore ...	1	7	110
p Nusseerabad (Rajpootana) ...	1	3	45
s Peshawur ...	1	4	106
Poona *r* ...	1	4	65
p Purneah ...	1	4	0
Rajkote Kattywar	1	3	120
p Rampore Beaulio	1	2	0
s Rawul Pindee	1	3	49
Setapore ...	1	4	11
p Silligoree ...	1	0	13
s Simla (about)	0	7	0
s Sonepere *r* ...	1	4	158
s Trichinopoly ...	1	2	85
s Umballa *l* ...	2	1	45
Vizianagram ...	1	3	107
s Wellington *r* ...	0	5	20

The letters *r* and *l* distinguish right and left handed courses, while the correct lengths of those marked *s* have been most kindly furnished to me by either the Honorary Secretaries or Stewards of these meetings, or by friends on the spot. Those marked *p* I have taken from published prospectuses, and the remainder from the *Oriental Sporting Magazine.*

CHAPTER VIII.

Trainers and Jockeys.

THE chief trainers, at the present time in India, are John Wheal, H. Ryder, H. Bowen, N. Vinall, T. Donaldson, and O. Dignum.

Wheal was formerly well-known in Ireland and Wales as a bold and finished steeplechase rider. Since then, he has spent a long and honorable career as a trainer in India. His natural cleverness, great experience, and the fact that he is never above personally looking after his horses, have made his success most marked.

Ryder, whose name has been so often coupled in victory with the celebrated Arab Anarchy, is second to none as a shrewd and able trainer. He rides well, and is an admirable judge of pace.

Unimpeachable probity and strict attention to his business have always characterised Bowen's connection with the Indian turf.

Vinall has been a successful trainer, and is one of the best jockeys we have ever had in India.

Donaldson has always maintained the most unblemished name as a jockey, and generally heads the list for winning mounts. His wonderful quickness in getting away at the start is well-known.

Dignum is a brilliant cross-country rider, and has been a fairly successful trainer.

The following is a list of the principal jockeys in India, with their lowest riding weights.

		st.	lbs.			st.	lbs.
H. Hackney	...	8	7	H. Ryder	...	8	0
T. Donaldson	...	7	8	T. Tingey	...	8	4
J. Irving	...	8	10	G. Gooch	...	7	10
W. Blackburn	...	7	12	H. Williamson	...	7	10
N. Vinall	...	7	12	H. Stratford	...	8	0
H. Bowen	...	8	0	R. Walker	...	6	10
H. Walsh	...	8	2	J. Cavanagh	...	9	0
T. Cozens	...	8	5	Robinson	...	8	10
C. Dewing	...	10	2	J. Gerard	...	7	7

Dewing and Tingey are the two foremost steeple-chase riders in India: they are both extremely good.

A first class jockey, who trains and rides, would expect a salary of about Rs. 150 a month, with winning and losing mounts, though the latter might not be charged for in small events.

On the flat, jockeys' fees are reckoned at Rs. 50 for a losing, and Rs. 80, sometimes Rs. 100, for a winning mount. Cross-country riders charge Rs. 100 and Rs. 200. Good native jockeys generally demand Rs. 25 and Rs. 50.

CHAPTER IX.

Wasting for Race Riding.

MEN waste for riding, either to keep down their weight for a considerable time, as jockeys have to do during the racing season, or for one particular race or meeting. In the first case, a man should rely on abstinence in the matter of food and drink, and exercise, as physic and heavy sweats continued for a long time would destroy his strength and nerve. In training, the diet should be limited to fresh meat boiled, grilled, or roast—on no account stewed or fried—plain boiled fish without sauce, dry, hard biscuit and toast, with a small variety of vegetables that do not put up weight, such as onions, which are particularly useful in this respect, but on no account should sauce or butter be used with them. Salt ought to be the only condiment allowed. Jockeys generally confine themselves to cold meat and biscuit, which food palls quickly on their appetite. Bread, potatoes, cauliflower, peas, rice, butter, milk, fat of every kind, soups, puddings, sugar, sweets, stews, minces, and everything containing an excess of fat, sugar or starch should be carefully avoided. It is a well-known fact, that to keep in good health one should eat daily a certain proportion of vegetables in order that certain salts, contained in them, may be furnished to the system. By cooking, a large proportion of these salts being lost, a man in training should eat every day, so to obviate the necessity of consuming a large bulk, a small quantity of lettuces, raw tomatos, onions, celery, cucumber, radishes or cress, or in their place a little fresh fruit, with the exception of plantains, custard apples, and other fruits containing much sugar or farinaceous matter.

When wasting, one should avoid eating large quantities of meat, for doing so produces great languor and depression. "The first effect of an excessive meat diet is not that of increased strength, but rather a feeling of heaviness and weariness in the muscles, with nervous excitation often rising to sleeplessness, which he [Ranke] attributes to the accumulation in the blood of the alkaline salts of the meat" (Carpenter).

The drink should be restricted to water, weak tea without milk or sugar, light claret and water, or very weak spirits and water. The weaker these are taken the better, for tea, coffee, and alcohol check waste of tissue. A man in strict training should on no account take aerated waters, for they are so refreshing that it is hard to resist taking more than is advisable. As fluid of any sort puts up weight, a man should only drink that kind of which a little will quench thirst. I need hardly say that the less spirits a man takes, the steadier will be his nerves. If this regimen be strictly adhered to, the jockey need do nothing further than to take lots of exercise. Riding four or five training gallops every morning will get a man fitter than anything I know; but this is a luxury heavy weights cannot indulge in, so they ought to walk, play racquets, cricket, and take all the healthy exercise they can get, whether on horseback or on foot, short of going in for regular sweats. A couple of Cockle's pills or a sedlitz powder may be necessary now and then.

In this climate, Cockle's pills are very apt to lose, to a great extent, their purgative properties, if kept for some time after the box containing them has been opened. Lamplough's pyretic saline is probably the most agreeable saline draught. Epsom salts are by far the most effectual aperient for getting off weight; their effect is less nauseating and weakening than that of Cockle's pills.

The following would be about the correct style of daily food: A steak or a couple of chops—done on the gridiron, but not on the frying pan—a couple of slices of dry crisp toast, a few plain boiled onions, a bunch of radishes or cress, or a stick of celery, or a couple of tomatos, and a cup of tea, without milk or sugar, for breakfast. A slice or two of cold meat, a hard biscuit, and a glass of water for lunch. A couple of slices from a joint, plain boiled onions, a biscuit, a stick of celery, and half a pint of claret with water for dinner. By pursuing this system, with plenty of ordinary exercise, a man, in a month or so, will gradually get down to within 5 or 6 lbs. of his lightest riding weight, which, if required, can be attained by a couple of sweats and a dose of physic.

But if a man has to get off, say 21 lbs. in ten days or a fortnight, stronger measures will have to be adopted. Banting, as before described, must be followed, though a man should dispense with his frugal lunch, and eat and drink as little as he can manage to do with at breakfast and dinner. The training should commence with a strong dose of physic, say three Cockle's pills at night and an ounce of Epsom salts next morning. On that day, nothing beyond a quiet walk should be done; but on the next and succeeding days he should take a sweat, and about every third day an ounce of salts the first thing in the morning. On the day physic is taken, a long walk without sweaters will be enough. The sweat should be arranged in something of the following fashion: A pair of long knickerbocker stockings, over which a pair of thick worsted ones and a pair of boots for the feet. A pair of drawers and a couple of pairs of thick cloth trousers for the legs. A jersey, three flannel shirts, a thick *kumurbund*, a couple of warm waistcoats, two shooting coats and a great coat for the body. A pair of warm gloves for the hands, a large woollen comforter wrapped round and round the neck, and a couple of large cloth caps pulled down over the ears, will do as far as clothing is concerned. A pair of thick woolen socks, folded as if they were about to be put on the feet, are a capital substitute for gloves. Great care should be taken that every part be protected from the air, for even if the hands or neck be left bare, perspiration will be materially checked. With this amount of clothes, on a warm day, most men will find that a sharp walk of four miles will be as much as they can do without overtaxing their strength; one should arrange, if possible, so as to have the wind at one's back when returning home. The walk being finished, the man in training should lie down with a lot of rugs heaped over him, and remain thus, as long as he can, which usually will not be more than ten minutes or a quarter of an hour. During this time, the heavy oppressed feeling about the heart is most trying.

After the rugs and clothes are taken off, the man should be quickly dried, and then have a warm bath, and after that he may have a cold douche if his liver be in good order. He should not dress till he is thoroughly cool, and ought to forbear taking anything to drink as long as he possibly can after a sweat, for the more heated the body is, the more rapidly will it absorb fluid.

If a man has to sweat often, instead of using waistcoats he should have a thick flannel jacket, made, for the purpose, to fit tight over the flannel shirts, and to button high and close under the chin.

If a man has hacks to ride, and is unable to walk, he can take a sweat on horseback by putting on clothes as before, and then going for a sharp ride; but this, though pleasanter, will not be as effective practice as walking.

A sweat, like that I have described, will take from 4 to 6 lbs. off an ordinary man, provided there be little or no wind, which most materially prevents perspiration. When taking a sweat in this country, one should avoid the sun as much as possible, for few things tend to make one so nervous, as hard exercise when exposed to its influence. Having one's nerves in good order is of far more consequence than being able to get the exact weight. This particularly applies to men who ride their own horses, for jockeys have little option in the matter, owners being often foolishly exacting on this point. I am quite certain that on the flat a jockey can ride quite 5 lbs. better when he is fit and well, than he can when he is weak from wasting, while in steeplechasing the difference is one of stones and not of pounds.

A lamp bath is often taken instead of a regular sweat, if the man in training be lazy, or not able to walk well. It is arranged thus: Three or four small saucers full of oil with lighted cotton wicks in them, are placed under a chair on which the man sits, care being taken that a couple of thick doubled towels are put under him. He should have no clothes on, but should have several rugs and blankets, wrapped round the chair and himself, and brought tight under it, so that the heated air may not escape. A waterproof sheet considerably assists this operation. A little practice is required to teach one how to get the rugs and blankets fixed. If the hot air be properly kept in, the person taking this bath will break out into a profuse perspiration in about ten minutes, while this may be continued for an hour, which will be about the limit that most men can bear.

A lamp bath will take little more than half the weight off that a regular sweat will do, for its action is confined to the pores of the skin alone, while in the other there is a general waste of the body, the lungs aiding very largely in carrying off the *debris*. By the quickened breathing disintegrated tissue is rapidly got rid of, and pure blood is sent to the heart, and from it to the system generally. In a lamp bath, the action of the heart, after a short time, becomes tumultuous and the breathing laboured, on account of the lungs being gorged with insufficiently aerated blood, while, if this be continued much further, its action will become more and more feeble, till at last faintness occurs. By persisting in these sweats, the heart is very liable to become permanently injured.

I have described wasting and Banting from a jockey's point of view, though I am well aware how injurious they are to health, which cannot be maintained, under ordinary conditions, without a due proportion of fat or oil, and starch or sugar in the food, along with an adequate supply of fresh vegetables. I would strongly advise any of my readers who, being inclined to put up weight, may wish to keep it permanently down, on no account to Bant, but to take lots of hard exercise, and to substitute for dinner, a light meal consisting of a little cold lean meat and some plain vegetables. This, with an ordinary breakfast at about 11 A. M., and a cup of tea and a slice of toast first thing in the morning, will be enough for any healthy man to keep "fit" on. Beer, butter, stews, and pastry should be avoided.

I need hardly say that, any mode of wasting, however good, must prove injurious if carried to excess or continued for any time. The quicker weight is got off under judicious conditions, and the sooner the system is allowed to return to its healthy normal state, the less strain will it experience from wasting.

The more a man trusts to *hard exercise and self-denial* the "fitter" will he be to ride; while Banting, sweats, and physic should only be employed when time is limited, or the amount to be got off is considerable.

A man in training should weigh himself every day to

see how the process of wasting procees. A Salter's spring balance, noting ½lbs., up to 200lbs. is a cheap and most portable machine.

A man can ride in a light saddle (2 or 2½lbs.) a little less than what he will weigh in ordinary clothes.

If a jockey be at all in hard condition, he need allow nothing for wasting during a race on a hot day, for the horse will sweat more into the saddle cloth or pannel than the jockey is likely to lose.

The following is a safe rule to adopt for weighing out before a race. Everything, including the bridle, being in the scales, put ½lb on the opposite side, and if the jockey can draw his weight with this ½lb, he is quite safe.

Weighing before a race is called " weighing out," and after a race it is termed " weighing in."

CHAPTER X.

Betting.

LOTTERIES—DOUBLE LOTTERIES—PARI MUTUELS—RACE POOLS.

Lotteries.—The number of tickets and their prices in lotteries vary, though at the principal meetings they are generally fixed at Rs. 100 and Rs. 10 respectively.

The Honorary Secretary of the races, or other person appointed to manage the lotteries, should, on commencing, first write down the tickets taken by single indiviiduals, and then those taken conjointly; the practice being to throw with dice for tickets, the loser paying for them, though both he and the winner of the toss equally share the amount obtained for any horse, which any of their tickets may draw. Not until all the tickets, that can be disposed of conjointly, are written down, should sweeps be allowed to take place, as they are a last resource to fill up a lottery paper: for somehow or other, people will rarely take tickets, either on their own account or conjointly, after sweeps have commenced. A lottery should be made out on a large sheet of foolscap. Generally on the first and part of the second page the tickets are written down. At the end of the second page there is a form for recording the result of the drawing, and on the third, one for showing the debit and credit of each person may be given.

I will now give an illustrative lottery paper for a race

in which we may assume that five horses, *viz.*, Mr. Johnson's Sam, Mr. Williams' Jack, Mr. Payne's Lucy, Mr. Thomson's Ruby, and Mr. Smith's Brilliant, are declared to start, that there are 50 tickets at Rs. 10 each, and that Lucy won. From the total amount of the lottery, 5 per cent. is deducted for the benefit of the Race Fund.

Cawnpore Spring Meeting—1878.

LOTTERY ON THE DERBY—PRICE OF TICKETS Rs. 10.

No.	Names.		No.	Names.
1	Jones (1–2)	To Williams (1–11)	26	Thompson, Jones. (26–30)
2			27	
3	Williams (3–4)		28	
4			29	
5	Simpson (5–6)		30	
6			31	Smith, Thompson. (31–35)
7	Payne (7–8)		32	
8			33	
9	Johnson (9–10)		34	
10			35	
11	Thompson		36	Williams.
12	Johnson		37	Simpson, Williams. (37–39)
13	Smith (13–14)	To Williams (13–15)	38	
14			39	
15	Thompson		40	Thompson, Smith.
16	Jones, Thompson		41	Thompson, Williams. (41–43)
17	Thompson, Williams		42	
18	Williams, Thompson		43	
19	Thompson, Williams (19–24)		44	Williams, Thompson. (44–46)
20			45	
21			46	
22			47	Thompson, Smith. (47–50)
23			48	
24			49	
25	Johnson		50	

This form usually occupies the first and part of the second pages of the lottery paper.

RESULT OF DRAWING.

No.	Names of Drawers.	Horses.	Buyers.	Owner's claim.	Price.
47	Thompson, Smith ...	Sam ...	Smith ...	½	120
21	Thompson, Williams ...	Jack ...	Thompson	,,	90
12	Johnson ...	Lucy ...	Williams...	,,	70
46	Williams, Thompson ...	Ruby ...	Thompson	,,	140
5	Simpson, Williams ...	Brilliant ...	Williams...	,,	40

Price of horses ...	460
Ditto tickets ...	500
Total ...	960
Less 5 per cent. ...	48
Actual value of lottery ...	912

The above form should be at the end of the list of tickets. It is generally at the bottom of the second page.

DEBITS AND CREDITS.

Names.	Price of Tickets.	Bought.	Drew.	Lottery.	+	−
Jones ...	30	......	......	......	...	30
Williams ...	70	220	135	912	757	...
Simpson ...	50	10	20	......	...	40
Payne ...	20	......	......	......	...	20
Johnson ...	40	120	70	......	...	90
Thompson ...	220	450	175	......	...	495
Smith ...	70	120	60	......	...	130
				Percentage	48	
	500	920	460	912	805	805

The above form is usually drawn out on the third page of the lottery paper.

On the lottery paper, which I have given as an illustration, we see that the Nos. 12, 25, and 36 were taken by single individuals, and that there was a sweep of two tickets per man for Nos. 1 to 11 and for 13, 14, and 15, the break having occurred by Johnson having taken No. 12 on first going off; while the remaining tickets were taken conjointly.

By the C. T. C. Rules an owner is entitled to claim one-fourth of his horse's chance (taking that proportion of risk as well as gain) immediately on its being sold. The owner's share is the only one allowed to be recorded on a lottery paper, whatever part be taken, it being optional to the buyer to give more than one-fourth if he chooses, to the owner, in case the latter asks for it.

In the "Debits and Credits" we see that half of Sam is debited to Johnson, the owner of that horse.

By using the form of "Debits and Credits" we ensure correctness, which is proved, firstly, by the addition of the column under "Price of tickets" amounting to their gross value, and secondly, by the total sum under column "Bought" being exactly double that under "Drew," for the purchaser of a horse's chance pays double the amount he is sold for, first to the drawer, and then into the lottery. The final step in proving the accounts, is to see that the total winnings, plus the percentage, is equal to the total losings. When this system is employed, a form like the following should be used to show the total debits and credits on each day's racing. I here assume that there were four lotteries held, and that twelve persons took part in them.

Account of Lotteries held on 1st Day's Racing.

Names.	1st Lottery.	2nd Lottery.	3rd Lottery.	4th Lottery.	+	−
Williams ...	− 90	+ 1,610	− 850	+ 300	980	...
Brown ..	− 10	− 40	− 50	− 800	...	900
Stone ...	− 500	− 320	− 100	+ 1,400	480	...
Thompson ...	+ 1,450	− 400	− 80	− 200	770	...
Lake ...	− 50	− 180	− 20	+ 400	150	...
Green ...	− 30	− 60	+ 400	− 400	...	90
Baker ...	− 100	− 10	− 100	− 150	...	360
Grey ...	− 200	− 300	− 40	− 400	...	940
Boyd ...	− 50	− 200	+ 750	− 150	350	...
Smith ...	− 320	+ 100	− 30	+ 100	...	150
Payne ...	− 50	− 50	− 50	− 100	...	250
Reid ...	− 50	− 230	− 10	− 100	...	390
				Total percentage.	350	
Percentage...	90	80	80	100	3,080	3,080

Nothing can be less liable to error than the system which I have described; while correctness is a most valuable quality, when a mass of accounts has to be got through in a short time, which is always the case at a race meeting. This system's only fault is that, at a settling, if persons are not acquainted with its working, reference to the different debits and credits of individuals cannot be so readily made, and explanation given, as by another system which I shall now describe and which was shown to me some time ago by the then Honorary Secretary at Meerut. The working of this latter system is so self-evident that I need only give the form for the accounts of each day's racing. Its only fault is that error cannot be readily checked. To save room, I give the form for only four lotteries, though of course it can be made out for any number.

In lottery accounts, the debits consist of price of tickets and purchase of horses; the credits, that of horses drawn, and lotteries or parts of lotteries won: by the following system (see next page) these items are arranged in the most simple manner for reference and computation:—

Dr. *Total account of Lotteries held on — Day's Racing.* **Cr.**

1st Lottery.		2nd Lottery.		3rd Lottery.		4th Lottery.					1st Lottery.		2nd Lottery.		3rd Lottery.		4th Lottery.		Grand Total.	
Price of Tickets.	Bought.	Price of Tickets.	Bought.	Price of Tickets.	Bought.	Price of Tickets.	Bought.	Total Dr.	Names.	Total Cr.	Drew.	Lottery.	Drew.	Lottery.	Drew.	Lottery.	Drew.	Lottery	Dr.	Cr.
																		Total Percentage ...		

An owner, who attends many lotteries, will find it convenient to have a lottery book, made in the following form, in which to record his transactions. The book may contain a couple of hundred pages, each one being about the size of a quarter of a sheet of foolscap.

Form for Lottery Book.————*Meeting*————18 .

No.————*Lottery on*————. *Date*————.

No.	Name of drawers.	Name of horse.	Name of purchaser.	Owner's claim.	Sold for	REMARKS.

Tickets taken ...
,, lost ...
,, won ...
,, shared ...

Name of winning horse ...
Number of tickets in lottery ...
Price of each ticket ...

Price of horses ...
Ditto tickets ...
Total ...
Less 5 per cent. ...
Actual value of lottery

Formerly the ledger system was in general use for keeping lottery accounts. It consisted of entering each person's name, who took part in the lotteries, in a ledger, giving one page to his debits, and the other to his credits. It is far too tedious, for by it accounts cannot be made up in sufficient time to allow of a settling immediately after a meeting is over: while every Honorary Secretary knows, if this be not done, how extremely difficult it is to subsequently square accounts satisfactorily. Among the residents of a station this remark does not apply, but at a large meeting, where the bulk of the plungers are here to-day and gone to-morrow, it is most essential that everything should be settled as quickly as possible, for absentees find it hard to believe that they have won so little, or lost so much.

The lottery odds against a horse will be:—Price of tickets + price of all the horses − discount − double price of the one particular horse, to that double price.

Thus in the case we have already given, the odds against Jack are 500 + 460 − 48 − 180 to 180, *viz.*, 732 to 180, or about 4 to 1.

Suppose, by a private arrangement the buyer of Lucy, who won the race, had given away one-fourth of her, then the quarter winnings would be thus calculated:—

Actual value of lottery	912
Lucy's doubled price	140
... ...	4)772
One-fourth share of winnings	193

Double lotteries—Are generally resorted to, when, from a paucity of horses in two races, speculation on either, separately, is checked. The chances of all the horses are combined together, and the buyer of the chance which contained the names of the winners of both events takes the lottery. Let us suppose that two races—The Planter's Cup and Selling Stakes—had each three entries as follows:—

Planter's Cup.	*Selling Stakes.*
Kingcraft.	Lurline.
Exeter.	Butterfly.
Chorister.	Brandy.

The combined chances would then be:—

1. Kingcraft and Lurline.
2. Kingcraft and Butterfly.
3. Kingcraft and Brandy.
4. Exeter and Lurline.
5. Exeter and Butterfly.
6. Exeter and Brandy.
7. Chorister and Lurline.
8. Chorister and Butterfly.
9. Chorister and Brandy.

These nine chances will be drawn for, and auctioned off, in the same manner as if they represented nine different horses entered for one particular race.

Pari Mutuels—Can never be an adequate substitute for lotteries in this country, for the simple reason that they entail the trouble of exercising one's judgment in trying to spot the winner, instead of leaving the matter to chance. Scores of men gamble in lotteries, who do not know one horse from another, possibly not even their names, but they like a quiet "punt" with the chance of drawing a horse; they are the true supporters of lotteries; but as they do not care for racing, it would afford no interest to them to back one horse, in preference to another, in a Pari Mutuel.

Pari Mutuels in India are usually managed in the following manner: near the Race Stand is fixed a long box divided into partitions, each of which has a slit like those in letter-boxes. On each partition is written the name of a race, in the order they are to be run. The person managing the Pari Mutuel is provided with cards printed in the following form:—

MEERUT AUTUMN MEETING—1878.

Tickets—Rs. 5.

Name of race____________________

Horse backed____________________

No. of tickets__________

Signature of backer____________________

Having received a card, the intending backer fills it in according to his fancy, and places it, through the slit, into the partition set apart for the race on which he wishes to invest. This partition is closed on the horses arriving at the starting post, after which no more cards can be put in. When the day's racing is finished, the amount invested on the losers in each event is divided among those who backed the winners of those respective races, after deducting a percentage, usually 5 per cent., for the benefit of the Race Fund. Let us assume that in one of the races the winner was backed by A for Rs. 10, by B for Rs. 25, and by C for Rs. 15, and that the other horses in the same race had been backed for Rs. 160. The total here would be Rs. 210, from which to calculate a percentage of Rs. 10 at 5 per cent. Deducting this Rs. 10 from Rs. 160 (amount lost), would leave Rs. 150 to be divided between A, B, and C, and they would get respectively Rs. 30, Rs. 75, and Rs. 45.

Race Pools—May be got up by any number of persons who bid for choice of horses entered for a race, the buyer of the winner of which takes the several amounts bid for the other horses. Say, for instance, that the horses Lancer, Gaylad, Breeze, and Phantom were entered for a certain race; the auctioneer would then ask, "How much for first choice?" Suppose A bid Rs. 50, B bid Rs. 70, and D finally got it for Rs. 500. D would then have the choice of any one of the four horses. Let us say that he took Gaylad. The second choice for Lancer, Breeze, and Phantom would, in the same manner, be put up to auction, and suppose A got it for Rs. 400 and took Lancer. Also that B got Breeze for Rs. 80, and that C bought Phantom for Rs. 120. The pool would thus stand:—

D pays for Gaylad	Rs.	500
A „ Lancer	„	400
B „ Breeze	„	80
C „ Phantom	„	120
If Gaylad wins, D will win	„	600
„ Lancer „ A „ „	„	700
„ Breeze „ B „ „	„	1,020
„ Phantom „ C „ „	„	980

HINDUSTANEE STABLE AND VETERINARY VOCABULARY.

The following, with the exception of names of diseases, colours, and some technical expressions, are words of common use in the stable which any syce will understand. In order to render the pronunciation easy to those unacquainted with the language, I have written the vowels as they are pronounced in the following words:—

a as in "star"	o as in "tore"	oo as in "poor"
é „ "écarté"	u „ "fun"	ow „ "town"
i „ "kin"	ú „ "pull"	y „ "by"

n should be pronounced like the French nasal n, as in "mon." The Hindee letters t, d, and r are pronounced hard as in English, and the th, dh, and rh like what these letters would sound if aspirated; kh and gh stand for these two guttural letters in Arabic.

PARTS, ETC., OF THE HORSE.

Abdomen, *Pét.*
Artery, *Shiryan.*
Back, *Peeth.*
Backbone, *Reerh.*
Back tendon, *Ghúr-nuss.*
Bars of the foot, *Dohree pútlee.*
Bile, *Pitta.*
Bladder, *Phúknee.*
Blood, *Khoon.*
Bone, *Huddee.*
Brain, *Mughz; bhéja.*
Cannon-bone, *Nullee.*
Cartilage, *Kurree huddee.*
Cheek, *Gal.*
Chest, *Chhatee; seena.*
Cleft of the frog, *Pútlee kee ghaee.*
Corners of the mouth, *Bachh.*
Coronet, *Súm kee mughzee* or *bhown.*
Crust of the hoof, *Shakh.*
Dock, *Saghiree.*
Ear, *Kan.*
Elbow, *Aglee kohnee.*
Eye, *Ankh.*
Eyelash, *Buronee.*

Eyelid, *Puluk.*

Feather (in the hair), *Bhownree.*
Fetlock joint, *Múttha.*
Flank, *Kohk.*
Fibre, a (of muscle, etc.), *Résha.*
Foot, *Pyr.*
Forearm, *Bazoo ;* dund.
Forehead, *Matha ; péshanee.*
Foreleg, *Hath.*
Forelock, *Chotee.*
Frog, *Pútlee.*
Foam (from the mouth), *Kuf.*

* Gullet, *Hulk*
Gums, *Musooré.*

Hair (of the mane or tail), *Bal.*
„ (of the body), *Roan ; rom.*
Haw (of the eye), *Butank.*
Head, *Sir.*
Heart, *Dil.*
Heel (of the hoof), *Khoontee.*
Hind leg, *Paon.*
„ quarters, *Pútha.*
Hip, *Koola.*
Hock, *Koonch.*
Hoof, *Súm.*

Intestines, *Ant ; unturee.*

Jaw, *Jubra.*
Joint, *Jor ;* ganth *; gira.*

Kidney, *Gúrda.*
Knee, *Ghútna ; zanoo.*

Lip, *Honth.*
Liver, *Kuléja.*
Loins, *Kumr.*
Lungs, *Phéphra*

Mane, *Yal.*
Mark of the teeth, *Dant kee seeahee.*
Membrane, *Jhillee.*
Mouth, *Moonh.*
Muscle, *Gosht.*
Muzzle, *Thoothun.*

Neck, *Gurdun.*
Nerve, *Usub.*
Nose, *Nak.*
Nostrils, *Nuthna.*

Palate, *Taloo.*
Pancreas, *Libba.*
Pastern, *Gamchee.*
Periosteum, *Huddee kee jhillee.*
Pores (of the skin), *Musam.*
Pulse, *Nubz.*
Pupil of the eye, *Ankh kee pútlee.*

Ribs, *Puslee.*
Rump, *Pútha.*

Saliva, *Ral.*
Scrotum, *Fota.*
Sheath, Ghi*laf.*
Shoulder, *Phur.*
Sinew, see Tendon.
Skeleton, Thuth*uree.*
Skin, *Chumra.*
Sole of the foot, *Dilla ; tulwa.*
Spinal cord, *Huram mughz.*
Spleen, *Tillee.*
Stifle, *Kúlaba.*

---

* In Hindustanee, the same word appears to be used without distinction to express both the gullet and windpipe.

Stomach, *Kotha.*
Synovia, *Jor ka tél.*
Tail, *Dúm.*
Tendon, *Py; nuss; puttha.*
Temple, *Kun-puttee.*
Thigh, *Ran.*
Throat, *Gula.*
Toe of the hoof, Tho*kur.*
Tongue, *Jeebh.*
Tooth (milk), *Doodh ka dant.*
" (molar), Darh.
" (nipper), *Dant.*
Tooth (permanent), *Pukka dant;* darh.
" (wolf's) *Chor dant.*
Tushes, *Nésh; khoontee.*

Urethra, *Nézé ké soorakh.*

Vein, *Rug; wureed.*
Vertebra, *Munka.*

Windpipe, *Hulk.*
Withers, *Mudow.*

Yard, *Néza.*

COLOURS OF THE HORSE.

Bay, *Kúmyt.*
" with legs black up to the knees, *Seeah zanoo kúmyt.*
" with belly and inside of legs light coloured, *Kéhur.*
Black, *Múshkee; kala.*
* Brown, or dark bay, *Téleeya kúmyt; lukhowree kúmyt.*
Chesnut (all over), *Súrung.*
" with dark mane and tail, *Kúmyt.*
" (dark), *Mowha súrung.*
" dark, with light mane and tail, *Chowdur súrung.*
Cream coloured, *Doodheeya shirgha.*
Dun, light, all over, *Shirgha.*
" with black mane and tail, *Summund.*
" (black stripe down back), *Sélee summund.*
" (dark with dark points and black horizontal stripes on forearms), *Kúla.*
" with zebra marks, *Kéhuree kúla.*
Dun, with legs black up to the knees, *Seeah zanoo summund.*
Grey or white, with dark mane and tail, *Subza.*
† Grey flea-bitten, *Mugsee.*
" dappled, *Gúldar subza.*
" dark iron, *Neela subza.*
" nutmeg, *Lal subza.*

---

* NOTE.—Natives rarely distinguish brown as a colour: if ordinary brown, they usually call it *Kumyt;* if dark brown, *Mushkee.*

† A horse is called Mugsee only after he is 12 years old and the grey in his coat has turned to white, leaving the black specks clearly visible.

Grey with skin black and white in patches, *Sunjaf*.
Mouse coloured, *Soor*.
Piebald, *Kala abluk*.
Roan, *Gurra*.
Skewbald, *Lal abluk*.
Strawberry roan (legs and muzzle white, coat ticked out with white), *Cheena*.
White (with white hoofs, mane and tail, and pink skin), *Núkra*.
White (mane and tail white, skin black), *Súrkha*.
Horse with four white stockings and blaze, *Puchkuleeyan*.

These are the correct Urdoo terms, that are in use among Native Cavalry, &c. Syces have very vague ideas on colour, and generally confine themselves to the following:—

Bay and chesnut, *Lal*.
Black, *Kala*.
Dun, *Sumund*.
Grey, *Subza*.
White, *Suféd*.

DISEASES, AILMENTS, DEFECTS, ETC., OF HORSES.

Anasarca, *Tubuk*.
Asthma, *Duma*.
Blind, *Andha*.
„ of one eye, *Kana*.
Barbs, or paps, *Unchhur*.
Blister, *Chhala*.
Boil, *Phora*.
Bots (eggs), *Leek*.
„ (larvæ), *Bur*.
Bronchitis, *Kuf*.
Brittle feet, *Súm khara*.
Bruise, *Chot*.
Brush, to, *Néwur lugna*.
Canker of the foot, *Kufgeera*.
Capped hock, *Kúhneea*.
„ knee, *Zanooa*.
Capped elbow, *Kheesa*.
Cataract, *Moteea-bind*.
Catarrh, *Zúkam; surdhee*.
Chest founder, *Chhatee bund*.
Cold, *Zúkam*.
Colic, *Kúrkúree*.
Consumption, *Khushkbél*.
Constipation, *Kubz*.
Corn, *Chhala*.
Cough, *Khansee*.
Cracked heels, *Gamchee men chheewur*.
Curb, *Bujr huddee*.
Cysts, *Jowa*.
Diarrhœa, *Zeeada dust*.
Dropped hip, *Kum koola*.

Dull, to be, *Sust hona.*
Dysentery, *Péchish ;* kh*oonee dust.*
Elephantiasis, *Feel-pa.*
Enteritis, *Boghma.*
Epilepsy, *Mirgee.*
Farcy, *Bél.*
Fever, *Tup ; bú*kh*ar.*
Fill, to (as a leg), *Py ajana.*
Fistula, *Nasoor.*
Flat feet, *Chúpatee súm.*
Flatulency, *Badee.*
Girthgall, *Zér tung zu*khm.
Glanders, Kh*unak ; seemba.*
Goose rumped, *Tubur goon.*
Granulate, to, *Angoor bhurna.*
Granulations, *Angoor.*
Hide bound, *Chirm* kh*úshk.*
Indigestion, *Budhuzmee.*
Inflammation, *Julun ; sozish.*
,, of the feet, see Laminitis.
,, ,, liver, *Kuléjá kee beemaree.*
,, ,, lungs, see Pneumonia.
Jaundice, *Yurkan ; kunwul bad.*
Lame, *Lungra.*
,, chronically, *Kuhna lung.*
Laminitis, *Súm ka tup.*
Lampas, *Talooa.*
Loins, gone in the, *Kumree.*
Loodiana disease (purpura), *Gutheea ; bhugona ; zuhurbad.*
Madness, *Deewangee.*
Maggots, *Keeré.*
Mange, *Khújlee ;* kh*arish.*
Megrims, *Mirgee.*
Mellanosis, *Bamunee.*
Moonblindness, *Ruttowndhee ; shub-koree.*
Mucus (from the eyes), *Keechur.*
,, (,, ,, nose), *Néta ; rént*
,, (,, ,, throat), *Khakhar.*
Navicular disease, *Súrun bad* (?)
Œdéma or swelled leg, *Feel-pa.*
Ophthalmia, *Ankh ú*th*na.*
Pain, *Durd.*
Parrot mouthed, *Toté duhun.*
Pneumonia, or inflammation of the lungs, *Phéphré kee beemaree.*
Proud flesh, *Bud-gosht.*
Pumiced feet, *Chúpatee súm.*
Pus, matter, *Peeb.*
Retention of urine, *Péshab-bund.*
Rheumatism, *Baee.*
Ringbone (on forefeet), *Chukrawul.*
Ringbone (on hindfeet), *Pústuk.*
Ringworm, *Dad.*
Roaring, *Shérdumee.*
Sandcrack, *Shikak súm.*
Sore back (to have), *Pee*th *lugna.*
Sore mouth, *Buchka.*
,, throat, *Gulsooa.*
Spavin (bog), *Motra.*
,, (bone), *Hudda.*
Speck (in the eye), *Chheent.*
Splint, *Bél* huddee *; bér* hud*dee.*

Splinter (of bone, etc.), *Kirich.*
Sprain, *Moch.*
Sprained tendon, *Py ajana.*
Strangles, *Húbuk.*
Stringhalt, *Jhunukbad.*
Suppression of urine, *Péshab bund.*
Surfeit, *Gurmee dané.*
Swelling, *Wurum; soojun.*
Tetanus, *Chandnee kee beemaree; pista duhun.*
Thorough pin, *Bhubhootura.*
Thrush, *Russ úturna.*
Tumour, *Rusaowlee.*
Tympanitis, *Badee.*
Upright pasterns, *Múrghpa.*
Wart, *Mussa.*
Weave, to, *Jhoomna.*
Windgall, *Byza.*
Worm in the eye, *Moonja.*
Worms (round), *Kénchooa.*
„ (thread), *Chúnchúna.*
Wound, *Zukhm.*

DISEASES OF CATTLE.

Foot and mouth disease, *Khúr-puka; khúrha.*
Hoven, *Badee.*
Pleuro pneumonia, *Pheepree.*
Quarter-ill, *Gutheea; goli.*
Rinderpest, *Mata; chéchuck; devi.*

AGES OF THE HORSE.

A colt, *Buchhéra.*
A filly, *Buchhéree.*
A colt up to one month old, *Kurra.*
Ditto four months old, *Sinaya.*
„ eight months old, *Wastat.*
One year old, *Surloo.*
Until two years old, *Nakund.*
„ three years old, *Doék.*
„ four years old, *Charsala.*
„ five years old, *Punjsala.*
Ten years old and upwards, *Mulé punj.*

MEDICINES, DRUGS, &c.

Acid (*s*), *Tézab.*
Aconite, *Seengeea bish.*
Aloes, *Elwa; músubbur.*
Alum, *Phitkurree.*
Anise seed, *Sownf.*
Antimony (black), *Súrma.*
Areca nut, *Súparee.*

Arsenic, white, *Sunkheea.*
„ yellow, *Hurtal.*
„ red, *Mynsil.*
Asafœtida, *Heeng.*

Blue stone, *Neela tooteea.*
Borax, *Sohaga.*

Camphor, *Kafoor.*
Carraway seed, *Ajwyn.*
Carbonate of soda, *Kharsujee.*
Castor oil, *Réndee ka tél.*
Catechu, *Kuth.*
Caustic, *Tooteea.*
Chalk, *Khuree mittee.*
Corrosive sublimate, *Ruskapoor.*
Croton bean, *Jumalgota.*
„ oil, *Jumalgoté ka tél.*

Ginger (green), *Udruk.*
„ (dry) *Sonth.*

Honey, *Shuhud.*
Hoof ointment, *Súm roghun.*

Indian hemp (leaves), *Bhung; subzee.*
„ „ (dried flowers), *Ganja.*
„ „ (resin), *Churus.*
Iron, sulphate of, *Huree kusees.*

Kerosine oil, *Mittee ka tél.*

Lard, *Soour kee churbee.*
Leech, *Jonk.*
Lime, *Choona.*
Linseed oil, *Ulsee*, or *teesee ka tél.*

Mercury, *Para.*
Mustard, *Rai.*
Mustard oil, *Surson ka tél.*

Neatsfoot oil, *Paé ka tél.*
Nitre, *Shora.*
Nux vomica, *Kúchla.*

Oakgalls, *Majoo.*
Ointment, *Murhum.*
Oil, *Tél.*
Opium, *Afeem.*

Pepper (red), *Lal mirch.*
„ (black), *Gol* „
Poppy heads, *Posta.*
Poultice, *Lúbdee.*

Resin, *Ral.*

Sal ammoniac, *Nowsadur.*
Salt, *Numuk.*
Salts (Epsom), *Júlabee numuk.*
Sesamum oil, *Til* or *jinjilee ka tél.*
Soap-nut, *Reeta.*
Sugar of lead, *Suféda.*
Sulphate of copper, *vide* Blue stone.
Sulphur, *Gunduk.*
Sweet oil, *Meetha tél.*

Turpentine, *Gunda birozé ka tél; tarpeen ka tél.*

Venice or crude turpentine, *Gundabiroza.*
Verdigris, *Jungal.*
Vinegar, *Sirka.*

Wax, *Moom.*

Zinc, sulphate of, *Suféd tootee*

SADDLERY, HARNESS, CLOTHING, STABLE GEAR, &c.

Backband, *Barkush.*
Balling iron, *Daroo-kush.*
Bandages, *Puttee.*
Bandage, a wet, *Pochara.*
Bearing rein, *Gol bag.*
Bedding, *Bichalee.*
Bellyband, *Pétee.*
Bit (curb), *Duhana.*
Blanket, *Kummul.*
Body-piece (clothing), *Gurdunnee.*
Breast-piece, *Chhatee-bund.*
Breast-plate, *Pésh-bund.*
Breechen, *Púshtung.*
Bridle, *Lugam.*
Broom, *Jharoo.*
Browband, *Kun sirra.*
Brush, *Broosh,* or *koochee.*
Bucket, *Baltee.*
Buckle, *Buksooa.*

Chamois leather, *Sabur.*
Clothing (light), Thunda *kupra.*
„ (warm), *Gurm kupra.*
Clyster pipe, *Pichkaree.*
Collar, *Hulka.*
Comb, *Kunghee.*
Crupper, *Dúmchee.*
Curb-chain, *Duhané-kee-zunjeer.*
Curry-comb, *Khurara.*

Girths, *Tung.*
Girth tugs, *Chheep.*
Gloves made of hair for grooming, *Huthee.*

Hames, *Huslee.*
Harness, *Saz.*
Harness, double, *Joree ka saz.*
„ single *Ekla saz.*
„ tandem, *Agul pichul saz.*
Head collar or halter, *Núkta.*
Head-ropes, *Agaree.*
Head stall (of a bridle), *Sirduwalee.*
Heel-ropes, *Pichharee.*
Hobbles, casting, *Ghúr puchhar; lungur.*
Hobbles (for the hind legs), *Mújuma.*
Hole (in a stirrup leather, &c.), *Ghur.*
Holsters, *Kuboor.*
Hood, *Kunsilla.*

Keeper (on reins, etc.), *Chhula.*

Leading rein, *Bagdoree.*
Lipstrap, *Buhadúree.*

Martingale, *Zérbund.*
Muzzle, *Chheeka.*

Nosebag, *Tobra.*
Nose band, *Nas bund.*

Pad (harness), *Chal.*
Pannel (of a saddle), *Guddee.*
Picker (hoof), *Súm-khúdnee.*
Port of a bit, *Jeebhee.*

Reins, *Ras.*

Ring (of martingale, &c.), *Chhula.*
Roller, *Furakhee.*
Rosette, *Kurn phool.*
Rowel, *Phirkee.*
Rubber, *Jharun.*

Saddle, *Zeen.*
Saddle-cloth, *Tuh-roo; uruk-geer; numda; myl-khora.*
Saddle covering, *Boghbund; zeen-posh.*
Saddle dressing, *Moomroghun.*
Saddle flaps, *Dawun.*
Saddler, *Zeen saz; zeen ka mochee.*
Saddle stand, *Ghoree.*
Scissors, *Kainchee.*
Shaft, *Bum.*
„ tugs, *Choongee.*
Sieve, *Chhulnee.*
Sling, *Jhola.*
Snaffle, *Kuzaee.*
Spurs, *Kanté; múmréz.*
Strap, *Tusma.*
Stirrups, *Rikab.*
Stirrup-leathers, *Rikab-duwal.*
Stirrup-locks, *Champ.*
Surcingle, *Balatung.*
Sweat-scrapers, *Puseena-kush.*

Tape, *Feeta.*
Throat-lash, *Gultunnee.*
Tongue of a buckle, *Buksooa kee sooee.*
Trace, *Jot.*
Trace-bearers, *Manik jot.*
Twitch, *Kúchmal; poozmal.*

Weight-cloth, *Seesa-guddee.*
Whip, *Chabúk.*
Winkers, *Putta.*
Wisp, *Koocha.*

FOOD.

Barley, *Jow.*
Beans, *Sém.*
Bran, *Chokur.*

Carrots *Gajur.*

Flour (coarse), *Ata.*
„ (fine), *Myda.*
„ (very fine), *Soojee.*

Gram, *Chuna.*
„ (Madras), *Kúlthee.*
Grass, *Ghas.*

Linseed, *Ulsee; teesee.*

Maize, *Mukaee.*

Oats, *Jy.*

Rice (in husk), *Dhan.*
„ (uncooked), *Chawul.*
„ (cooked), *Bhat.*
Rice gruel, *Kanjee.*
Rock salt, *Numuk sung.*

Salt, *Numuk.*
Sugarcane, *Gunna; ookh; eekh.*

Wheat, *Géhoon.*

RELATING TO SHOEING.

Anvil (a blacksmith's), *Nihai.*
„ (shoeing-smith's, small), *Sindan.*

Bar shoe, *Gol nal.*
Buttress, *Súm turash.*

Calkin, *Khoonta.*
Clench, a, *Púchee.*
„ a nail, to, *Mékh hopúchee kurna.*
Clips, *Killif* or *thokur.*
Cold chisel, *Chhénee.*
Drawing knife, *Chhúree.*

Forge, *Mistree-khana.*
Fullering, *Punalee.*

Hammer, *Huthowree.*

Nail, *Prég ; mékh.*

Pincers, *Zumboor ; sunrsee.*
Punch, *Súmba ; pogur.*

Rasp, *Rét.*
Removing, *Kholbundee.*

Shoe, *Nal.*
Shoe with calkins (also with thickened heels), *Khoontee-dar nal.*
Shoe with clips, *Thokur-dar nal.*
Shoeing, *Nalbundee.*
„ smith, *Nal-bund.*

MISCELLANEOUS.

Amble, to, *Ruhwar chulna.*
Arab, an, *Tazee* or *urubee ghora.*

Bag (for oats, &c.), *Bora.*
Ball (physic), *Duwa-kee-golee.*
Bite, to, *Katna.*
Biter (a horse), *Kuttur.*
Bleed, to, *Fusd kholna.*
Bobtailed horse, *Bunda*, or *lun-doora ghora.*
Bolt, to, *Phutjana.*
Breeding district, *Khét.*
Brook (water jump,) *Nala.*
Buck, to, *Kandhee marna.*

Canter, to, *Poya chulna.*
Caster, a, *Nuzuree ghora.*
Chaff, *Bhoosa.*
Clean, *Saf.*

Cold (*adj.*). *Thunda,*
Colours, *Ghúrdowree Kupra.*
Colt, *Buchhéra.*
Condiment, *Musala.*
Country-bred horse, *Désee ghora.*
Cowdung, *Gobur.*
Cowkick, to, *Kainchee marna.*
Crib-biter, *Howapeené-wala.*

Dandruff, *Roosee.*
Defect (in a horse), *Ayb.*
Digest, to (food), *Huzm kurna.*
Dirty, *Myla.*
Dismount, to, *Uturna.*
Ditch, *Khaee.*
Door, *Durwaza.*
Double bank, *Dumduma.*
Drench, to, *Duwa pilana.*

Drink, to, *Peena.*
Drive, to, *Hankna.*
Dung, *Leed.*

Eat, to, *Khana.*
English horse, *Bilayutee ghora.*
Entire (as a horse), *Andoo.*

Fast (swift), *Téz.*
Fat (*s*), *Churbee.*
Fat (*adj.*), *Mota; furba.*
Farrier, *Saloturee.*
Feeder, a bad, *Kum* khor.
Filly, *Buchhéree.*
Fire, *Ag.*
Fire, to, *Daghna.*
Flat (as a race), *Suffart.*
Fleam, *Nushtur.*
Foment, to, *Séukna.*
Forage, *Chara.*
Forage (daily allowance of), *Ratib.*

Gallop, to, *Dowrna; surput phénkna.*
Garron, a (a raw-boned horse), *Dugga.*
Geld, to, Akh*ta kurna.*
Gelding, Ahk*ta.*
Godown (of water), *Ghoont.*
Grass cutter, *Ghuseeara.*
Grass lands (preserved for grass and hay), *Rukh.*
Graze, to, *Churna.*
,, to send to, *Churana.*
Grind coarsely, to, *Dulna.*
,, finely, to, *Peesna.*
Groom, *Saees.*
,, to, *Mulish kurna.*

Half-bred, *Doghla.*
Handful (double), *Unjul.*
,, (single) *Mútthee.*
Hand-rub, to, *Hath sé mulna.*
Hard-mouthed, *Moohzor.*
Head groom, *Jumedar saees.*
Hedge, *Bar.*
High couraged, *Jan baz.*
Hill pony, T*anghun.*
Hollow-backed horse, *Kuchhee,* or *zeen púsht ghora.*
Horse, *Ghora.*
,, to, *Gurm hojana; bég lana; alung hona.*

Horse-fly, Dans.
Hot, *Gurm.*
Hurdle, *Phoos kee tuttee.*

Jade, a, *Khullur.*
Jib, to, Urh*-jana.*
Jockey, *Coachwan.*
Jump, to, *Koodna; phandna.*

Kick, to, *Púshtuk-marna; lat chulana.*
Kick, to (with both hind feet at once), *Dúluttee marna.*
Kicker, *Luttur.*

Lead a horse, to, *Tihlana.*
Leather, *Chumra.*
Livery stables, *Urgurra.*
Litter (manure,) *Khad.*
Lotion, *Dhone kee duwa.*
Lunge to, a horse, *Kawa déna.*

Mare, *Ghoree; madwan.*
Mill (hand), *Chukkee.*
Mount, to, *Suwar-hona.*
Neigh, to, *Hinhinana.*

Ointment, *Murhum.*

Once round (race course), *Poora chukkur.*

Pant, to, *Hampna.*

Paw, to (from impatience), *Tapna.*

Paw, to (strike out with the fore-leg), *Tap marna.*

Pestle and mortar, *Hawun dista.*

Physic (*s*), *Duwa.*

" to, *Duwa dêna.*

" " (purge), *Júlab dêna.*

Pinch (of salt, etc.), *Chútkee.*

Plunge, to, *Lumbeean kurna.*

Pony, *Yaboo; tattoo.*

Post and rails, *Jungla.*

Pot (cooking), *Dégchee.*

Powder (medicine given dry), *Súfoof.*

Powder, a (medicine wrapped up in paper), *Púreea.*

Prance, to, *Nachna.*

Quiet (as a horse), Gh*ureeb.*

Race, *Bazee.*

Race course, *Chukkur; ghúrdowr.*

Race horse, *Ghúrdowree* ghora,

Rear, to, *Alifhona.*

Ride, to, *Suwaree kurna.*

Rig, a, *Ek andeea.*

Roar, to (as a horse), *Shêrdumee kurna.*

Rope, *Russee.*

Rough-rider, *Chabúk suwar.*

Run away, to, *Bhagjana.*

Saddle, to, *Zeen bandhna.*

Scales, *Turazoo.*

Selling race, *Leelameebazee.*

Sheaf, *Poola.*

Shy, to, *Bhurukna.*

Skittish, *Chunchul.*

Slow (as a horse), *Dheema; mutha.*

Slight built, *Chhuréra budun.*

Snort, to, *Furfur kurna.*

Soap, *Sabun.*

Sound (as a horse), *Bé ayb.*

Stable, *Istubbul; than; tubéla.*

Stack (of hay, etc.), *Gurree.*

* Star (on forehead), *Sitara.*

Steeple-chase, *Tuttee bazee.*

Stomachic, *Pachuk.*

Straw, *Púwal.*

" (a single), *Tinka.*

" (for bedding), *Bichalee.*

Stripe down back (like that of a donkey), *Sélee.*

Stud-bred, a, *Lumburee ghora.*

Stumble, to, Th*okur khana.*

Sweat, *Puseena.*

Tan, *Bukla.*

Thick (as gruel, &c.), *Garha.*

Thorough-bred, *Useel.*

Tired, *Thuk gya.*

---

* NOTE.—If the star be so small that it can be covered by the thumb is called *Sittara péshanee,* and is considered among natives to be a most unlucky mark.

Tow, *Sun.*
Trough (feeding), *Kuthra.*
Trot, to, *Dúlkee chulna.*
Unsound, *Aybee.*
Underbred, *Kumzat.*
Veterinary Manual, *Furus nama.*
Vicious, *Budzat.*
Walk, to (as a horse), *Kudum kudum chulna.*
Walk, to (lead a horse out for a), *Rowl kurna.*
Wall, *Deewal.*
Walleyed (one eye), *Takee.*
Walleyed (both eyes), *Súlymanee.*
Water, *Panee.*
„ boiling, *Khowlta* or *josh panee.*
„ lukewarm, *Sheer gurm panee.*
Weaver (a horse), *Jhoomnéwala.*
Weighing house, *Tol ghur.*
Window, *Khirkee.*
Wind-sucker, *Howa peené wala.*
Winning post, *Jeet kee luhree.*

PHRASES.

The *abscess* has come to a head	*Phora puk gya.*
The horse has a sore *back* ...	*Ghorê kee peeth lugee hy.*
The horse *bolted* off the course...	*Ghora chukkur sé phut gya.*
My horse *bores* to the right ...	*Humara ghoradahiné ko bag kurta*
Where was that horse *bred*? ...	*Wuh his khét ka ghora hy?*
The horse is not properly *broken* in	*Ghoré ka mooh huchcha hy.*
The horse has cut himself *brushing*	*Ghoré ko néwur luga hy.*
The horse has a *cataract* in his off eye	*Ghoré kee duhinee ankh men moteea-bind hy.*
The horse is in hard *condition* ...	*Ghora ka budun gutheela hy.*
The horse is a *crib-biter* (or *wind sucker*)	*Ghora kowa peeta.*
Wash the horse's *dock* and sheath	*Ghoré kee saghiree aur fota dho.*
The horse looks *dull*	*Ghora sust maloom déta hy.*
He *fell* off the horse	*Wuh ghoré pur sé gira.*
The horse's leg is *filled* ...	*Ghoré ko py agyee.*
Put the shoe *firmly* on ...	*Nal jikkur ke bandho.*
The mare is in *foal*	*Ghoree gabhin hy.*
Foment the horse's leg with hot water for half an hour ...	*Ghoré ké pyr ko gurm panee sé adhe ghunté tuk sénko.*
Slaken the *girths*	*Tung* dheelé *kuró.*
Tighten the *girths*	*Tung kuso.*

Give your horse two or three *go-downs* of water	*Apné ghore ko do teen ghoont panee do.*
The horse chucks his *head* (when being ridden)	*Ghora sir marta.*
The horse has cracked *heels* ...	*Ghoré kee gamchee men chheewur ho gya.*
Hold my horse	*Humara ghora thamo.*
He *hogged* the mane of his pony	*Usné apné* tattoo *kee yal ko bubree keeya.*
The jockey was not able to *hold* the horse	*Coachwan ghoré ko nuheen rok sukka.*
Lengthen the stirrups one *hole* ...	*Rikab ko ék ghur aur lumba kuro.*
Shorten the stirrups two *holes* ..	*Rikab ko do ghur churhao.*
The horse's *hoof* slopes too much, take more off the toes...	*Ghoré ka súm zeeada sulamee hy, punjé ké neeché sé aur cheelo.*
The horse has *hurt* his leg ...	*Ghoré ke pyr ko chot lugee.*
Don't *jerk* the reins	*Rus ko jhutka mut do.*
The horse has clean *legs* ...	*Ghoré ké hath pyr durust hyn.*
The horse has got *lockjaw* ...	*Ghoré ko chandnee né mara.*
Make much of your horse ...	*Apné ghoré ko dilasa do.*
He can't *master* the horse ...	*Ghora is sé nuheen dubta.*
That horse is difficult to *mount*	*Wuh ghora bud rikab hy.*
The mare has a light *mouth* ...	*Madwan ka moonh nurm hy.*
How *old* is that horse ...	*Us ghoré kee úmr kya hai.*
The horse has *ophthalmia* ...	*Ghoré kee ankh ú*thee.
Tell me the good and bad *points* of that horse	*Us ghoré ké ayb aur húnur hum sé kuho.*
The horse *pulls* a great deal ...	*Ghora buhút moonh zor hy.*
The grey horse *refused* the water jump	*Subza ghora nalé sé phut gya.*
Your horse is a *roarer* ...	*Túmhara ghora shérdumee kurta.*
He has a strong *seat* ...	*Uska asun kura hy.*
He has a weak *seat*	*Uska asun* dheela *hy.*
Ride the horse at a *smart* walk...	*Ghoré ko chutuk sé kudum kud-um chullao.*

Take the horse once round at half *speed*	*Ghoré ho ék chukhur* ath *anné ka do.*
The horse has *sprained* his leg...	*Ghoré ké pyr men moch aya.*
I will give the horse a *sweat* to-morrow morning	*Hum kul 'fujjur ghoré sé pusseena nikalengé.*
The horse goes *tender* on the near foreleg	*Ghora apné bayan hath ko kuchh manta hy.*
The horse has *thrush* ...	*Ghoré ké súm men rus útura hy.*
Don't put on the bandages too *tight*	*Puttee zeeada tung mut bandho.*
The horse *trips*	*Ghora* thokur *khata.*
The horse *turns out* his toes ...	*Ghoré ké pyr men tao hy.*
The horse is a *weaver* ...	*Ghora humésha jhoomta.*
The horse's *withers* are galled...	*Ghoré ka mudow sooja hy.*
The horse's *wind* is good ...	*Ghoré ka dum* khoob *bund hy.*
The horse's *wind* is bad ...	*Ghoré ka dum juldee* toot *jata.*
Wisp down the horse ...	*Ghoré ké kooncha maro.*

Appendix.

CALCUTTA TURF CLUB TABLES

FOR

Weight for Age and Class.

JANUARY.

½ A Mile.

	3 years. st.	lbs.	4 years. st.	lbs.	5 years. st.	lbs.	6 and aged. st.	lbs.
English ...	8	5	9	10	10	0	10	0
Australians...	8	11	9	5	9	7	9	7
Capes ...	7	11	8	5	8	7	8	7
Country-breds	6	0	7	2	7	7	7	7
Arabs ...	5	0	6	2	6	7	6	7

¾ of a Mile.

	3 years. st.	lbs.	4 years. st.	lbs.	5 years. st.	lbs.	6 and aged. st.	lbs.
English ...	7	12	9	7	10	0	10	0
Australians...	8	1	9	1	9	6	9	7
Capes ...	7	1	8	1	8	6	8	7
Country-breds	5	4	6	12	7	5	7	7
Arabs ...	4	4	5	12	6	5	6	7

1 Mile.

	st.	lbs.	st.	lbs.	st.	lbs.	st.	lbs.
English ...	7	6	9	4	10	0	10	0
Australians...	7	11	8	13	9	5	9	7
Capes ...	6	11	7	13	8	5	8	7
Country-breds	4	11	6	6	7	4	7	7
Arabs ...	3	11	5	6	6	4	6	7

1¼ Mile.

	st.	lbs.	st.	lbs.	st.	lbs.	st.	lbs.
English ...	7	4	9	3	9	13	10	0
Australians...	7	9	8	12	9	4	9	7
Capes ...	6	9	7	12	8	4	8	7
Country-breds	4	7	6	4	7	3	7	7
Arabs ...	3	7	5	4	6	3	6	7

1½ Mile.

	st.	lbs.	st.	lbs.	st.	lbs.	st.	lbs.
English ...	7	2	9	2	9	12	10	0
Australians...	7	6	8	11	9	4	9	7
Capes ...	6	6	7	11	8	4	8	7
Country-breds	4	3	6	1	7	1	7	7
Arabs ...	3	3	5	1	6	1	6	7

1¾ Mile.

	st.	lbs.	st.	lbs.	st.	lbs.	st.	lbs.
English ...	7	0	9	1	9	11	10	0
Australians...	7	4	8	10	9	3	9	7
Capes ...	6	4	7	10	8	3	8	7
Country-breds	3	13	5	11	6	13	7	7
Arabs ...	2	13	4	11	5	13	6	7

2 Miles.

	st.	lbs.	st.	lbs.	st.	lbs.	st.	lbs.
English ...	6	13	9	0	9	11	10	0
Australians...	7	2	8	9	9	3	9	7
Capes ...	6	2	7	9	8	3	8	7
Country-breds	3	9	5	9	6	12	7	7
Arabs ...	2	9	4	9	5	12	6	7

2½ Miles.

	st.	lbs.	st.	lbs.	st.	lbs.	st.	lbs.
English ...	6	10	8	11	9	10	10	0
Australians...	6	11	8	8	9	3	9	7
Capes ...	5	11	7	8	8	3	8	7
Country-breds	3	5	5	3	6	10	7	7
Arabs ...	2	5	4	3	5	10	6	7

3 Miles.

	st.	lbs.	st.	lbs.	st.	lbs.	st.	lbs.
English ...	...	...	8	9	9	10	10	0
Australians...	...	...	8	7	9	2	9	7
Capes ...	...	...	7	7	8	2	8	7
Country-breds	...	...	4	11	6	7	7	7
Arabs ...	...	...	3	11	5	7	6	7

4 Miles.

	st.	lbs.	st.	lbs.	st.	lbs.	st.	lbs.
English ...	...	...	8	8	9	7	10	0
Australians...	...	...	8	2	9	1	9	7
Capes ...	...	...	7	2	8	1	8	7
Country-breds	...	...	4	3	6	0	7	7
Arabs ...	...	...	3	3	5	0	6	7

FEBRUARY.

	½ A Mile.								¾ of a Mile.							
	3 years.		4 years.		5 years.		6 and aged.		3 years.		4 years.		5 years.		6 and aged.	
	st.	lbs.	st.	lbs.	st.	lbs.	st.	lbs.	st.	lbs.	st.	lbs.	st.	lbs.	st.	lbs.
English ...	8	7	9	11	10	0	10	0	8	1	9	8	10	0	10	0
Australians ...	8	12	9	5	9	7	9	7	8	3	9	1	9	6	9	7
Capes ...	7	12	8	5	8	7	8	7	7	3	8	1	8	6	8	7
Country-breds	6	2	7	2	7	7	7	7	5	6	6	13	7	5	7	7
Arabs ...	5	2	6	2	6	7	6	7	4	6	5	13	6	5	6	7
	1 Mile.								1¼ Mile.							
	st.	lbs.	st.	lbs.	st.	lbs.	st.	lbs.	st.	lbs.	st.	lbs.	st.	lbs.	st.	lbs.
English ...	7	9	9	5	10	0	10	0	7	7	9	4	9	13	10	0
Australians ...	7	13	9	0	9	5	9	7	7	11	8	13	9	4	9	7
Capes ...	6	13	8	0	8	5	8	7	6	11	7	13	8	4	8	7
Country-breds	5	0	6	9	7	4	7	7	4	9	6	6	7	3	7	7
Arabs ...	4	0	5	9	6	4	6	7	3	9	5	6	6	3	6	7
	1½ Mile.								1¾ Mile.							
	st.	lbs.	st.	lbs.	st.	lbs.	st.	lbs.	st.	lbs.	st.	lbs.	st.	lbs.	st.	lbs.
English ...	7	5	9	3	9	13	10	0	7	3	9	2	9	12	10	0
Australians ...	7	9	8	12	9	4	9	7	7	7	8	11	9	3	9	7
Capes ...	6	9	7	12	8	4	8	7	6	7	7	11	8	3	8	7
Country-breds	4	5	6	3	7	2	7	7	4	2	5	13	7	0	7	7
Arabs ...	3	5	5	3	6	2	6	7	3	2	4	13	6	0	6	7
	2 Miles.								2½ Miles.							
	st.	lbs.	st.	lbs.	st.	lbs.	st.	lbs.	st.	lbs.	st.	lbs.	st.	lbs.	st.	lbs.
English ...	7	1	9	1	9	12	10	0	6	12	8	13	9	12	10	0
Australians ...	7	5	8	10	9	3	9	7	7	1	8	9	9	3	9	7
Capes ...	6	5	7	10	8	3	8	7	6	1	7	9	8	3	8	7
Country-breds	3	12	5	11	6	13	7	7	3	8	5	5	6	11	7	7
Arabs ...	2	12	4	11	5	13	6	7	2	8	4	5	5	11	6	7
	3 Miles.								4 Miles.							
	st.	lbs.	st.	lbs.	st.	lbs.	st.	lbs.	st.	lbs.	st.	lbs.	st.	lbs.	st.	lbs.
English ...	...	...	8	11	9	11	10	0	...	...	8	10	9	8	10	0
Australians ...	...	...	8	8	9	2	9	7	...	...	8	4	9	2	9	7
Capes ...	...	...	7	8	8	2	8	7	...	...	7	4	8	2	8	7
Country-breds	...	...	4	13	6	8	7	7	...	...	4	5	6	2	7	7
Arabs ...	...	...	3	13	5	8	6	7	...	...	3	5	5	2	6	7

MARCH.

	½ A MILE.								¾ OF A MILE.							
	3 years.		4 years.		5 years.		6 and aged.		3 years.		4 years.		5 years.		6 and aged.	
	st.	lbs.	st.	lbs.	st.	lbs.	st.	lbs.	st.	lbs.	st.	lbs.	st.	lbs.	st.	lbs.
English ...	8	10	9	12	10	0	10	0	8	4	9	9	10	0	10	0
Australians ...	8	13	9	5	9	7	9	7	8	5	9	2	9	6	9	7
Capes ...	7	13	8	5	8	7	8	7	7	5	8	2	8	6	8	7
Country-breds	6	3	7	3	7	7	7	7	5	8	6	13	7	5	7	7
Arabs ...	5	3	6	3	6	7	6	7	4	8	5	13	6	5	6	7
	1 MILE.								1¼ MILE.							
	st.	lbs	st.	lbs.	st.	lbs.	st.	lbs.	st.	lbs.	st.	lbs.	st.	lbs.	st.	lbs.
English ...	7	12	9	6	10	0	10	0	7	10	9	5	10	0	10	0
Australians ...	8	1	9	0	9	5	9	7	7	13	8	13	9	4	9	7
Capes ...	7	1	8	0	8	5	8	7	6	13	7	13	8	4	8	7
Country-breds	5	2	6	11	7	4	7	7	4	11	6	8	7	3	7	7
Arabs ...	4	2	5	11	6	4	6	7	3	11	5	8	6	3	6	7
	1½ MILE.								1¾ MILE.							
	st.	lbs.	st.	lbs.	st.	lbs.	st.	lbs.	st.	lbs.	st.	lbs.	st.	lbs.	st.	lbs.
English ...	7	8	9	4	10	0	10	0	7	6	9	3	9	13	10	0
Australians ...	7	11	8	13	9	4	9	7	7	10	8	12	9	3	9	7
Capes ...	6	11	7	13	8	4	8	7	6	10	7	12	8	3	8	7
Country-breds	4	7	6	5	7	2	7	7	4	4	6	1	7	1	7	7
Arabs ...	3	7	5	5	6	2	6	7	3	4	5	1	6	1	6	7
	2 MILES.								2½ MILES.							
	st.	lbs.	st.	lbs.	st.	lbs.	st.	lbs.	st.	lbs.	st.	lbs.	st.	lbs.	st.	lbs.
English ...	7	4	9	3	9	12	10	0	7	1	9	1	9	12	10	0
Australians ...	7	8	8	10	9	3	9	7	7	4	8	10	9	3	9	7
Capes ...	6	8	7	10	8	3	8	7	6	4	7	10	8	3	8	7
Country-breds	4	1	5	13	7	0	7	7	3	10	5	7	6	12	7	7
Arabs ...	3	1	4	13	6	0	6	7	2	10	4	7	5	12	6	7
	3 MILES.								4 MILES.							
	st.	lbs.	st.	lbs.	st	lbs.	st.	lbs.	st.	lbs.	st.	lbs.	st.	lbs.	st.	lbs.
English ...	...	...	8	13	9	11	10	0	...	...	8	12	9	9	10	0
Australians ...	...	...	8	9	9	3	9	7	...	...	8	6	9	3	9	7
Capes ...	...	...	7	9	8	3	8	7	...	...	7	6	8	3	8	7
Country-breds	...	...	5	1	6	9	7	7	...	...	4	7	6	4	7	7
Arabs ...	...	...	4	1	5	9	6	7	...	...	3	7	5	4	6	7

APRIL.

	½ A Mile.				¾ of a Mile.			
	3 years.	4 years.	5 years.	6 and aged.	3 years.	4 years.	5 years.	6 and aged.
	st. lbs.	st. lbs.	st. lbs.	st. lbs.	st. lbs.	st. lbs.	st. lbs.	st. lbs.
English ...	8 13	9 13	10 0	10 0	8 7	9 10	10 0	10 0
Australians ...	8 13	9 5	9 7	9 7	8 7	9 3	9 6	9 7
Capes ...	7 13	8 5	8 7	8 7	7 7	8 3	8 6	8 7
Country-breds	6 4	7 3	7 7	7 7	5 10	7 0	7 5	7 7
Arabs ...	5 4	6 3	6 7	6 7	4 10	6 0	6 5	6 7

	1 Mile.				1¼ Mile.			
	st. lbs.	st. lbs.	st. lbs.	st. lbs.	st. lbs.	st. lbs.	st. lbs.	st. lbs.
English ...	8 1	9 8	10 0	10 0	7 13	9 7	10 0	10 0
Australians ...	8 3	9 1	9 5	9 7	8 1	9 0	9 4	9 7
Capes ...	7 3	8 1	8 5	8 7	7 1	8 0	8 4	8 7
Country-breds	5 4	6 12	7 4	7 7	4 13	6 9	7 4	7 7
Arabs ...	4 4	5 12	6 4	6 7	3 13	5 9	6 4	6 7

	1½ Mile.				1¾ Mile.			
	st. lbs.	st. lbs.	st. lbs.	st. lbs.	st. lbs.	st. lbs.	st. lbs.	st. lbs.
English ...	7 11	9 6	10 0	10 0	7 9	9 5	10 0	10 0
Australians ...	8 0	9 0	9 4	9 7	7 13	8 13	9 4	9 7
Capes ...	7 0	8 0	8 4	8 7	6 13	7 13	8 4	8 7
Country-breds	4 9	6 6	7 3	7 7	4 6	6 3	7 2	7 7
Arabs ...	3 9	5 6	6 3	6 7	3 6	5 3	6 2	6 7

	2 Miles.				2½ Miles.			
	st. lbs.	st. lbs.	st. lbs.	st. lbs.	st. lbs.	st. lbs.	st. lbs.	st. lbs.
English ...	7 7	9 5	9 12	10 0	7 4	9 4	9 12	10 0
Australians ...	7 11	8 13	9 4	9 7	7 7	8 12	9 4	9 7
Capes ...	6 11	7 13	8 4	8 7	6 7	7 12	8 4	8 7
Country-breds	4 4	6 1	7 1	7 7	3 12	5 9	6 13	7 7
Arabs ...	3 4	5 1	6 1	6 7	2 12	4 9	5 13	6 7

	3 Miles.				4 Miles.			
	st. lbs.	st. lbs.	st. lbs.	st. lbs.	st. lbs.	st. lbs.	st. lbs.	st. lbs.
English ...	... ...	9 2	9 11	10 0	... ...	9 0	9 10	10 0
Australians ...	... ...	8 10	9 3	9 7	... ...	8 7	9 3	9 7
Capes ...	... ...	7 10	8 3	8 7	... ...	7 7	8 3	8 7
Country-breds	... ...	5 3	6 10	7 7	... ...	4 9	6 5	7 7
Arabs ...	... ...	4 3	5 10	6 7	... ...	3 9	5 5	6 7

MAY.

½ A MILE.

	3 years. st.	lbs.	4 years. st.	lbs.	5 years. st.	lbs.	6 and aged. st.	lbs.
English ...	9	1	10	0	10	0	10	0
Australians ...	9	0	9	5	9	7	9	7
Capes ...	8	0	8	5	8	7	8	7
Country-breds	6	5	7	4	7	7	7	7
Arabs ...	5	5	6	4	6	7	6	7

¾ OF A MILE.

	3 years. st.	lbs.	4 years. st.	lbs.	5 years. st.	lbs.	6 and aged. st.	lbs.
English ...	8	9	9	12	10	0	10	0
Australians ...	8	9	9	4	9	7	9	7
Capes ...	7	9	8	4	8	7	8	7
Country-breds	5	11	7	1	7	5	7	7
Arabs ...	4	11	6	1	6	5	6	7

1 MILE.

	st.	lbs.	st.	lbs	st.	lbs.	st.	lbs.
English ...	8	4	9	10	10	0	10	0
Australians ...	8	5	9	2	9	6	9	7
Capes ...	7	5	8	2	8	6	8	7
Country-breds	5	6	6	12	7	4	7	7
Arabs ...	4	6	5	12	6	4	6	7

1¼ MILE.

	st.	lbs	st.	lbs.	st.	lbs.	st.	lbs.
English ...	8	1	9	9	10	0	10	0
Australians ...	8	3	9	1	9	5	9	7
Capes ...	7	3	8	1	8	5	8	7
Country-breds	5	1	6	10	7	4	7	7
Arabs ...	4	1	5	10	6	4	6	7

1½ MILE.

	st.	lbs.	st.	lbs.	st.	lbs.	st.	lbs.
English ...	8	0	9	8	10	0	10	0
Australians ...	8	2	9	0	9	5	9	7
Capes ...	7	2	8	0	8	5	8	7
Country-breds	4	11	6	7	7	3	7	7
Arabs ...	3	11	5	7	6	3	6	7

1¾ MILE.

	st.	lbs	st.	lbs.	st.	lbs.	st.	lbs.
English ...	7	12	9	7	10	0	10	0
Australians ...	8	1	8	13	9	5	9	7
Capes ...	7	1	7	13	8	5	8	7
Country-breds	4	8	6	4	7	2	7	7
Arabs ...	3	8	5	4	6	2	6	7

2 MILES.

	st.	lbs.	st.	lbs.	st.	lbs.	st.	lbs.
English ...	7	10	9	6	9	12	10	0
Australians ...	8	0	8	13	9	5	9	7
Capes ...	7	0	7	13	8	5	8	7
Country-breds	4	6	6	2	7	1	7	7
Arabs ...	3	6	5	1	6	1	6	7

2½ MILES.

	st.	lbs.	st.	lbs.	st.	lbs.	st.	lbs.
English ...	7	7	9	4	9	12	10	0
Australians ...	7	10	8	12	9	5	9	7
Capes ...	6	10	7	12	8	5	8	7
Country-breds	4	0	5	11	6	13	7	7
Arabs ...	3	0	4	11	5	13	6	7

3 MILES.

	st.	lbs.	st.	lbs.	st.	lbs.	st.	lbs.
English ...	...	...	9	3	9	11	10	0
Australians ...	...	...	8	11	9	4	9	7
Capes ...	...	...	7	11	8	4	8	7
Country-breds	...	...	5	5	6	11	7	7
Arabs ...	...	...	4	5	5	11	6	7

4 MILES.

	st.	lbs.	st.	lbs.	st.	lbs.	st.	lbs
English ...	...	...	9	2	9	11	10	0
Australians ...	...	...	8	8	9	4	9	7
Capes ...	...	...	7	8	8	4	8	7
Country-breds	...	...	4	11	6	6	7	7
Arabs ...	...	...	3	11	5	6	6	7

JUNE.

	½ A MILE.								¾ OF A MILE.							
	3 years.		4 years.		5 years.		6 and aged.		3 years.		4 years.		5 years.		6 and aged.	
	st.	lbs.	st.	lbs.	st.	lbs.	st.	lbs.	st.	lbs.	st.	lbs	st.	lbs.	st.	lbs.
English ...	9	3	10	0	10	0	10	0	8	12	9	13	10	0	10	0
Australians ...	9	0	9	5	9	7	9	7	8	10	9	4	9	7	9	7
Capes ...	8	0	8	5	8	7	8	7	7	10	8	4	8	7	8	7
Country-breds	6	5	7	4	7	7	7	7	5	12	7	1	7	5	7	7
Arabs ...	5	5	6	4	6	7	6	7	4	12	6	1	6	5	6	7
	1 MILE.								1¼ MILE.							
	st.	lbs.	st.	lbs.	st.	lbs.	st.	lbs.	st.	lbs.	st.	lbs.	st.	lbs.	st.	lbs.
English ...	8	7	9	11	10	0	10	0	8	5	9	10	10	0	10	0
Australians ...	8	7	9	2	9	6	9	7	8	5	9	1	9	6	9	7
Capes ...	7	7	8	2	8	6	8	7	7	5	8	1	8	6	8	7
Country-breds	5	8	6	13	7	5	7	7	5	3	6	11	7	4	7	7
Arabs ...	4	8	5	13	6	5	6	7	4	3	5	11	6	4	6	7
	1½ MILE.								1¾ MILE.							
	st.	lbs.	st.	lbs.	st.	lbs.	st.	lbs.	st.	lbs.	st.	lbs.	st.	lbs.	st.	lbs.
English ...	8	3	9	9	10	0	10	0	8	1	9	8	10	0	10	0
Australians ...	8	4	9	1	9	6	9	7	8	3	9	0	9	6	9	7
Capes ...	7	4	8	1	8	6	8	7	7	3	8	0	8	6	8	7
Country-breds	4	13	6	8	7	3	7	7	4	10	6	5	7	2	7	7
Arabs ...	3	13	5	8	6	3	6	7	3	10	5	5	6	2	6	7
	2 MILES.								2½ MILES.							
	st.	lbs.	st.	lbs.	st.	lbs.	st.	lbs.	st.	lbs.	st.	lbs.	st.	lbs.	st.	lbs.
English ...	8	0	9	7	9	13	10	0	7	11	9	5	9	12	10	0
Australians ...	8	2	9	0	9	6	9	7	7	13	8	13	9	6	9	7
Capes ...	7	2	8	0	8	6	8	7	6	13	7	13	8	6	8	7
Country-breds	4	8	6	3	7	1	7	7	4	2	5	12	7	0	7	7
Arabs ...	3	8	5	3	6	1	6	7	3	2	4	12	6	0	6	7
	3 MILES.								4 MILES.							
	st.	lbs.	st.	lbs.	st.	lbs.	st.	lbs.	st.	lbs.	st.	lbs.	st.	lbs.	st.	lbs.
English ...	...	...	9	4	9	12	10	0	...	...	9	4	9	12	10	0
Australians ...	...	...	8	12	9	5	9	7	...	...	8	8	9	4	9	7
Capes ...	...	...	7	12	8	5	8	7	...	...	7	8	8	4	8	7
Country-breds	...	...	5	7	6	12	7	7	...	...	4	13	6	8	7	7
Arabs ...	...	...	4	7	5	12	6	7	...	...	3	13	5	8	6	7

JULY.

	½ A MILE.				¾ OF A MILE.			
	3 years.	4 years.	5 years.	6 and aged.	3 years.	4 years.	5 years.	6 and aged.
	st. lbs.	st. lbs.	st. lbs.	st. lbs.	st. lbs.	st. lbs.	st. lbs.	st. lbs.
English ...	9 4	10 0	10 0	10 0	9 0	10 0	10 0	10 0
Australians...	9 1	9 5	9 7	9 7	8 11	9 4	9 7	9 7
Capes ...	8 1	8 5	8 7	8 7	7 11	8 4	8 7	8 7
Country-breds	6 6	7 5	7 7	7 7	6 0	7 2	7 6	7 7
Arabs ...	5 6	6 5	6 7	6 7	5 0	6 2	6 6	6 7

	1 MILE.				1¼ MILE.			
	st. lbs.	st. lbs.	st. lbs.	st. lbs.	st. lbs.	st. lbs.	st. lbs.	st. lbs.
English ...	8 11	9 12	10 0	10 0	8 8	9 11	10 0	10 0
Australians...	8 9	9 3	9 6	9 7	8 7	9 2	9 6	9 7
Capes ...	7 9	8 3	8 6	8 7	7 7	8 2	8 6	8 7
Country-breds	5 10	6 13	7 5	7 7	5 5	6 11	7 5	7 7
Arabs ...	4 10	5 13	6 5	6 7	4 5	5 11	6 5	6 7

	1½ MILE.				1¾ MILE.			
	st. lbs.	st. lbs.	st. lbs.	st. lbs.	st. lbs.	st. lbs.	st. lbs.	st. lbs.
English ...	8 7	9 10	10 0	10 0	8 5	9 9	10 0	10 0
Australians...	8 6	9 1	9 6	9 7	8 5	9 0	9 6	9 7
Capes ...	7 6	8 1	8 6	8 7	7 5	8 0	8 6	8 7
Country-breds	5 1	6 8	7 4	7 7	4 12	6 6	7 3	7 7
Arabs ...	4 1	5 8	6 4	6 7	3 12	5 6	6 3	6 7

	2 MILES.				2½ MILES.			
	st. lbs.	st. lbs.	st. lbs.	st. lbs.	st. lbs.	st. lbs.	st. lbs.	st. lbs.
English ...	8 4	9 8	9 13	10 0	8 1	9 6	9 13	10 0
Australians...	8 4	9 0	9 6	9 7	8 2	9 0	9 6	9 7
Capes ...	7 4	8 0	8 6	8 7	7 2	8 0	8 6	8 7
Country-breds	4 10	6 4	7 2	7 7	4 4	5 13	7 1	7 7
Arabs ...	3 10	5 4	6 2	6 7	3 4	4 13	6 1	6 7

	3 MILES.				4 MILES.			
	st. lbs.	st. lbs.	st. lbs.	st. lbs.	st. lbs.	st. lbs.	st. lbs.	st. lbs.
English ...	... ...	9 5	9 13	10 0	... ...	9 4	9 12	10 0
Australians...	... ...	8 13	9 6	9 7	... ...	8 9	9 5	9 7
Capes ...	... ...	7 13	8 6	8 7	... ...	7 9	8 5	8 7
Country-breds	... ...	5 9	6 13	7 7	... ...	5 1	6 9	7 7
Arabs ...	... ...	4 9	5 13	6 7	... ...	4 1	5 9	6 7

AUGUST.

	½ A Mile.								¾ of a Mile.							
	3 years.		4 years		5 years.		6 and aged.		3 years.		4 years.		5 years.		6 and aged.	
	st.	lbs.	st.	lbs.	st.	lbs.	st.	lbs.	st.	lbs.	st.	lbs.	st.	lbs.	st.	lbs.
English ...	9	5	10	0	10	0	10	0	9	1	10	0	10	0	10	0
Australians...	8	1	9	3	9	6	9	7	7	8	8	13	9	5	9	7
Capes ...	7	1	8	3	8	6	8	7	6	8	7	13	8	5	8	7
Country-breds	6	7	7	5	7	7	7	7	6	2	7	2	7	6	7	7
Arabs ...	5	7	6	5	6	7	6	7	5	2	6	2	6	6	6	7

	1 Mile.								1¼ Mile.							
	st.	lbs.	st.	lbs.	st.	lbs.	st.	lbs.	st.	lbs.	st.	lbs.	st.	lbs.	st.	lbs.
English ...	8	12	9	13	10	0	10	0	8	10	9	12	10	0	10	0
Australians...	7	2	8	11	9	4	9	7	6	12	8	9	9	3	9	7
Capes ...	6	2	7	11	8	4	8	7	5	12	7	9	8	3	8	7
Country-breds	5	11	6	13	7	5	7	7	5	7	6	11	7	5	7	7
Arabs ...	4	11	5	13	6	5	6	7	4	7	5	11	6	5	6	7

	1½ Mile.								1¾ Mile.							
	st.	lbs.	st.	lbs.	st.	lbs.	st.	lbs.	st.	lbs.	st.	lbs.	st.	lbs.	st.	lbs.
English ...	8	9	9	11	10	0	10	0	8	8	9	10	10	0	10	0
Australians...	6	9	8	8	9	2	9	7	6	5	8	7	9	1	9	7
Capes ...	5	9	7	8	8	2	8	7	5	5	7	7	8	1	8	7
Country-breds	5	3	6	9	7	4	7	7	5	0	6	7	7	3	7	7
Arabs ...	4	3	5	9	6	4	6	7	4	0	5	7	6	3	6	7

	2 Miles.								2½ Miles.							
	st.	lbs.	st.	lbs.	st.	lbs.	st.	lbs.	st.	lbs.	st.	lbs.	st.	lbs.	st.	lbs.
English ...	8	7	9	9	10	0	10	0	8	4	9	7	9	13	10	0
Australians...	6	2	8	6	9	1	9	7	5	8	8	5	9	1	9	7
Capes ...	5	2	7	6	8	1	8	7	4	8	7	5	8	1	8	7
Country-breds	4	12	6	5	7	2	7	7	4	6	6	1	7	1	7	7
Arabs ...	3	12	5	5	6	2	6	7	3	6	5	1	6	1	6	7

	3 Miles.								4 Miles.							
	st.	lbs.	st.	lbs.	st.	lbs.	st.	lbs.	st.	lbs.	st.	lbs.	st.	lbs.	st.	lbs.
English ...	...	...	9	5	9	13	10	0	...	...	9	4	9	12	10	0
Australians...	...	...	8	4	9	1	9	7	...	...	7	6	8	10	9	7
Capes ...	...	...	7	4	8	1	8	7	...	...	6	6	7	10	8	7
Country-breds	...	...	5	11	7	0	7	7	...	...	5	3	6	11	7	7
Arabs ...	...	...	4	11	6	0	6	7	...	...	4	3	5	11	6	7

SEPTEMBER.

½ A MILE.

	3 years. st.	lbs.	4 years. st.	lbs.	5 years. st.	lbs.	6 and aged. st.	lbs.
English ...	9	6	10	0	10	0	10	0
Australians ...	8	3	9	3	9	6	9	7
Capes ...	7	3	8	3	8	6	8	7
Country-breds	6	8	7	5	7	7	7	7
Arabs ...	5	8	6	5	6	7	6	7

¾ OF A MILE.

	3 years. st.	lbs.	4 years. st.	lbs.	5 years. st.	lbs.	6 and aged. st.	lbs.
English ...	9	3	10	0	10	0	10	0
Australians ...	7	9	8	13	9	5	9	7
Capes ...	6	9	7	13	8	5	8	7
Country-breds	6	3	7	3	7	6	7	7
Arabs ...	5	3	6	3	6	6	6	7

1 MILE.

	st.	lbs.	st.	lbs.	st.	lbs.	st.	lbs.
English ...	9	0	10	0	10	0	10	0
Australians ...	7	3	8	11	9	4	9	7
Capes ...	6	3	7	11	8	4	8	7
Country-breds	5	12	7	0	7	5	7	7
Arabs ...	4	12	6	0	6	5	6	7

1¼ MILE.

	st.	lbs.	st.	lbs.	st.	lbs.	st.	lbs.
English ...	8	12	9	13	10	0	10	0
Australians ...	7	0	8	9	9	3	9	7
Capes ...	6	0	7	9	8	3	8	7
Country-breds	5	9	6	12	7	5	7	7
Arabs ...	4	9	5	12	6	5	6	7

1½ MILE.

	st.	lbs.	st.	lbs.	st.	lbs.	st.	lbs.
English ...	8	11	9	12	10	0	10	0
Australians ...	6	11	8	8	9	2	9	7
Capes ...	5	11	7	8	8	2	8	7
Country-breds	5	5	6	10	7	4	7	7
Arabs ...	4	5	5	10	6	4	6	7

1¾ MILE.

	st.	lbs.	st.	lbs.	st.	lbs.	st.	lbs.
English ...	8	10	9	11	10	0	10	0
Australians ...	6	7	8	7	9	1	9	7
Capes ...	5	7	7	7	8	1	8	7
Country-breds	5	2	6	8	7	3	7	7
Arabs ...	4	2	5	8	6	3	6	7

2 MILES.

	st.	lbs.	st.	lbs.	st.	lbs.	st.	lbs.
English ...	8	9	9	10	10	0	10	0
Australians ...	6	4	8	6	9	1	9	7
Capes ...	5	4	7	6	8	1	8	7
Country-breds	4	2	6	6	7	2	7	7
Arabs ...	3	2	5	6	6	2	6	7

2½ MILES.

	st.	lbs.	st.	lbs.	st.	lbs.	st.	lbs.
English ...	8	6	9	8	9	13	10	0
Australians ...	5	11	8	5	9	1	9	7
Capes ...	4	11	7	5	8	1	8	7
Country-breds	4	8	6	3	7	2	7	7
Arabs ...	3	8	5	3	6	2	6	7

3 MILES.

	st.	lbs.	st.	lbs.	st.	lbs.	st.	lbs.
English ...	...	...	9	6	9	13	10	0
Australians ...	...	...	8	4	9	1	9	7
Capes ...	...	...	7	4	8	1	8	7
Country-breds	...	...	5	13	7	1	7	7
Arabs ...	...	...	4	13	6	1	6	7

4 MILES.

	st.	lbs.	st.	lbs.	st.	lbs.	st.	lbs.
English ...	...	...	9	5	9	12	10	0
Australians ...	...	...	7	8	8	11	9	7
Capes ...	...	...	6	8	7	11	8	7
Country-breds	...	...	5	5	6	13	7	7
Arabs ...	...	...	4	5	5	13	6	7

OCTOBER.

	½ a Mile.				¾ of a Mile.			
	3 years.	4 years.	5 years.	6 and aged.	3 years.	4 years.	5 years.	6 and aged.
	st. lbs.	st. lbs	st. lbs.	st. lbs.	st. lbs.	st. lbs.	st. lbs.	st. lbs.
English ...	9 7	10 0	10 0	10 0	9 4	10 0	10 0	10 0
Australians ...	8 5	9 3	9 6	9 7	7 10	8 13	9 5	9 7
Capes ...	7 5	8 3	8 6	8 7	6 10	7 13	8 5	8 7
Country-breds	6 8	7 5	7 7	7 7	6 5	7 3	7 6	7 7
Arabs ...	5 8	6 5	6 7	6 7	5 5	6 3	6 6	6 7

	1 Mile.				1¼ Mile.			
	st. lbs.	st. lbs.	st. lbs.	st. lbs.	st. lbs.	st. lbs.	st. lbs.	st. lbs.
English ...	9 1	10 0	10 0	10 0	9 0	9 13	10 0	10 0
Australians ...	7 5	8 11	9 4	9 7	7 2	8 9	9 3	9 7
Capes ...	6 5	7 11	8 4	8 7	6 2	7 9	8 3	8 7
Country-breds	5 13	7 1	7 6	7 7	5 11	6 12	7 5	7 7
Arabs ...	4 13	6 1	6 6	6 7	4 11	5 12	6 5	6 7

	1½ Mile.				1¾ Mile.			
	st. lbs.	st. lbs.	st. lbs	st. lbs.	st. lbs.	st. lbs.	st. lbs	st. lbs.
English ...	8 13	9 12	10 0	10 0	8 12	9 11	10 0	10 7
Australians ...	6 13	8 8	9 2	9 7	6 9	8 7	9 1	9 7
Capes ...	5 13	7 8	8 2	8 7	5 9	7 7	8 1	8 7
Country-breds	5 7	6 10	7 4	7 7	5 4	6 9	7 3	7 7
Arabs ...	4 7	5 10	6 4	6 7	4 4	5 9	6 3	6 7

	2 Miles.				2½ Miles.			
	st. lbs.	st. lbs.	st. lbs.	st. lbs.	st. lbs.	st. lbs.	st. lbs.	st. lbs.
English ...	8 11	9 11	10 0	10 0	8 8	9 9	9 13	10 0
Australians ...	6 6	8 6	9 1	9 7	6 0	8 5	9 1	9 7
Capes ...	5 6	7 6	8 1	8 7	5 0	7 5	8 1	8 7
Country-breds	5 2	6 7	7 2	7 7	4 10	6 5	7 2	7 7
Arabs ...	4 2	5 7	6 2	6 7	3 10	5 5	6 2	6 7

	3 Miles.				4 Miles.			
	st. lbs.	st. lbs.	st. lbs.	st. lbs.	st. lbs.	st. lbs.	st. lbs.	st. lbs.
English ...	... ...	9 7	9 13	10 0	... ...	9 6	9 13	10 0
Australians ...	... ...	8 4	9 1	9 7	... ...	7 10	8 12	9 7
Capes ...	... ...	7 4	8 1	8 7	... ...	6 10	7 12	8 7
Country-breds	... ...	6 1	7 2	7 7	... ...	5 7	7 1	7 7
Arabs ...	... ...	5 1	6 2	6 7	... ...	4 7	6 1	6 7

NOVEMBER.

	½ A Mile.				¾ of a Mile.			
	3 years.	4 years.	5 years.	6 and aged.	3 years.	4 years.	5 years	6 and aged.
	st. lbs.	st. lbs.	st. lbs.	st. lbs.	st. lb	st. lbs.	st. lbs.	st. lbs.
English ...	9 8	10 0	10 0	10 0	9 5	10 0	10 0	10 0
Australians ...	8 7	9 4	9 6	9 7	7 11	9 0	9 5	9 7
Capes ...	7 7	8 4	8 6	8 7	6 11	8 0	8 5	8 7
Country-breds	6 11	7 6	7 7	7 7	6 6	7 4	7 7	7 7
Arabs ...	5 11	6 6	6 7	6 7	5 6	6 4	6 7	6 7

	1 Mile.				1¼ Mile.			
	st. lbs.	st. lbs.	st. lbs.	st. lbs.	st. lbs.	st. lbs	st. lbs.	st. lbs.
English ...	9 2	10 0	10 0	10 0	9 1	9 13	10 0	10 0
Australians ...	7 7	8 12	9 4	9 7	7 4	8 10	9 3	9 7
Capes ...	6 7	7 12	8 4	8 7	6 4	7 10	9 3	8 7
Country-breds	6 1	7 2	7 6	7 7	5 13	7 0	7 6	7 7
Arabs ...	5 1	6 2	6 6	6 7	4 13	6 0	6 6	6 7

	1½ Mile.				1¾ Mile.			
	st. lbs.	st. lbs.	st. lbs	st. lbs	st. lbs.	st. lbs.	st. lbs.	st. lbs.
English ...	9 0	9 12	10 0	10 0	8 13	9 11	10 0	10 0
Australians ...	7 1	8 9	9 3	9 7	6 12	8 8	9 2	9 7
Capes ...	6 1	7 9	8 3	8 7	5 12	7 8	8 2	8 7
Country-breds	5 9	6 12	7 5	7 7	5 6	6 10	7 4	7 7
Arabs ...	4 9	5 12	6 5	6 7	4 6	5 10	6 4	6 7

	2 Miles.				2½ Miles.			
	st. lbs.	st. lbs.	st. lbs.	st. lbs	st. lbs.	st. lbs.	st. lbs.	st. lbs.
English ...	8 12	9 11	10 0	10 0	8 9	9 9	10 0	10 0
Australians ...	6 9	8 7	9 2	9 7	6 3	8 6	9 2	9 7
Capes ...	5 9	7 7	8 2	8 7	5 3	7 6	8 2	8 7
Country-breds	5 4	6 9	7 4	7 7	4 12	6 7	7 4	7 7
Arabs ...	4 4	5 9	6 4	6 7	3 12	5 7	6 4	6 7

	3 Miles.				4 Miles.			
	st. lbs.	st. lbs.	st. lbs.	st. lbs	st. lbs.	st. lbs.	st. lbs.	st. lbs.
English ...	... ...	9 8	10 0	10 0	... ...	9 6	9 13	10 0
Australians ...	... ...	8 5	9 1	9 7	... ...	7 12	8 13	9 7
Capes ...	... ...	7 5	8 1	8 7	... ...	6 12	7 13	8 7
Country-breds	... ...	6 3	7 4	7 7	... ...	5 9	7 3	7 7
Arabs ...	... ...	5 3	6 4	6 7	... ...	4 9	6 3	6 7

DECEMBER.

	½ A Mile.				¾ of a Mile.			
	3 years.	4 years.	5 years.	6 and aged.	3 years.	4 years.	5 years.	6 and aged.
	st. lbs.	st. lbs.	st. lbs.	st. lbs.	st. lbs.	st. lbs.	st. lbs.	st. lbs.
English ...	9 9	10 0	10 0	10 0	9 6	10 0	10 0	10 0
Australians...	8 9	9 4	9 6	9 7	7 13	9 0	9 5	9 7
Capes ...	7 9	8 4	8 6	8 7	6 13	8 0	8 5	8 7
Country-breds	6 13	7 6	7 7	7 7	6 7	7 5	7 7	7 7
Arabs ...	5 13	6 6	6 7	6 7	5 7	6 5	6 7	6 7

	1 Mile.				1¼ Mile.			
	st. lbs.	st. lbs.	st. lbs.	st. lbs.	st. lbs.	st. lbs.	st. lbs.	st. lbs.
English ...	9 3	10 0	10 0	10 0	9 2	9 13	10 0	10 0
Australians...	7 9	8 13	9 5	9 7	7 7	8 11	9 4	9 7
Capes ...	6 9	7 13	8 5	8 7	6 7	7 11	8 4	8 7
Country-breds	6 4	7 3	7 7	7 7	6 2	7 2	7 7	7 7
Arabs ...	5 4	6 3	6 7	6 7	5 2	6 2	6 7	6 7

	1½ Mile.				1¾ Mile.			
	st. lbs.	st. lbs.	st. lbs.	st. lbs.	st. lbs.	st. lbs.	st. lbs.	st. lbs.
English ...	9 1	9 12	10 0	10 0	9 0	9 11	10 0	10 0
Australians...	7 4	8 10	9 3	9 7	7 1	8 9	9 3	9 7
Capes ...	6 4	7 10	8 3	8 7	6 1	7 9	8 3	8 7
Country-breds	5 11	7 0	7 6	7 7	5 9	6 12	7 6	7 7
Arabs ...	4 11	6 0	6 6	6 7	4 9	5 12	6 6	6 7

	2 Miles.				2½ Miles.			
	st. lbs.	st. lbs.	st. lbs.	st. lbs.	st. lbs.	st. lbs.	st. lbs.	st. lbs.
English ...	8 13	9 11	10 0	10 0	8 10	9 10	10 0	10 0
Australians...	6 12	8 8	9 2	9 7	6 7	8 7	9 2	9 7
Capes ...	5 12	7 8	8 2	8 7	5 7	7 7	8 2	8 7
Country-breds	5 7	6 11	7 6	7 7	5 1	6 9	7 6	7 7
Arabs ...	4 7	5 11	6 6	6 7	4 1	5 9	6 5	6 7

	3 Miles.				4 Miles.			
	st. lbs.	st. lbs.	st. lbs.	st. lbs.	st. lbs	st. lbs.	st. lbs.	st. lbs.
English ...	... ...	9 9	10 0	10 0	... ...	9 7	9 13	10 0
Australians...	... ...	8 6	9 1	9 7	... ...	8 0	9 0	9 7
Capes ...	... ...	7 6	8 1	8 7	... ...	7 0	8 0	8 7
Country-breds	... ...	6 6	7 6	7 7	... ...	5 12	7 5	7 7
Arabs ...	... ...	5 6	6 6	6 7	... ...	4 12	6 5	6 7

Lowest weight allowed.

Note.—5 st. 7 lbs. is the lowest weight allowed under any circumstances, and lower weights are only entered with reference to the clauses about raising the weights when Country-breds and Arabs run together without any other class, and in weight for age races. By making the additions of 1 st., 2 st., or 3 st. to the weights shown in this table, the proper weights will be found; but it must in no case be less than 5 st. 7 lbs.

(2.) When English and Colonial horses run together without any other class, the foregoing table is reduced 7 lbs.

(3.) When Country-breds and Arabs run together without any other class, the foregoing table is raised 2 st.

(4.) The weight for age is, for English horses, the foregoing table reduced 1 st.: for Australians, the foregoing table reduced 7 lbs.: for Capes, the foregoing table raised 7 lbs.: for Country-breds, the foregoing table raised 1 st. 7 lbs.; and for Arabs the annexed table raised 2 st. 7 lbs.

(5.) Weight for class is the weight for aged horses in the foregoing table.

(6.) When English and Colonial horses run together without any other class in a weight for class race, the weight is reduced 7 lbs.; and when Country-breds and Arabs run together without any other class, the weight is raised 2 st.

(7.) Welter weight for age and class, weight for age, and weight for class are found by adding 2 st. to the foregoing table and applying the preceding clauses.

Two-year olds to carry three-year old weights.

(8.) If any person wishes to run a two-year old, he can do so, the horse running on the same terms as a three-year old.

(9.) If any one wishes to run a three-year old for a race exceeding 2½ miles, he can do so, the horse running on the same terms as a four-year old.

(10.) When the terms of a race are weight for age and

inches, the foregoing table of weight for age and class, and clauses (2), (3), and (4) of this rule apply, the weights fixed thereby being the standard for 14 hands, and 4 lbs. being added or deducted for each half-inch above or below 14 hands.

(11.) If the terms of a race are weight for inches, the standard for 14 hands will be the weight for class scale, the preceding clauses of this rule being applicable.

English, Country-bred, and Arab horses take their age from January 1st; Australians and Capes from August 1st.

The Field.—"The scope of the little work before us may be indicated in few words: Captain Hayes put himself under the teaching of the principal and professors of the new Edinburgh Veterinary College; and he implies that the present book is the outcome of his studies there, added to his own practical observations. Most of the ordinary diseases of horses are concisely described, and a course of treatment laid down for the guidance of the amateur.

"In the pathology and treatment, the author quotes from 'Stone-henge,' Percival, Gamgee, Dick, and frequently from Professor William's book on veterinary medicine and surgery. The whole result is so far satisfactory that the book may be consulted with advantage by those for whom it is intended—by the owners of horses who may find themselves with sick animals on their hands without the means of obtaining the assistance of an experienced Veterinary Surgeon."

Irish Sportsman. — "We can safely recommend Captain Hayes' new work. . . . . . In the pages of 'Veterinary Notes' there is a vast quantity of useful information of a practical kind, which the horse-owner will be wise to read, study, and inwardly digest. The plan of the work is excellent and practical; the various diseases are treated of in a plain and simple manner; symptoms are closely described, and the remedies are within easy reach."

Veterinary Journal.—"A handy little book for the use of horse-owners, which may prove of much service to them when they cannot obtain the assistance of a Veterinary Surgeon, as well as afford them some notion of many of the ailments to which the horse is exposed, and the manner in which they may be best treated . . . . The book has several well drawn woodcuts; and the frontispiece, giving a representation of good fore-legs, is particularly well executed. Altogether we think the 'Notes' will fully serve the end for which they were intended."

Broad Arrow.—"A book which owners of horses will find truly valuable. It is a treatise on the pathology, treatment of the more frequent diseases of horses, written in a concise and popular form. Non-professional readers are specially addressed, the author's object being to inculcate a rational method of treatment, and not to furnish them with any vaunted nostrums or specifics, which, as he says, constitute the stock in trade of the quack and empiric."

Land and Water.—"It is necessary that every owner of a horse should understand something of the diseases to which it is subject, and the remedies for those diseases, and to such as these, the book will be both useful and salutary. The arrangement is excellent, the several organs being taken in physiological order."

U

BOOKS ON THE HORSE:

VETERINARY AND DESCRIPTIVE,

SOLD BY

THACKER, SPINK, AND COMPANY,

CALCUTTA.

THE EVERY-DAY HORSE BOOK: VETERINARY NOTES for Horse Owners: with a Hindustanee Veterinary Vocabulary. By CAPT. M. HORACE HAYES, B.S.C. Rs. 5.

VETERINARY MEDICINES: THEIR ACTIONS AND USES. By FINLAY DUN. Fifth Edition, Revised and Enlarged, 1878. 8vo. Rs. 10.

ILLUSTRATED HORSE DOCTOR. Being an accurate and detailed account, accompanied by more than 400 Pictorial Representations, characteristic of the various Diseases to which the Equine Race are subjected, &c. By EDWARD MAYHEW, M.R.C.V.S.

ILLUSTRATED HORSE MANAGEMENT, containing descriptive remarks upon Anatomy, Medicine, Shoeing, Teeth, Food, Vices, Stables: likewise a plain account of the situation, nature, and value of the various points: together with Comments on Grooms, Dealers, Breeders, Breakers, and Trainers. 400 Engravings. By E. MAYHEW. New Edition, Revised. By J. I. LUPTON, M.R.C.V.S. 8vo. Rs. 8-8.

HORSES AND STABLES. By COLONEL F. FITZWYGRAM. With 24 Plates of Illustrations. 8vo. Rs. 7-8.

YOUATT ON THE HORSE. Revised and Enlarged by W. WATSON, M.R.C.V.S. 8vo. Woodcuts. Rs. 8-14.

THE BOOK OF THE HORSE: Thorough-bred, Half-bred, Cart-bred, Saddle and Harness, British and Foreign: with Hints on Horsemanship, the management of the Stable, Breeding, Breaking, and Training for the Road, the Park, and the Field. By SAMUEL SIDNEY. With 25 Coloured Plates from Original Paintings and 100 Wood Engravings. Demy 4to., cloth gilt. Rs. 22-8.

BOOKS ON THE HORSE.—Continued.

EVERY MAN HIS OWN HORSE DOCTOR. By GEORGE ARMATAGE, M.R.C.V.S., in which is embodied Blaine's Veterinary Art. Illustrated. Rs. 15.

A MANUAL OF VETERINARY SANITARY SCIENCE AND POLICE. By GEORGE FLEMING, F.R.G.S. 2 vols. Illustrated. Rs. 25-14.

A TEXT-BOOK OF VETERINARY OBSTETRICS; including the Diseases and Accidents incidental to Pregnancy, Parturition, and Early Age in the Domesticated Animal, with 212 Illustrations. By GEORGE FLEMING. 8vo. Rs. 21-8.

THE PRINCIPLES AND PRACTICE OF VETERINARY MEDICINE. By WILLIAM WILLIAMS, M.R.C.V.S., &c. Rs. 20.

THE PRINCIPLES AND PRACTICE OF VETERINARY SURGERY. By WILLIAM WILLIAMS, M.R.C.V.S. Illustrated. Rs. 21-8.

LECTURES ON THE EXAMINATION OF HORSES AS TO SOUNDNESS. With an Appendix on the Law of Horses and Warranty. By WILLIAM FEARNLEY, M.R.C.V.S. Rs. 5-6.

ON HORSE-BREAKING. By ROBERT MORETON, M.R.C.V.S. 8vo. Rs. 3-8.

HORSES AND RIDING. By GEORGE NEVILE, M.A. Second Edition. Rs. 4-4.

THE POCKET AND THE STUD; or, Practical Hints on the Management of the Stable. By HARRY HIEOVER. Rs. 1-12.

PURDONS' VETERINARY HANDBOOK. The Diseases of Cattle, Horses, Sheep, Swine, Dogs, and Poultry. By R. O. PRINGLE. Fifth Edition. Rs. 1-12.

HORSE-SHOES AND HORSE-SHOEING: their Origin, History, Uses, and Abuses. By GEORGE FLEMING, F.R.G.S. Illustrated. Rs. 15.

PRACTICAL HORSE-SHOEING. By G. FLEMING, F.R.G.S. Illustrated. Rs. 1-6.

NOTES ON SHOEING HORSES. By LIEUT.-COL. F. FITZWYGRAM. Second Edition. Rs. 3-8.

RURAL SPORTS, COACHING, HORSEMANSHIP, &c.

AN ENCYCLOPÆDIA OF RURAL SPORTS; or, Complete Account of Hunting, Shooting, Fishing, Racing, &c., &c. By DELABERE P. BLAINE. New Edition, Revised and Corrected. 600 Engravings. Royal 8vo., cloth. Rs. 15.

BRITISH RURAL SPORTS, comprising Shooting, Hunting, Coursing, Fishing, Hawking, Racing, Boating, and Pedestrianism. By STONEHENGE. Thirteenth Edition. Illustrated. Royal 8vo. Rs. 15.

BRITISH SPORTS AND PASTIMES. Edited by Anthony Trollope. Rs. 7-8.

THE SPORTSMAN'S GAZETTEER and General Guide. The Game Animals, Birds, and Fishes of North America: their Habits and various Methods of Capture. By CHARLES HALLOCK. Rs. 10-12.

DOWN THE ROAD; or, Reminiscences of a Gentleman Coachman. Illustrated. By C. T. S. BIRCH REYNARDSON. Second Edition. Rs. 15.

ANNALS OF THE ROAD; or, Notes on Mail and Stage Coaching in Great Britain. By Capt. MALET. Illustrated. Rs. 15.

HORSEMANSHIP; or, The Art of Riding and Managing a Horse. Illustrated. By Capt. RICHARDSON. Rs. 6-8.

HINTS ON HORSEMANSHIP; or, Common Sense and Common Errors in Common Riding. By Col. G. GREENWOOD. Rs. 1-12.

THREE LETTERS ON THE HORSE, MASTER, AND DONKEY. By 'BLUNT SPURS.' Illustrated. Re. 1.

THE DOG IN HEALTH AND DISEASE, comprising the various modes of Breaking and Training him for Hunting, Coursing, Shooting, &c. By STONEHENGE. Illustrated. Rs. 5-6.

YOUATT ON THE DOG. Revised and Enlarged. By W. WATSON. 8vo. Illustrated. Rs. 4-4.

THE DOG, with simple Directions for his Treatment and notices of the best Dogs of the Day and their Breeders or Exhibitors. By 'IDSTONE.' Illustrated. Rs. 1-12.

THE PRACTICAL KENNEL GUIDE, with plain Instructions how to rear and breed Dogs for Pleasure, Show, and Profit. By GORDON STABLES, M.D. Rs. 2-8.

DOGS: THEIR POINTS, WHIMS, INSTINCTS, AND PECULIARITIES. Edited by HENRY WEBB. Illustrated. Rs. 4.

THE TREATMENT OF THE DOMESTICATED DOGS. By 'MAGENTA.' Rs. 1-12.

THE OX: HIS DISEASES AND THEIR TREATMENT. With Essay on Parturition in the Cow. By J. R. DOBSON. Illustrated. Rs. 5-6.

THE COMPLETE GRAZIER and Farmers' and Cattle-Breeders' Assistant: a Compendium of Husbandry. By WILLIAM YOUATT and ROBERT SCOTT BURN. 8vo. Rs. 15.

EVERY MAN HIS OWN CATTLE DOCTOR. By FRANCIS CLATER and E. MAYHEW. Rs. 4-4.

POPULAR BOOKS ON SPORT, &c.

THIRTEEN YEARS AMONG THE WILD BEASTS OF INDIA. Their Haunts and Habits from personal observation, with an account of the modes of Capturing and Taming Elephants. By G. P. SANDERSON, Officer in charge of the Government Elephant-catching Establishment in Mysore. With 21 full-page Illustrations and 3 Maps. Small 4to. Rs. 17-14.

NATURAL HISTORY, SPORT, AND TRAVEL. By EDWARD LOCKWOOD, Bengal Civil Service, late Magistrate of Monghyr. Crown 8vo. Rs. 7-8.

THE LARGE AND SMALL GAME OF BENGAL and the North-Western Provinces in India. By Capt. J. H. BALDWIN, F. Z. S., Bengal Staff Corps. Second Edition. With numerous Illustrations. 4to., cloth. Rs. 15.

SEONEE; or, Camp Life on the Satpura Range: A Tale of Indian Adventure. By ROBERT ARMITAGE STERNDALE, F.R.G.S. Illustrated by the Author. Second Edition. Demy 8vo., cloth. Rs. 15.

LARGE GAME SHOOTING IN THIBET and the North-West. By Major ALEXANDER A. KINLOCH, C.M.Z.S., 60th Rifles. Illustrated with Photographs. First and Second Series. Demy quarto, cloth. Each Rs. 15.

THE ORIENTAL SPORTING MAGAZINE, from June, 1828, to June, 1833, reprinted in 2 vols. 8vo., cloth. Rs. 20.

These Volumes contain the well-known contributions to Sporting Literature published under the title of "Tales of a Tinker," and numerous exciting descriptions of Tiger Hunting, Quail Shooting, Hog Hunting, Fox Hunting, &c.

SPORT IN MANY LANDS: EUROPE, ASIA, AFRICA, AND AMERICA. By H. A. LEVESON, the Old Shikarry, Author of "The Forest and the Field." With Illustrations. 2 vols. 8vo., cloth. Rs. 8-8.

THE LARGE GAME and Natural History of South and South-East Africa. From the Journals of the Hon'ble W. H. DRUMMOND. With Illustrations. Demy 8vo., cloth. Reduced to Rs. 10-8. *(Published at 21s.)*

CONTENTS:—Buffalo—Rhinoceros—Eland—Elephant—Lions—Leopards—Hunting with Dogs—Anecdotes of Antelopes—Game Birds.

THE OLD FOREST RANGER; or, Wild Sports of India on the Neilgherry Hills, in the Jungles, and on the Plains. By Major WALTER CAMPBELL, of Skipness. New Edition. With Illustrations on steel. Crown 8vo. Rs. 3-8.

BOOKS ON SPORT.—Continued.

MELINDA THE CABOCEER; or, Sport in Ashanti: a Tale of the Gold Coast. By J. A. SKERTCHLEY. With eight Illustrations. Crown 8vo. Reduced to Rs. 3-4. *(Published at 8s.)*

HUNTING, SHOOTING, AND FISHING; A Sporting Miscellany with Anecdotic Chapters about Horses and Dogs. Numerous Illustrations. Crown 8vo. Rs. 5-6.

A MANUAL OF INDIAN SPORT. (Reprinted from the 'TIMES OF INDIA.') 12mo., cloth. Rs. 1-8.

A useful and handy *vade mecum* for the use of Indian Sportsmen in the jungle.

WRINKLES; or, Hints to Sportsmen and Travellers upon Dress, Equipment, Armament, and Camp Life. By the Old Shikarry. Illustrated. Post 8vo. Rs. 2-8.

THE FOREST AND THE FIELD. By the Old Shikarry. With Eight Illustrations. Crown 8vo. Rs. 2-8.

THE WILD SPORTS OF INDIA: With detailed Instructions for the Sportsman. By Major HENRY SHAKESPEAR. Crown 8vo. Rs. 3-8.

THE HUNTING GROUNDS OF THE GREAT WEST: A Description of the Plains, Game, and Indians of the Great North American Desert. By RICHARD IRVING DODGE, Lieutenant-Colonel, United States Army. With an Introduction by W. BLACKMORE. With numerous Illustrations by Ernest Griset. 8vo., cloth. Rs. 17-2.

OVER TURF AND STUBBLE. By "Old Calabar." Crown 8vo., cloth. Rs. 8-8.

WOLF HUNTING AND WILD SPORT IN LOWER BRITANNY. By the Author of "Paul Pendril," &c., &c. With Illustrations by Col. H. H. CREALOCKE, C.B. 8vo. Rs. 8-8.

PAST DAYS IN INDIA; or, Sporting Reminiscences of the Valley of the Soane and the Basin of Singrowlee. By a late Customs Officer. Reduced to Rs. 3-8. *(Published at 10s. 6d.)*

THE GREAT THIRST LAND: a Ride through Natal, Orange Free State, Transvaal, Kalahari. By PARKER GILLMORE, ("Ubique") 8vo., cloth. Rs. 15.

THE ROD IN INDIA: being Hints how to obtain Sport, with remarks on the Natural History of Fish, Otters, etc., and Illustrations of Fish and Tackle. By HENRY SULLIVAN THOMAS, M.C.S. 8vo. boards. Rs. 5.

HANDBOOK OF THE FRESHWATER FISHES OF INDIA, giving the characteristic peculiarities of all the Species at present known, and intended as a guide to Students and District Officers. By Capt. R. BEAVAN, F R.S.S. 8vo., cloth. Rs. 7-8.

BOOKS ON SPORT.—Concluded.

THE MOOR AND THE LOCH. Containing Minute Instructions in all Highland Sports. By JOHN COLQUHOUN. Fourth Edition, enlarged. 2 vols. Rs. 17-2.

TRIVIATA; or, Crossroad Chronicles of Passages in Irish Hunting History during the season of 1875-76. With Illustrations. Rs. 11-6.

SPORT AND WAR; or, Recollections of Fighting and Hunting in South Africa. By Major-General BISSETT, C. B. Illustrated. Rs. 10.

FLOOD, FIELD, AND FOREST. By GEORGE ROOPER. Fourth Edition. Illustrated. Rs. 3-8.

THE SCIENCE OF FOX-HUNTING and Management of the Kennel. By SCRUTATOR. Rs. 3-8.

EIGHT YEARS IN CEYLON. By SAMUEL W. BAKER. New Edition. Illustrated. Rs. 5-6.

THE MODERN PRACTICAL ANGLER, a complete Guide to Fly-fishing, Bottom-fishing, and Trolling. By H. CHOLMONDELEY PENNELL. Illustrated. Rs. 4-4.

SPORTING SKETCHES AT HOME AND ABROAD. By the OLD BUSHMAN. Illustrated. Rs. 2-8.

LIFE WITH THE HAMRAN ARABS, an account of a Sporting Tour of some Officers of the Guards in the Soudan. By ARTHUR B. R. MYERS. Photographs. Rs. 8-8.

THE WILD ELEPHANT and the method of Capturing and Taming it in Ceylon. By SIR J. EMERSON TENNENT, Bart. Rs. 2-8.

CAMP NOTES: STORIES OF SPORT AND ADVENTURE in Asia, Africa, and America. By F. BOYLE. Rs. 7-8.

THE SAVAGE LIFE, a second series of "Camp Notes." By F. BOYLE. Rs. 8-8.

GUN, ROD, AND SADDLE: Personal Experiences. By 'UBIQUE.' Rs. 5-6.

WANDERINGS OF A NATURALIST IN INDIA: The Western Himalays and Cashmere. By A. L. ADAMS, M.D. 8vo. Rs. 7-8.

THE FOX AT HOME, AND OTHER TALES. By GEORGE ROOPER. Illustrated. Rs. 3-8.

SPORT IN ABYSSINIA; or, The Mareb and Tackazzee. By the EARL MAYO. Rs. 8-8.

THE RIFLE AND THE HOUND IN CEYLON. By SIR SAMUEL BAKER, Bart. Illustrated. Rs. 5-6